NICHOLS:
A COLLEGE FOR THE HILL
1931~1996

∾

VOLUME II IN A BICENTENNIAL HISTORY

JAMES L. CONRAD JR., PH.D.

PUBLISHED BY NICHOLS COLLEGE, 2013
PRINTED BY THE BASSETTE COMPANY, SPRINGFIELD, MASSACHUSETTS

Published by Nichols College, 2013
123 Center Road, Dudley, Massachusetts 01571

Copyright © 2013, by Nichols College

All rights reserved. No part of the book may be reproduced,
stored in a retrieval system, or transmitted, in any form or by any means,
electronic, mechanical, photocopying, recording, or otherwise,
without the written permission of Nichols College.

Printed in the United States of America
Book cover and design by Patricia Korch, Creative Director, Nichols College
Book interior production by Darcy Adshead, Adshead Graphics, Auburn, MA
Printed by Bassette Company, Springfield, Massachusetts

ISBN: 978-0-981-5664-2-9

Cover: Budleigh Hall
Source: Photograph taken by Justin Dolan '09

TABLE OF CONTENTS

List of Illustrations .... v–viii
Preface .... xi–xii
Introduction 1–9
Chapter 1. Roots for the Beginning 11–30
      "The Beautiful Old Campus of Nichols Academy" 12
         Hezekiah Conant's New Academy Buildings, 1881–1885 ... 15
         The Academy Seeks a Tenant 19
      "The Course of Study Developed so Successfully" 20
      Toward the Development of the All-Male Private School 24
      James L. Conrad, Coach and Business Program Director 26
      A Junior College Program in New Hampshire 28
Chapter 2. Building the College, 1931–1943 31–58
      Before the Start, April to September, 1931 33
      September 21, 1931 40
      "From an Absolute Beginning" 42
         The Two-Year College Emerges 44
      College and Campus Become One 50
         An Academy Decision 55
Chapter 3. "Ye Strong Sons of Nichols," 1931–1946 59–81
      The Pioneers 61
         Athletics 63
         Other Extra-Curricular Activities 68
      With War on the Horizon, 1938–1941 72
      The College Faces War, December 1941–June 1943 74
      "The Winter of Despair," 1943–1946 78
Other Notable Events, People, Items, and Pictures 1931–1946 83–88
Chapter 4. "Redesigning the Historic Campus" 1946–1958 89–116
      Resetting the Plan 90
         The Alumni Memorial Hall 93
         The Post-War Nichols Student 96
      James L. Conrad at Mid-Point 100
         1950s – Adjustments for Growth 102
      A New Campus Emerges from the Old 105
         The Enlisted Reserve Corps 108
         A Conservation and Forestry Program 110
         To a Four-Year Program in Business 111
      The Nichols Man 112

CHAPTER 5. NICHOLS COLLEGE OF BUSINESS ADMINISTRATION, 1958–1966. . 117–140
    Business Education in 1958 119
    The "Momentum of Growing" 120
        "4-Year Program Oked for Nichols". 121
        A New Athletic and Recreational Center. 125
        Other Needs 127
        Conservation and Forestry – A Four-Year Program. 132
    Milestone Events at Mid-Decade 134
        Sesquicentennial Celebration. 135
        Accreditation. 137
        A President Retires. 137

OTHER NOTABLE EVENTS, PEOPLE, ITEMS, AND PICTURES 1946–1966 141–149

CHAPTER 6. THE COLLEGE "TRANSFORMING," 1966–1978 151–179
    The Great Transformation, 1960–1980 152
    Gordon B. Cross and a "Rush of Decisions," 1966–1971 154
        Changes Begin 155
        "Widen the Horizon," A New Curriculum, 1971–1973 159
    Life in an Atmosphere of Change and Innovation 163
        Student Activism and New Social Rules 164
        Coeducation 168
        A Continuing Commitment to Intercollegiate Athletics 171
        A Crossroads. 174
    Darcy C. Coyle and an Age of Survival, 1973–1978 174
        The MBA Program. 176

AERIAL VIEWS OF THE NICHOLS CAMPUS, 1975 180–183

CHAPTER 7. BEYOND THE PAST, 1978–1996 185–214
    Lowell C. Smith, the Fourth President of Nichols. 186
        Internal Reorganization and Redesign, 1978. 189
    Advancing the College, 1978–1996. 191
        Institute for American Values (Robert C. Fischer
          Policy and Cultural Institute) 191
        The Computer at Nichols 196
        New Facilities and the "Campaign for Nichols" 198
    Reactions to Problems of Growth. 201
        Nichols Students Entering a New World. 204
        Blue Ribbon Committee on the Future of Nichols Athletics 207
    "Nichols Nighttime". 209
    Lowell C. Smith, in Retrospect 211

OTHER NOTABLE EVENTS, PEOPLE, ITEMS, AND PICTURES 1967–1996 215–223

CHAPTER 8. AT THE END OF THE TWENTIETH CENTURY 225–234

ENDNOTES 235–260

APPENDIXES A, B, C, D, E, F 261–273

INDEX. 275–290

ILLUSTRATIONS

Introduction
Nichols Academy Campus, circa 1900. 1
"Announcement," circa May 1931. 3

Chapter 1
Nichols emblem, 1931 11
A pre-1895 picture of Dudley Hill looking south along Center Street. . . 13
Conant-built Academy buildings, 1881–1885 16
Roger Conant Hall, circa 1905 16
A view of Budleigh Hall from the south and a point overlooking
  the Quinebaug River Valley, circa 1895 17
Hezekiah Conant Courtyard 18

Chapter 2
Nichols Junior College Seal, 1932 31
Upper Budleigh Gates 32
James L. Conrad, B.B.A., President. 33
Quincy H. Merrill, M.D. 33
Nichols Dining Hall, 1933–1934 40
The Class of 1932. 42
Bradford M. Kingman, A.B., A.M., Dean. 49
Wesley G. Spencer, BPE, Ed.M., Dean 49
Merrill Hall, completed in 1937 52
Damage on Dudley Hill caused by the Hurricane of 1938 53
New Budleigh Hall, 1933 57

Chapter 3
Nichols Junior College Seal, 1937 59
Nichols Student Body, 1931–1932 60
Hal Chalmers '36 64
Buffalo Nickel, 1936. 65
Hockey on Conant Pond 66
View of Nichols athletic fields and campus in mid-1930s 66–67
Nichols CPT students at North Grafton Airport, 1941 75
Colonel James L. Conrad, circa 1945 80
Hal Chalmers, Chief Specialist Physical Instructor, circa 1945 80
Other Notable Events, People, Items, and Pictures 1931–1946 83–88

v

Chapter 4
    Nichols Junior College Seal, 1942 89
    Campus Signs, 1957. 91
    Gilbert C. Garland, B.S., M.Ed., Dean 92
    This bell, a gift to the Academy by the Class of 1884 94
    Alumni Hall and its tower. 95
    Colonel and Mrs. James L. Conrad 103
    Charles E. Leech, B.S., M.C.S., Dean 104
    Everett R. Nordstrom, B.B.A., Dean of Men. 104
    James L. Conrad Hall 107
    Construction underway for new athletic fields 107
    Nichols Own Third Battalion 108
    The Colors. 109
    Foresters demonstrate their skills. 110
    "Range" of heights for Nichols Students, Class of 1955 114
    Graduation 1959. ("Neath Copper Beeches") 116

Chapter 5
    Nichols College of Business Administration Seal, 1959 117
    Academy Building with new frontage, 1958. 118
    Photo of *Bison*. 121
    Library Building, 1962 124
    Interfaith Chapel, 1963 125
    View of field house from the east. 126
    New Auditorium, 1965. 126
    Merrill Infirmary, 1962–1997 126
    Charles M. Quinn, B.S., M.B.A., Dean of Faculty,
        Executive Vice President 128
    George F. Chisholm, A.B., M.A., Dean of Students 128
    Robert H. Eaton, A.B., M.A., Dean of Men/Registrar. 128
    Nichols students tour foreign facility 129
    Records for Nichols Fall Athletic Teams, 26–1, 1965. 131
    Paul White, A.B., M.A., Ph.D., Director, Forestry Program 133
    Foresters in action 133
    Crowd enjoying the Brothers Four concert in Field House, 1965. 135
    Academic Convocation for Sesquicentennial Celebration
        held in Field House, 1965. 136
    Graduation 1966 – A Final Degree 139
    Other Notable Events, People, Items, and Pictures 1946–1966 141–149

Chapter 6
    Nichols College Seal, 1972 151
    Gordon B. Cross, B.A., M.B.A., Ph.D., President 154
    No More Foresters 156
    Administrative Committee, 1969 157
    A Bison statue 158
    IBM 1130, the first Nichols Computer System 163
    Alex Gottfried, "Nichols is [in 1969]." 165
    Part of first group of seven women to graduate from
        Nichols College in 1974 169
    New Athletic Fields and Field House, 1976 171
    West entrance to Chalmers Field House, dedicated 1968 172
    First Women's Basketball Team, 1978 173
    Darcy C. Coyle, B.S., M.B.A., D.B.A., President 175
    James L. Conrad Jr., A.B., A.M., Ph.D., Dean of Faculty 178
    Albert J. Sargent, B.S.B.A., M.B.A., Ph.D., Vice President 178
    Thomas F. McClutchy, B.S.B.A., M.B.A., Bursar 178
    Michael J. Vendetti, B.S., M.Ed., Athletic Director 178
    The "Blizzard of 1978" 179
    Aerial Views of the Nichols Campus, 1975 180–183

Chapter 7
    Lowell C. Smith, B.S.B.A., M.B.A., Ph.D., President 187
    Peter R. Savage, B.A., M.A., Ph.D., Dean of Academic Affairs 191
    Edward G. Warren, B.A., M.A., Ph.D., Dean of Academic Affairs 191
    Governor George Romney gives the inaugural address of
        the Institute for American Values 194
    Robert C. Fischer, A.B., M.A., Director of the Institute for
        American Values 194
    "Circus in America," Institute Program at Nichols on football field ... 195
    "College Dedicates New Davis Information Center" 197
    Davis Hall 199
    Shamie Hall 200
    Francis W. Robinson, Jr. '38 Tennis Courts 201
    Student Services Center Ribbon Cutting Ceremony 203
    Floyd N. Franke, B.A., M.Ed., Ph.D., Dean of Student Affairs 205
    Kenneth E. Grant, B.S., Bursar 205
    Roger F.X. Carney, B.S., M.S.I.A., M.A., Dean of Student Affairs 205
    The Old Man (Lowell C. Smith) and His Challengers 212
    Other Notable Events, People, Items, and Pictures 1967–1996 215–223

Charts
    Chart 2.1. Operating Philosophies and Responsibilities
        at Nichols in 1940 38
    Chart 2.2. Nichols Junior College, Enrollment, 1931–1943 43
    Chart 4.1. Geographical Distribution of Nichols Student Body
        in 1957, 1960, 1963, 1974 97
    Chart 4.2. Major Acquisition and Construction Projects, 1950–1958 ... 106
    Chart 5.1. Major Plant Acquisitions and Construction
        Projects, 1958–1966 123
    Chart 6.1. Nichols Curriculum, 1969 160
    Chart 6.2. A Chronology of Change, 1971–1974 161
    Chart 6.3. The Curricula, 1974–1975 162

Maps
    Map 1. First Map of the Nichols Junior College Campus, 1931 35
    Map 2. Nichols Campus, 1965 140
    Map 3. Aerial Views of the Nichols Campus, 1975 180

Appendixes
    Appendix A. Programs in Business Administration:
            New Hampton (1930–1931) and Nichols
            Junior College (1933–1934 and 1942–1943) 261
    Appendix B. Memories of the Hurricane of '38 263
    Appendix C. Statement of Institutional Purpose as Described in
            Applicable Charters: 1941, 1958, 1971, 1974 265
    Appendix D. Nichols College Athletic Hall of Fame Members, 1972– .. 267
    Appendix E. Four-Year Curriculum for Bachelor's Degree in
            Business Administration, 1960 271
    Appendix F. Major Institutional, Organizational, Academic
            Restructuring Issues Discussed, 1958–1966 273

To all members of the Nichols community,
past, present, and future, near and far,
without whom this book could
not have been written.

PREFACE

This is the second part of the bicentennial history of Nichols. The first volume in this series — *Nichols Academy: The Spring on the Hill, 1815–1931* — was published in 2008.[1] This second volume — *Nichols: A College for the Hill, 1931–1996* — begins with the emergence of Nichols as a two-year college in 1931 and continues to the end of the administration of the fourth Nichols President, Lowell C. Smith.

The period in the history of Nichols from 1931 to 1996 has significant personal meaning for me. I was born in 1932, one year after Nichols Junior College of Business Administration and Executive Training was established. As the son of the College's first president whose administration lasted for 35 years, I had a close personal view of the College's early development. I gained yet another perspective as a Nichols College administrator and a faculty member for 43 years. On various occasions between 1957 and 2000, I served as director of admissions, department chair, dean of the faculty, and vice president of external academic affairs. I also was a member of the Nichols College Board of Trustees from 2000 to 2008. In fact, however, a closeness to one's story may not always be helpful. According to Clark Kerr, former Chancellor of the University of California, "It is difficult to be in the battle and yet to stand above it."[2]

With academic degrees in history from Dartmouth College, Clark University, and the University of Connecticut, I was thoroughly introduced to the historian's craft. My opportunity to write a formal history of Nichols appeared when I retired as a professor emeritus of history from Nichols in 1999. What follows here is a result of my personal and long-time attachment to the institution and its area, an appreciation of sound administrative practices, and a substantial background and training as an historian.

As I dealt with this history, I was reminded of a story told by Dean Acheson, former United States Secretary of State, to Arthur M. Schlesinger Jr., the pre-eminent American historian. Acheson told Schlesinger of his experience when he was writing his memoirs and attempting to describe a critical meeting he had with President Franklin Delano Roosevelt and Secretary of State, Cordell Hull, just prior to World War II. Acheson stated that he had a vivid recollection of their meeting and wrote at length about the ensuing discussion. However,

xi

when Acheson's fact-checkers went over his account, they found that Hull had been ill that day and was not in Washington. This meeting did not occur as Acheson recalled it.[3] As a result of this reminder, I have made every effort to check the facts presented here.

This is written for those who have been part of the nearly two hundred year history of Nichols as well as for others who wish to understand its story better. Numerous people have helped me throughout this project. It has been accomplished primarily due to the commitment, encouragement and support of Robert Kuppenheimer, Nichols College Class of 1969 and Nichols College Board of Trustees member, and with the assistance of Nichols College Presidents Debra Townsley, Susan West Engelkemeyer, and interim president, Gerald Fels, as well as former president, Lowell C. Smith. I also owe much to a large number of Nichols people who contributed to this work. Thanks again go to Conant Library Director, Jim Douglas, and to Evelyn Nieszczezewski, Rosalba Onofrio and other members of the Library staff. I am indebted also to my longtime colleague at Nichols, Professor Thomas G. Smith, for significant editorial advice and support. I am most appreciative of the cooperation extended to me by the staff of the Currier Center including Len Harmon, Blanche Milligan, Kathy Sandstrom, and Diane Perry. Also my thanks for support go to the members of the Nichols Historical Project Committee and to members of the Nichols Information Technology Department. And, since the beginning of the entire history project, Patricia Korch, the College's creative director, has been by my side with wise council, direction, and much skill. She deserves much credit for what has resulted.

I also am indebted to a talented and impressive number of Nichols student newspaper and yearbook editors and writers who provided excellent material for this history. Their writings gave me important insights that are not available elsewhere. Also in this category are the many Nichols alumni who completed "Historical Questionnaires" sent to them several years ago. I carefully read all their responses. They too contributed much to this history.

A host of others made special contributions and must be thanked. Some who read or made significant contributions to this manuscript include: Dr. Edward Warren; Robinson V. Smith; Ms. Norma Jean Moore; T. Holmes Moore; David Lombard '65; Dr. Faythe Turner; Thomas McClutchy '75; Dr. Brian McCoy; Dr. Alan Reinhardt; Richard Scheffler '63; Cynthia Brown '11; Justin Dolan '09; and Jacquelyn Khillah '15. Whatever errors that exist here are mine entirely.

On a more personal note, the help of my wife, Bunny and two sons, Michael and Jeffrey, was of great importance in completing this work. So too was the support that I received from the College community during periods of trial and illness. Especially critical was the help provided me on one occasion by the Nichols public safety officers who made it possible for me to continue on.

INTRODUCTION

Nichols Academy Campus, circa 1900.
Left to right: Conant Library and Observatory, Academy building and Hall, and Roger Conant Hall, The Village Grammar School (partially hidden), and Conant Memorial Church are adjacent to the campus.
Source: Nichols Junior College of Business Administration and Executive Training, "Announcing – A NEW EDUCATIONAL PLAN," Folder 513, Nichols College Archives (hereafter NCA).

In its collective historical sense, Nichols – the Academy, the two-year or Junior College, the College of Business Administration, and the College – will be 200 years old in 2015. The celebration of its bicentennial will soon begin. Situated on a lovely hilltop in south central Massachusetts, this small, private and long-independent institution has experienced extensive challenges over the years. Amasa Nichols constructed his first Academy building in 1815 and Hezekiah Conant built his still-standing Academy buildings in the early 1880s on Dudley Hill. When the Nichols Academy Board of Trustees gave James L. Conrad the opportunity to establish a new college in the Academy buildings in 1931, they came together to rededicate the place and purpose of the institution Amasa Nichols introduced.

The objective here is to tell the Nichols College story from 1931 to 1996. Aristotle, the Greek philosopher and scholar, once gave seemingly simple advice for this task. He said: "If you would understand anything . . . observe its beginning and its development."[1] A corollary to Aristotle's opinion adds that all events also have both a history and a context. Together these suggestions offer directions for getting off to a good start. Compounding the task, however, is the fact that Nichols has a number of documented beginnings: 1815, 1819, 1823, 1871, 1881, 1931, 1946, 1958, 1971 and 1974.

A book-length history of Nichols has not been written despite its long, colorful, and sometimes difficult journey through the frontiers of America's educational past.[2] Consequently, to correct this omission, a plan for writing a Nichols history was developed in the office of then Nichols President, Debra Townsley, discussed by a committee established for this purpose, and accepted in 2003. Shortly thereafter, I was selected to write this history.

Because of its nature and complexity, the writing of the Nichols history was divided into two parts. The first volume of the Nichols bicentennial history, *Nichols Academy: The Spring on the Hill, 1815 – 1931*, was published in 2008.[3] The second, or this volume, is titled, *Nichols: A College for the Hill, 1931 – 1996*.

First and foremost, this is an institutional history. In its broadest sense, it contains the complex story of dynamic interactions between vision and reality and between purpose and necessity that continually test an institution's resolve. Not surprisingly, its course also reflects national conditions and the evolving state of higher education. And, in yet another sense, this is the story of a small, rural, private and independent Massachusetts institution and the people who supported it, assumed its leadership, enrolled in its classes, and generally became part of its structure throughout the years – and centuries. This odyssey takes its students from a beginning in a rural, Universalist academy and its learning village on Dudley Hill through America's early national period to a professionally-oriented college featuring business education and offering graduate degrees as it enters the 21st century.

Initially Nichols Academy received adequate support until 1909. The "old" Academy was assisted by the town of Dudley when it served as Dudley High School from 1871 to 1909. Great assistance also came from Hezekiah Conant and his three "modern" buildings constructed in the 1880s. During this period, however, the Academy began to struggle with declining support and attendance. It was difficult for its trustees to work around the growth of free secondary or public high schools established in Massachusetts by the 1860s. This resulted in a general decline in Academy boarding enrollments and forced the school to rely on only one significant source (Hezekiah Conant) for funds and leadership. This was not enough.

When the first formal announcement regarding Nichols Junior College of Business Administration and Executive Training appeared in 1931, much changed for Dudley Hill. This announcement introducing the new institution's style, direction and purpose is reproduced here:

Announcing –
A NEW EDUCATIONAL PLAN
Nichols Junior College of Business Administration and Executive Training
Dudley, Massachusetts

HE old Nichols Academy at Dudley, Massachusetts, founded in 1815, but inoperative for the last few years, will be reopened next fall as the Nichols Junior College of Business Administration and Executive Training. James Lawson Conrad, head of the Junior College of Business Administration department at New Hampton School for Boys, New Hampton, N.H., has been elected president of the college and begins his duties at once.

The new school will be the first eastern junior college exclusively for men, and it also will be the first institution of junior college rank in the East to offer business administration courses with full campus and dormitory equipment.

Nichols Academy was founded in Dudley in 1815 by Amasa Nichols, an energetic business man. Among the early trustees of influence was Samuel Slater, "The Father of Cotton Manufacture in the United States." Hezekiah Conant, a native of Dudley, took an active interest in the academy during the latter part of the last century and he gave the Academy its present buildings.

As in the case of many other New England schools, the local high school has taken over the functions of the Academy, and for the last few years the buildings have been vacant with the endowment accumulating to be put to some educational use.

The new junior college program is in keeping with the trend of the times. Ten years ago junior colleges were practically unknown in this country. Now they number 430 and enroll 67,000 students. Only recently have they made their first inroads in New England, but at present all the junior colleges are for girls, with the exception of one which is co-educational. Nichols will be the first junior college in the East for men only.

The decision to reopen Nichols Academy as a Junior College for boys exclusively was largely influenced by the success of Mr. Conrad in developing the Junior College of Business Administration department at New Hampton. The New Hampton School, due to the increased demand for her facilities as a preparatory school, is cooperating in the transfer of the Junior College of Business Administration department to Nichols. . . .

"Announcement," circa May 1931.
Source: Nichols Junior College,
Folder 513, Nichols College Archives.

There is little question that the old Dudley academy, an institution of the past, experienced a life-giving infusion in 1931 when it joined with essentially a school of the future – a specialized two-year college. This resulted in an uneasy partnership in which a two-year college program in business administration began on a long-existing campus owned by a virtually inactive academy. This relationship lasted about ten years and was extremely beneficial for both, although it ultimately had to end.

At least two slightly different but equally legitimate views exist regarding the new college's beginning. In the first, and from the standpoint of Academy supporters and nearby people, a two-year or junior college was being transferred to Dudley and the Academy campus. The local newspaper, the *Webster Evening Times*, applauded the Academy's work in achieving this "transfer."[4] According to the Junior College's first official announcement, the New Hampton School in New Hampton, New Hampshire, where the program then existed, was "cooperating in the transfer of the Junior College of Business Administration department to Nichols."[5] In short, this decision was seen saving the Academy – with the addition of a new and successful program.

In its initial announcement in the late spring of 1931, however, the Junior College stated that the Academy was being "reopened" as Nichols Junior College of Business Administration and Executive Training. In effect, this was a second interpretation of the College's beginning. The trustees of the old Academy immediately announced that James L. Conrad and his partner, Frederick Smith of the New Hampton School, agreed to keep the "Nichols" name for the new College's title and to retain some of the traditions and relationships previously established by Nichols Academy.[6] Consequently, when the leasing agreement with the Academy was signed, the new junior college received a name, a campus, and a past, to go along with its new plan.

By declaring the beginning of the school to be a reorganization, President Conrad was able not only to create a new school but to acquire a past as well.[7] The first catalogues of Nichols Junior College of Business Administration and Executive Training stress this point. Clearly this was an important condition of the leasing agreement. With time, this latter explanation of its beginning in 1931 became a vital part of the College's history.

The May, 1931 announcement suggests how the Junior College intended to utilize the Academy's historic past. Although brief, it points out that Academy founders, early benefactors, and trustees included prominent business men and industrialists of national stature. Since Nichols Junior College was a two-year college of business administration, historic ties with Academy benefactors such as Amasa Nichols and Hezekiah Conant, and trustees like Samuel Slater, all well-known 19th century leaders of commerce and industry, were important. They immediately became part of a new institutional history.

⁓ Introduction

President Conrad was pleased that his program was to be associated with an institution that provided an image and history of long-existing accomplishment.[8] It also presented a scene of rural beauty and an elegance originating in the previous century. At the same time, the Nichols Academy trustees received what they wanted and needed: a tenant who could protect the school's past and perpetuate its future. They managed better than they knew.

More specifically, the new institution's purpose was spelled out by its President, James L. Conrad, as it opened in 1931:

> Nichols Junior College of Business Administration and Executive Training was established to meet a very definite educational need . . . . It incorporates a new idea in education – a junior college for men only, and an institution where a student can secure a college education in business administration and executive training and at the same time enjoy the advantages of dormitory and campus life. . . .[9]

Its program of study, according to President Conrad, was to combine courses in business education, similar to those offered in the third and fourth years of four-year colleges and universities, with necessary electives and selected cultural subjects. This was to occur in a two-year format and this was new.

To understand the forces that gave direction and content to Nichols Junior College of Business Administration and Executive Training in 1931, it is important to consider its institutional development. As straightforward as this "new idea" regarding two-year colleges may seem today, this was not the case in 1931. Nonetheless, by keeping its original educational plan in sight while considering the College's years from 1931 to 1996, it is possible to determine the nature and extent of the changes experienced at Nichols. Its new approach to business education and executive leadership introduced an evolving institutional experience in always changing times.

Contrary to Aristotle's opinion, describing growth and development is not a simple matter. For instance, not to be ignored in this evolution of Nichols is the role played by a grander context – the nature and events of America throughout the 20th century. For evidence of this phenomenon, one only need consider the affects of cataclysmic occurrences that were to befall American society between 1931 and 1996: the Great Depression; World War II; the Cold War, including Korea and Vietnam; a prolonged period of prosperity and recession; social crisis, segregation, demographic and gender issues; and eventually crisis and war in the Middle East. Each impacted on the course and character of higher education in America – and touched the essential nature of Nichols.

Not surprisingly, however, the introduction of the junior college was not without challenges in 1931. While many applauded the two-year college's virtues and possible contributions, others warned about its potential weaknesses. It took the New England Association of Colleges and Secondary Schools until 1929 before it acknowledged the existence of area junior colleges.[10] Walter Eells, a careful observer of these new institutions, concluded in 1931 that the majority of junior colleges in the nation were less than ten years old and that no standards for them existed. He saw these schools possessing a "wide diversity" of purpose.[11]

Twenty junior colleges were located in New England at the end of 1931, the year Nichols Junior College was established.[12] Ten, including Nichols, were in Massachusetts, four in Connecticut, three in Maine, and one each in Rhode Island, Vermont, and New Hampshire. Only Nichols was all male and featured a two-year approach to business education. This new program did not follow the usual junior college model which tended to focus on thirteenth and fourteenth grade levels. It was unique.

Nichols Junior College of Business Administration and Executive Training clearly was affected by the state and stature of higher education in Massachusetts. The fact that the new school initially had been well received in New Hampshire between 1928 and 1931 had little meaning for Massachusetts political leaders and educators. The first challenge for the new Dudley school was to gain acceptance from institutions and educators long-associated with higher education in the Bay State.

Massachusetts boys and their parents generally preferred a four-year college featuring a liberal arts curriculum. Some thought that the new two-year colleges simply were not equal to long-existing four-year schools; for them, junior college classification meant inferior status.[13] Established Massachusetts colleges actually seemed to be "deterrents" to two-year college growth since the "prestige value" of four-year colleges exceeded that of all other schools.[14] One voice went further by direly predicting that junior colleges were about to bring an end to "the quiet spread of civilization over the dark places in our land..." and would take "learning away from the common people...."[15] Without question, the thinking and receptiveness of the Massachusetts educational community was to be important in shaping the new junior college.

Much of the underlying difficulty regarding the recognition of junior colleges in the Commonwealth of Massachusetts also stemmed from a basic academic concern: many in higher education refused to recognize non-liberal arts courses. Professional or business courses such as offered by Nichols Junior College fell into this category. One long-accepted tenet of traditional educational thinking held that only liberal arts courses could be the basis for a bachelor's degree. A report on college standards by a New England Association committee in 1920 indicated that standards then being discussed were intended only for an "acceptable college of liberal arts."[16] This issue was seen by another observer as an argument taking place regarding the relative merits of "old, honored, and entrenched general liberal arts subjects" and "applied or specialized subject matter."[17] Some were concerned as well that the intellectual level of a college education was being lowered by increasing social motives.[18] This issue was extremely important for those involved in higher education in the post-World War I years.

One result of this negative perception of junior colleges in Massachusetts was the Commonwealth's delay in public funding for two-year public or community colleges. Initial studies supporting a need for such schools in the Bay State were first available in the 1920s. However, funding of public junior colleges in the Commonwealth was delayed until 1957.[19] And, when public junior colleges or community colleges were finally approved, they offered a challenge to private junior colleges similar to what was originally faced by Nichols Academy in the 1850s – the presence of free (or nearly so) competitive public education.

But there was much on the side of the young two-year college. The development of American higher education that occurred during the years after 1931 was supported by an expanding need for business education and an increasing acceptance of its potential value. This period also saw the beginning of an era of family businesses despite the Great Depression. Furthermore, the economic crisis of the 1930s documented the need for a better business education. An institution that focused on only two years also was most acceptable to an economically distressed society. Nichols, therefore, was in the vanguard of an era of educational expansion necessary to supply the needs of an emerging business society. In the process, the Nichols story also helps to introduce a new picture of business education that emerges in 1931 – the specialized two-year college.

Nevertheless, to survive, Nichols Junior College had to endure a difficult beginning, build a larger and stronger institution despite almost non-existent initial capitalization, and overcome the need to deal with an educational context that required time to recognize its strengths. Because of long-prevailing attitudes in 1931, an independent, private, two-year college in Massachusetts specializing in business education probably began with two strikes against it.

The intention here is to examine the College's history from its widest perspective. A broad brush approach can be applied to its period from 1931 to 1996 because of the full range of available primary sources and other resources. As a result, an all-encompassing description of the College's growth, goals, progress and educational environment can be developed. This history could not be complete without noting the contributions of all presidents and their administrations as well as those of the least noticeable Nichols students who passed through the portals of the Nichols Auditorium, formerly a barn built in the 1880s.

NICHOLS: A COLLEGE FOR THE HILL

The following chapters in the history of Nichols generally correspond with College administrations between 1931 and 1996. Historically, presidents of small colleges establish objectives and directions. Nichols has not been different. The first chapter here examines the College's roots. The four chapters that follow focus on the efforts of President James L. Conrad, the first Nichols president, to establish a two-year college of business administration, to survive World War II, and then to achieve four-year college status. This latter event occurred in 1958 with the recognition of Nichols College of Business Administration by the Board of Collegiate Authority of the Commonwealth of Massachusetts followed by this new four-year College's first commencement in 1961. The 35-year administration of President Conrad ended with his retirement in 1966.

Under the leadership of Dr. Gordon B. Cross, the second Nichols president, the College adopted a more traditional, university, coeducational, and comprehensive curriculum model with the creation of additional degree-granting programs, including some in the liberal arts. This was the formal beginning of a new Nichols College. A Master of Business Administration degree (MBA) followed and was first awarded by Nichols in 1977 during the administration of Dr. Darcy C. Coyle, the third President of Nichols. The next to the last chapter covers the administration of President Lowell C. Smith from 1978 to 1996 and considers the College's development and growth both on and beyond the Dudley Hill campus. This brings us to nearly 2000 and the third century of the school begun in 1815.

Primary archival support for this history generally comes from material in the extensive Nichols College Archives. These include the minutes of meetings of the Academy, Junior College, and College Boards of Trustees, student newspapers, yearbooks, catalogs, institutional records, and alumni responses to "Historical Questionnaires." Local newspapers, records of the Worcester County Registry of Deeds, and general educational histories make contributions as well.

Two brief earlier histories of Nichols College also are available and helpful since they present views from two separate College administrations. The first was written by Dr. Darcy C. Coyle, third president of Nichols College, and delivered as an address to the Newcomen Society in 1975.[20] The second was published on the occasion of the 175th anniversary of Nichols in 1990 during the administration of Dr. Lowell C. Smith, the fourth college president.[21] These histories, however, do not concentrate to any great extent on earlier periods in Nichols history or do they provide a historical perspective of the institution's course over time, as is the purpose here.

Although Nichols received national acknowledgment on occasion, only a few will recognize Nichols as a nationally known college. No one will remember Nichols as a large institution since it did not reach an enrollment of over 1,000 undergraduate day students until 2007. And, while a number of Nichols teams and their athletes have gained national recognition, no one will identify them as perennial national champions.

The College is known and appreciated best by those who attended it and truly benefited from their experiences and the institution's contributions. Within its areas of self-selected responsibilities and classifications, Nichols, in all its various forms and confronted by immense challenges, has traveled a long and remarkable journey. Over this time, the institution has emerged with an enduring sense of pride and being. In the process, its story helps to detail the emergence of business education in twentieth century America.

CHAPTER 1

ROOTS FOR THE BEGINNING

Nichols emblem, 1931.
This image of the Academy building's tower appears on the cover of the first catalog of Nichols Junior College in 1931. It then became part of the first College seal which was introduced the next year.
Source: Nichols Junior College of Business
Administration, *Catalog*, 1931–1932, front cover, NCA.

Nichols Junior College of Business Administration and Executive Training was introduced on Dudley Hill in south-central Massachusetts in 1931. Its founders correctly termed it "the first junior college exclusively for men" in the East, "a new idea in education" and "the first institution of junior college rank to offer business administration courses with full campus and dormitory equipment."[1] The new Junior College featured a two-year program of studies considered "fundamental to business and life."[2] Institutional announcements acknowledged the new junior college's prior ties with two New England private, secondary schools: The New Hampton School in New Hampton, New Hampshire; and Nichols Academy in Dudley, Massachusetts.

Its new beginnings can best be understood by examining the institution's intertwining features. In 1931, Nichols Junior College offered five distinct elements. These included a newly designed two-year program emphasizing college-level business administration courses located on a non-urban campus with college-provided housing, an all-male student body, and a commitment to an extensive athletic program all brought together by a new president in a private and independent institution. They provided historic and lasting cornerstones for the new college – they are the founding features of Nichols Junior College.

Higher education in the United States prior to the Civil War was composed of small collegiate institutions and universities, usually denominational in nature, offering classical courses with few distinct major areas of study or concentration. These institutions traditionally focused on building moral character, strengthening individual values, and developing intellectual foundations for professional activities. After the war ended, however, higher education experienced advancing change with the emergence of state-supported colleges and universities along with the development of curricula more responsive to evolving economic and societal needs. It was clear by World War I that the future was going to belong to experts. One aspect of this development was the appearance of a "managerial revolution" signaling the coming of professionalism to the American business scene.

By the 1880s, discussions in educational circles focused on the significant potential for growth and learning in the thirteenth and fourteenth grades, normally the first two years of college. Many institutions concentrating on two-year programs became known as junior colleges. Yet another feature of the expansive nature of this post Civil War education was the emergence of business education, although the difficult times of the 1930s slowed its growth.[3] Nevertheless, the substantial forces introduced by a complex wave of educational expansion appeared on the campus of the former Nichols Academy in the form of a "new educational plan."

"THE BEAUTIFUL OLD CAMPUS OF NICHOLS ACADEMY"[4]

Nichols Junior College of Business Administration and Executive Training, like the numerous copper beech trees on its Dudley, Massachusetts, campus, has deep and tangled roots. Historical accounts of the new college on Dudley Hill must begin with Amasa Nichols, a local manufacturer, merchant, speculator and a fervent Universalist, who constructed the first academy building in 1815 on his land in Dudley.[5] Initial support and encouragement for this school came from New England Universalists who applauded the idea of a secondary school available for their educational needs. The school on Dudley Hill was named Nichols Academy after its builder who gave the land and building to the Academy's board of trustees believing it was going to be supported by

A pre-1895 picture of Dudley Hill looking south along Center Street.
From *right to left* are the Conant Memorial Church, the town's Village
School, and Nichols Academy: Roger Conant Hall, the Academy
building and Hall, and the Conant Library and Observatory.
Source: "Nichols Academy looking down [south] Center Street," NCA.

New England Universalists. The new institution received its charter from the Commonwealth of Massachusetts in 1819.

The Academy building was a significant and determining gift. It cost Nichols $5,000, which must be added to the $10,000 he spent on his first academy building destroyed by fire three years before. These first Academy buildings were constructed next to the Dudley Town Common and the First Congregational Church. Amasa Nichols originally intended that his school building serve as a secondary school for Universalists, function as a meeting house for a small, local community of Universalists, and ultimately become a Universalist college.[6] His dream of such an institution collapsed by 1823 when the General Convention of New England Universalists was unable to provide necessary financial support for the Academy. Amasa Nichols then resigned as secretary of the Nichols Academy Board of Trustees in part because the Academy Board found it necessary to accept non-universalists as trustees. He also was on the verge of bankruptcy.[7] Nonetheless, his building and its Universalist-designed curriculum remained. They provided the beginning base – the place and purpose – for what was to follow.

Affectionately termed the "old" Academy, pre-Civil War Nichols Academy became a rural, private, independent, tuition-supported coeducational academy of significant regional stature. It offered a secondary school education that featured dual programs. Its Classical Course was composed of Latin, Greek, and higher mathematics subjects intended for those interested in enrolling in a university or school of theology. A second course, the so-called common English Course, featured subjects in English that included grammar and literature, as well as geography, arithmetic, the History of the United States, philosophy, geology, astronomy, logic, and moral philosophy, among others.[8] This dual offering was an important feature of early American secondary education. The Academy's students, male and female, ranged from 12 to 21 years of age.

Nichols Academy was led by a series of dedicated and well-educated preceptors who stayed for several years and then went on to the next institution. They received support from an active group of trustees and income from tuition. In its early years, the Academy attracted students from a 100-mile radius that extended through Massachusetts, Connecticut, Rhode Island, and into New York. Each year, twenty-five to fifty "scholars" enrolled for one or more terms lasting ten or eleven weeks. Like many early academies, Nichols admitted young men and women who came from near and far to board either in a few small rooms in the Academy building or in available, less-expensive locations on Dudley Hill. In effect, the Hill community rightly can be understood as a learning village since the Academy closely interacted with the everyday activities of those who surrounded it.[9]

A number of significant forces challenged the Academy's existence by the end of the Civil War. Time had left the wooden Academy building badly in need of repairs. Beyond this, private academies were threatened by the emergence of free public high schools. Such public schools appeared by 1860 in the communities surrounding Dudley including Webster, Oxford, and Southbridge, as well as throughout the entire state. Powerful arguments favoring state control of secondary education were introduced in Massachusetts by Horace Mann and in Connecticut by Henry Barnard, both leaders in the development of early public secondary schools. Not surprisingly, tuition-dependent academies found enrollments dropping significantly; some schools simply disappeared.

Fortunately for Nichols Academy, help arrived in the early 1870s in the form of two important yet separate developments. The first occurred in 1871 when Nichols Academy and the Town of Dudley agreed that the Academy was to serve as "Dudley High School." This assured the Academy of a constant number of local students while it could continue to function as a preparatory or "fitting" school for college-bound students. Nichols Academy's arrangement with the Town of Dudley continued until 1909.[10] As a result, the town did not have to construct its own high school.[11]

Second, industrialist Hezekiah Conant of Pawtucket, Rhode Island, returned to Dudley in 1874. A former resident who had attended Nichols Academy, Conant joined the Nichols Academy Board of Trustees and virtually rebuilt the old Academy, as well as Dudley Hill, over the next 20 years. Conant's contributions to his old school and to the Hill community were life-giving.

Virtually all the buildings available to the future Nichols Junior College in 1931 were constructed, financed, or redesigned in the 1880s and early 1890s by Hezekiah Conant with regionally recognized architects Elbridge Boyden and Son of Worcester, Massachusetts, and Charles F. Wilcox of Providence, Rhode Island. In 1874, with the Academy in desperate straits, Conant acquired a mortgage on the Academy land and its two small buildings: the Academy school house (the former Universalist Meeting House), and a boarding house built in 1873. Conant developed a campus for Nichols Academy on a plateau he built that required the construction of a high retaining wall located to the west of Center (or Dudley Hill or County) Road, north of Healy Road, and to the rear of the first Nichols Academy building. He moved thousands of yards of dirt to the top of Dudley Hill for fill.

Hezekiah Conant's New Academy Buildings, 1881~1885

Conant next built a new Academy building in 1881 to replace the Academy school house (former Universalist Meeting House which had replaced the original Nichols Academy building) at a cost of approximately $13,000. An irregular structure of gothic design, the new Academy building with a large hall, was 88 feet by 61 feet with a 76 foot high massive tower. It immediately was given by Conant to the Academy's trustees. A small gymnasium was added by Conant to the rear of this building in 1896 in response to increasing post Civil War interest in physical exercise and gymnastics.

Again, with Elbridge Boyden and Son, in 1882 Conant erected a smaller building, Conant Library and Observatory, just to the south of the newly built Academy building. It immediately became available as a library for both the Academy and the town while providing a functioning observatory and a weather station. Although small, the observatory was described as the "best equipped" of any similar structure, except for those in New England colleges – and this probably was the case.[12] Hezekiah Conant's famous astronomical clock also was housed in his library.

When the Academy's boarding house, constructed only ten years before, burned in 1883, Conant responded by erecting a new, three-story, brick boarding house in its place. He named this building for Roger Conant, an early ancestor. It was intended to be a commercial hotel or inn as well as a boarding house for as many as 36 Academy students. Ten years later he built a stable or carriage house to the rear of Conant Hall. In 1900, Hezekiah Conant gave this property – the Conant Library and Observatory and the Roger Conant Inn – to the Academy.

Conant Hall remains the most intriguing and significant of the three buildings completed on the Academy campus between 1881 and 1885. Beyond its utilitarian role for Hezekiah Conant, it is an architectural gem. Constructed in 1885 in American Queen Anne style, this building has a heavy symmetrical

Conant-built Academy buildings, 1881–1885.
At *left*, Conant Library and Observatory; *in center*, Academy Building, Hall, and Gymnasium and, *on right*, Roger Conant Hall.
Source: Dudley Centennial Committee, *A Commemorative Profile of Dudley, Massachusetts: 1776 United States Bicentennial 1976*, 10.

outline with a subtle but powerful asymmetrical facade best seen by examining the decorative work just beneath its third floor as well as its left and right gables. Its monumental chimneys further testify to its impressive Queen Anne style although pillars later added to Conant Hall may detract from the building's appearance for some.

Conant's reconstruction of Dudley Hill did not stop there. After completing the buildings on Academy Row, he immediately financed the rebuilding of the First Congregational Church on Dudley Hill after a fire destroyed the previous

Roger Conant Hall, circa 1905.
Source: Nichols Academy, *Annual Catalog, 1907–1908* (Dudley, Mass., 1907), 9.

A view of Budleigh Hall from the south and a point overlooking the Quinebaug River Valley, circa 1895.
Source: Notebook, Hezekiah Conant, Conant Folio, American Antiquarian Society. Courtesy American Antiquarian Society, Worcester, MA.

church in 1890. He also named this structure after Roger Conant. Designed by architect Charles F. Wilcox of Providence, Rhode Island, Conant Memorial Church also is an architectural masterpiece.[13] Wilcox then assisted the town of Dudley in the construction of the small village school between the Church and Conant Hall.

Soon after he became committed to the Academy in the early 1880s, Hezekiah Conant decided to establish his summer residence in Dudley. He purchased a number of properties on Dudley Hill, some around the Academy, while retaining control of the Academy and its land. As a final step in 1888 he acquired the property of Austin C. Burnett on the eastern side of Dudley Hill (now Center) Road for his summer estate.[14] The Conants tore down the Burnett house and erected a magnificent summer home. This new structure, named Budleigh Hall after a Conant ancestral home in England, majestically overlooked three states and the French and Quinebaug River Valleys in Massachusetts and Connecticut. Designed by architect Wilcox and constructed in Queen Anne style, it contained more than twenty-seven rooms and featured the latest in interior designs and furnishings. Its full dimensions, including piazzas and porte-cochere, measured 82 by 130 feet.[15] This new summer home was located on approximately 70 acres of well-landscaped grounds that included, at one time or another, five other homes, four barns, one cider mill, store houses, one mill, one water tank, and several tennis courts.[16] Hezekiah Conant died in 1902 in Rhode Island.[17]

One building on the Conant estate destined to have lasting importance for the new college was the former Burnett barn. Although the Conants tore down Burnett's house to construct Budleigh Hall, they decided in 1889 merely to remodel the old barn.[18] According to the *Nichols Alumni Magazine*, its lower level held a large head of cattle, the ground floor was used for storage of farm equipment, with the hayloft above.[19] Architect Wilcox's efforts created a stable with a main section of 48 feet by 50 feet, a carriage room of 30 feet by 37 feet, and a stud and harness room. Nine horses could be stabled in the redesigned structure.[20]

Another shed-like building on the Conant estate, originally deemed "unfit" for use, was located between Budleigh Hall (later Budleigh Towers) and the gymnasium (formerly the Burnett stables of the Conant estate). This was to be converted into a dining hall with a modern kitchen. The first Nichols catalog described it as spacious and attractive with room to accommodate the entire student body, the faculty, and possible guests to "sit-down" meals.[21] Actually, it was just large enough for 75 people.

Also being readied for use was the club house of the former Conant estate. This structure first called the Club or "Casino," soon became "Pop's," much later, "Bazzies." Located on the west side of Center Road, the club house had been the center for social activities on the Conant estate. Its interior featured a large fireplace along with a bowling alley, a room for pool and billiards, a lunch room and reading room. It soon was to overlook the new college athletic fields. The Club House became a much-appreciated and heavily utilized activity center for the small college community until 1972.

Hezekiah Conant Courtyard.
On left is the front or south side of the Conant stables, later to be the Nichols gymnasium (now Daniels Auditorium). *On the right* is a shed renovated in 1931 to become the first college dining hall. It was destroyed by fire in 1937. This picture is taken from the northwest corner of Budleigh Hall.
Source: Notebook, Hezekiah Conant, Conant Folio, American Antiquarian Society. Courtesy American Antiquarian Society, Worcester, MA.

The Academy Seeks a Tenant

After the Academy closed its doors in 1909 due to a lack of students, its trustees sought to put its three brick hilltop buildings to good use. Initially this seemed a simple task. These buildings were still relatively new and, although small, were impressive. Then too, the school's ideal location had been acclaimed by many Academy leaders over the previous century. Dudley's "pure air" was lauded in Academy catalogs which boasted of the town's reputation as one of the healthiest communities in the Commonwealth. According to one, its "retired situation renders it especially favorable to diligent study and good morals."[22]

Between 1909 and 1923, the Conant-built Academy building was used by the Town of Dudley as a lower-level or junior high school while the Conant Library was opened to townspeople and the inn remained available to Dudley visitors. This changed in 1923 when the Bethel Bible Institute, then located in Spencer, Massachusetts, leased the Academy buildings and purchased the buildings and land of the Conant estate. Named the "Dudley Bible Institute and Nichols Academy," this new institution combined the former Conant estate which it now owned, with land leased from the Academy.[23] The arrangement between the Academy trustees and Bethel Bible Institute was not long-lasting; the three leased Academy buildings were returned to the Academy Board of Trustees by 1926 after some trying times. The Dudley Bible Institute, as it then was called, remained on the former Conant estate for five more summers before moving to Providence, Rhode Island.[24]

After the former Bethel Bible Institute left the three Academy buildings, the Nichols Academy Board of Trustees renewed its efforts to find another tenant. Dr. Quincy H. Merrill, a long-time resident of Dudley, and a leading member of the Academy trustees, worked with the well-known educational bureau of Porter Sargent in Boston to bring a school to Dudley Hill.[25] In early 1931, after several years of effort, disappointment, and much anxiety, the Academy trustees began to discuss their property with two administrators from a New Hampshire preparatory school: Frederick Smith, the headmaster of The New Hampton School for Boys; and James L. Conrad, a coach and director of the New Hampton Junior College of Business Administration program, then part of the preparatory school. Smith and Conrad were interested in relocating their junior college program.

While searching for a new tenant, Dr. Merrill and his Academy committee talked with the Dudley Bible Institute's directors regarding the purchase of the former Conant estate to be added to the Academy's Conant-built structures. This property, including Budleigh Hall, was acquired by Nichols Academy in July 1931 for $5,000 and then leased to Smith and Conrad in September along with the original Academy hilltop property.[26] In all, the improvements and remodeling required to attract the new junior college were projected by some to cost as much as $45,000, mostly to be borne by the Academy. This included the construction of new athletic fields.

Despite a logical sense of urgency, Nichols Academy had specific conditions for the leasing of its buildings and campus. For one, the Academy trustees insisted that its property was to be used "in conformity with the [1819] Charter of Nichols Academy" and in a manner generally consistent with the wishes of Hezekiah Conant.[27] This included the use of the "Nichols" name. Smith and Conrad agreed to all conditions. Specifically, this also meant Conant Library was to be open for Dudley townspeople and the Academy Hall was to be ready for town use when needed. The College also was required to keep "intoxicating liquor" off the campus.

When the lease was signed in 1931, very real ties were established between the Academy and the new College. Furthermore, several Academy trustees were to be on the board of advisors of Nichols Junior College. In actuality, the agreement establishing Nichols Junior College in the buildings of Nichols Academy differed little from the Academy's previous leasing agreement with the Bethel Bible Institute. As some observers saw it, the Academy simply was being reopened in 1931.[28] This time, however, the outcome was to be different.

"The Course of Study Developed so Successfully"[29]

The Nichols Academy Board of Trustees' decision to lease its buildings was the direct result of this program's success at the New Hampton School for Boys in New Hampton, New Hampshire. This program in business administration, offered for several years at the New Hampton School, an independent, private preparatory school, was coming to Dudley with eleven former New Hampton students in their second or last years of the two-year program. The junior college program's move was assisted by the New Hampton School and by Headmaster Smith who joined the new Junior College's Board of Advisors.

Without question, this New Hampshire program's contribution to the beginning of Nichols Junior College was immensely important. It included a number of special features: a business program with a successful history that included courses generally taught on the third and fourth years of a college business program in a traditional university; an all-male environment, and an approach to student living and learning originating in a progressive, yet long-existing rural New Hampshire preparatory school; and several New Hampton trained faculty and staff, including the new president. Several graduates of this program had already earned transfer credits. They all easily meshed with Nichols Academy's history, traditions, and recent campus renovations.

Some commercial or business subjects, such as seen in the New Hampton junior college program, had been found at a few academies and preparatory schools. For instance, early New England academies offered bookkeeping as part of their common English courses. So did most 19th century public schools. After the Civil War, American lives and culture reflected a quickly expanding practical bent that closely paralleled America's industrial success. Furthermore, more and more Americans appreciated the potential of education to contribute to individual social and political success. In turn, the American educational system was greatly expanding.[30]

Some formal approaches to business education were established at a number of places in America's receptive 19th century environment. In its early formal use, business education was defined as "that area of education which develops skills, attitudes, and understandings essential for the successful direction of business relationships."[31] In contrast, vocational education was seen as a "program of education organized to prepare the learner in a particular chosen vocation or to upgrade employed workers."[32]

Arguably, the first early private commercial college in America was started by James Gordon Bennett in New York City in 1824. Three years later, Foster's Commercial School began in Boston.[33] They generally offered many practical courses including reading, elocution, penmanship, arithmetic, algebra, astronomy, history and geography, moral philosophy, and even counting-house procedures.

Another New York City school, Dolber's Commercial College, started in 1835, appears to have been the first "solely dedicated" to business education.[34] This was a critical event as it demonstrated that clerical training and other phases of business activity could be taught economically and effectively in a strictly educational setting.[35] Interestingly, few women attended these first business schools since employment for them was not available in American business houses.

Chains of specialized schools, such as Bryant and Stratton, located at nearly 50 different locations, also served as sources of business education.[36] These schools generally were established in urban areas such as Cleveland, Boston, Providence, Philadelphia, New York, Pittsburgh, Providence, and Rochester in New York state. The backbone of the business curriculum that evolved in these programs included penmanship (typewriting after 1885), shorthand, and bookkeeping. The success of these chains was vital in convincing Americans that office work could be learned more rapidly in a classroom environment than in apprentice programs in actual businesses. These schools demonstrated that business-related skills could be reduced to systems and effectively taught outside the workplace thus quickly fulfilling the needs of the business community along with those of potential employees or students.[37] Numbers of later well-known business leaders attended such schools. They included John

D. Rockefeller, who took courses in bookkeeping and "business computation" at Folsom's Commercial College in Cleveland and Henry Ford, who received a similar education at the Detroit Business Institute.[38]

Another quite different approach to business education was being introduced at established colleges and universities. After the Civil War, professional programs, such as engineering, agriculture, and architecture, among others, were emerging at American universities. Business education soon joined this group. The first collegiate school of business was established in 1881 at the University of Pennsylvania's Wharton School of Finance and Commerce in Philadelphia. Following Wharton in developing business programs based on a university model were the Universities of California and Chicago. These university programs featured two years of liberal arts or general education courses followed by two years of a major or professional study such as business.[39] Most university-based business programs were initiated through departments of economics. According to one study of Wharton's approach, "businessmen could best be prepared for their work by a liberal arts program to which some technical business subjects were added."[40] This approach became known as the "traditional" or university business school model.[41]

The introduction of business programs in established major universities was a significant endorsement for business education. By 1900, at least seven colleges and universities had departments offering a business program.[42] One supporter, Edmund J. James, then a director at Wharton in 1890, said of the business college: "They have done and are doing and are destined to continue doing, a great and useful work."[43]

Wharton's approach, however, was not the only four-year model available at the university level. New York University offered a program in 1900 "almost entirely" made up of technical business subjects.[44] While these and the programs that followed worked to establish a balance between their liberal arts courses and technical subjects, agreement on the exact nature of this relationship has been difficult to achieve. Nonetheless, all accepted that a core body of business courses had to be part of their programs.

Business education eventually became one of the faster growing segments of higher education. At least 180 universities were committed to such programs by 1935.[45] Course offerings in these early university-based schools of business administration usually were similar to the Wharton or university model and organized around broad objectives. These included the fundamentals of business administration, training in specialized fields, preparation for business leadership, and an understanding of cultural and ethical foundations necessary for the business world.[46]

A primary focus of these schools was to educate potential business leaders to make decisions based on economics, sociology, psychology, and related fields, as well as business courses. According to one interesting description of business education's historical development, "the drivers of business education evolved from craftsmen and merchants to accountants to colleges of arts and sciences and then to economic departments."[47] Beyond this, a master's program in management was introduced first in 1900 at Dartmouth College in Hanover, New Hampshire. Others quickly followed. Not surprisingly, this general expansion of business education eventually pointed to a need for standards in the "new" industry. As a consequence, the American Association of Collegiate Schools of Business, later expanded and renamed the Association to Advance Collegiate Schools of Business (AACSB), was founded in 1916 and became the first accrediting agency for undergraduate and graduate programs in business.

Yet another significant but frequently overlooked source of business education existed outside both the early commercial colleges and the university or "traditional" models. Nineteenth century private New England academies and preparatory schools sometimes offered practical subjects such as bookkeeping long before the Civil War. This interest led to the introduction of advanced business courses in some preparatory schools that then became another source of business education to appear on the college level.

It was just such a program that originally was transferred to Nichols and Dudley in 1931 from the New Hampton School for Boys in New Hampton, New Hampshire.[48] In fact, this specific program had evolved over the course of more than a half a century.[49] Interestingly, its genesis significantly differed from the "traditional" or university model in that a private, secondary school's interest in commercial courses led to the creation of a two-year college of business administration. Whereas the traditional university approach or model for business programs featured a liberal arts program to which technical business courses were added in the third and fourth years, the two-year college business program at New Hampton School and Nichols immediately offered business courses that generally were found in third and fourth years of the university model.

The New Hampton School, earlier named the New Hampton Literary and Biblical Institution, a Baptist-supported preparatory school, was located in central New Hampshire between Concord and Plymouth. It took its commercial or business program far beyond the one or two commercial subjects offered at other early academies. In 1868, to augment New Hampton's Classical or college preparatory program, its trustees created a Commercial Department that they said was "as thorough a course of instruction as can be obtained in any Business College in the country."[50] This business program featured practical training in every department of "actual business."[51]

New Hampton's Commercial College program began in the 1870s as a one-year course at the thirteenth grade level. The school was quick to claim that its program was "not one of the chain of business colleges . . . which sprang up like mushrooms and perished almost as quickly." New Hampton trustees in 1881 saw its commercial college inviting "comparison with the oldest and the best."[52] Its subjects included commercial law, penmanship, and a strong emphasis on "Book-keeping." Courses such as telegraphy were added as was instruction in the freight and express business. A practical training phase was introduced featuring an "actual" technical experience through the operation of an on-campus banking room and savings bank. Students managed a wholesale store at the school as well. When functioning as intended, the commercial department occupied a floor in a New Hampton School building.

This program experienced early success. By 1886, the trustees of New Hampton confidently claimed there was "no other Commercial College in the U.S. so thorough, so practical, so nearly resembling actual business" as their school.[53] It added phonography (the use of recording devices), typewriting, political economy, spelling, and business correspondence to its commercial program. Eventually, however, like many other private schools of the period, the New Hampton School experienced difficulties with declining enrollment, faltering patronage, and insufficient endowment. In 1917, at the request of the state of New Hampshire, New Hampton restructured its Commercial program leading to the creation of a secondary school course of four years and a Commercial College program of two years. This later course, resulting in a diploma, prepared its students for clerical positions or roles designed for the execution of one's business affairs.[54]

Change soon came to the New Hampton institution believed to be at its "nadir" in 1926.[55] When a new administration arrived that year, the school became "New Hampton, A New Hampshire School for Boys," an independent, private, all-male college preparatory school. As for the commercial program, very little remained in 1927 although the new preparatory school curriculum included an "intensive course in Business Method."[56] Nonetheless, several years later, and with little fanfare, New Hampton School reintroduced its two-year college program.

Toward the Development of the All-Male Private School

Most academies and preparatory schools of the post World War I era faced reduced enrollments following the emergence of free public schools. However, the public school system, as democratic as it appeared to be, was not acceptable to everyone. Some Americans were concerned about its secular nature. Others, parents of both males and females, were uncomfortable with certain features of public coeducation and the context it seemed to be creating. Some were interested in enrolling their children in institutions such as private preparatory schools that focused on the development of moral character. Still other parents were upset because they believed the public school system did not maintain sufficiently high academic standards.

The situation itself was somewhat different for young men and women. In fact, more young women were attending public high schools than were young men who frequently went to work on farms and in early mills. Young women also were seen doing better academically than their male classmates. It was not unusual for this distinction to be blamed by sensitive parents of males on the presence in public secondary education of large numbers of female teachers (generally nine out of ten were women).

Then too, some believed that males experienced a loss of masculinity in what might be seen as a feminine-guided learning environment.[57] This thinking was given credibility by psychologists such as G. Stanley Hall, president of Clark University in Worcester, Massachusetts, who declared that "sexual identity was an achievement shaped by circumstance and not a fixed characteristic." The desired image for males was projected by President Theodore Roosevelt, known for his "gladiatorial spirit."[58] A solution for some was an all-male educational experience that provided the opportunity to develop "male" characteristics through athletic competition and rural living.

Coeducation's impact on young women was of similar concern for the parents involved. The belief that young women might be adversely affected by the rigors of increased academic competition was common. Both male and female parents could be upset that their young daughters might be tempted to venture beyond traditional roles such as wives and homemakers if they excelled in new public secondary schools. The development of single-sex preparatory schools resulted from combined concerns about secularism, unacceptable academic standards, and co-education.

New Hampton's decision in 1926 to become all-male was in response to these concerns and the expressed needs of a number of parents. When this school was reorganized in 1926 under new headmaster Frederick Smith, the New Hampton School for Boys became a preparatory school with an all-male student body.[59] A similar approach was taken by other small New Hampshire and Vermont private preparatory schools such as Kimball Union Academy, Proctor, Tilton, and Vermont Academy. In a like fashion, Colby Academy, once a coeducational academy in New London, New Hampshire, became Colby School for Girls in 1928.

Headmaster Smith's aggressive plan to expand New Hampton's enrollment was successful. His assessment of parental concerns was on target. Small classes, emphasis on the out-of-doors, and the creation of an athletic program designed for all students combined to raise institutional numbers and school spirit. According to a 1927 New Hampton announcement, "Hard work and hard play under careful guidance and supervision fits the New Hampton boy to enter college or business with the mental, moral, and physical equipment to compete successfully and to work harmoniously."[60] This was the aim. As for Headmaster Smith, he was in the center of things, overseeing all events, cheering for all teams, and committed to knowing the names of every one of his students. His leadership style brought more students and additional success to his institution.

James L. Conrad, Coach and Business Program Director

With previous administrative experience as superintendent of the American School Foundation in Mexico City and principal of a Massachusetts high school, Headmaster Smith was faced with the challenge in 1926 of rebuilding the New Hampton School.

One of his younger assistants was James L. Conrad. He was born in Fitchburg, Massachusetts, in 1900. His parents, Thomas H. Conrad, a paper mill worker, and Catherine Kane Conrad, came from Nova Scotia and the Irish Free State, respectively. During his early years, he displayed an extremely competitive spirit. At 16 years of age, he was wrestling at many regional county fairs competing in the 150–160 pound class.[61]

In his later teens, he was recognized as a superb, all-around athlete in high school and YMCA circles. He received letters in football and baseball at Fitchburg High School in Fitchburg, Massachusetts.[62] There were, however, few other suggestions of later accomplishments. After high school, he began with single semesters at Fitchburg Normal School, where he played football, and at the University of New Hampshire.[63] At some point he also demonstrated an interest and talent in drawing.[64] When not in college, he worked on streetcars and in local paper mills.

In 1922, he enrolled in Villanova College (now University) where he registered in its newly organized College of Commerce and Finance. There Conrad developed into a superior college athlete excelling in three sports: football, basketball, and baseball. After one basketball game against then Rhode Island State (now the University of Rhode Island), he was acclaimed by the Kingston, Rhode Island, press as having "the greatest long shot [two-handed set shot] ever seen on the Rhode Island State court" when he made six consecutive baskets from center court.[65]

Aside from his athletic success at Villanova, Conrad began to develop an approach to business education based on his experience at its school of business. One account of this school, then in its first year, recognized it as "known for creativity and innovation, hands-on and service learning opportunities, an outstanding liberal arts foundation; a firm grounding in ethics, and an applied education that prepares leaders and global citizens within the ever-changing, complex, and fast-paced world of business." The need for ethical decision-making was central in everything they did.[66]

He then transferred to the College of Business Administration at Boston University due to financial difficulties. When the transfer rule did not allow him to play sports there, he coached freshman basketball and assisted the varsity basketball coach.[67] His long-term goals remained consistent: to obtain a coaching position after graduation.[68] Conrad completed his academic program by 1926 and graduated from Boston University with a Bachelor of Business Administration degree (BBA). His Boston University experience also introduced him to a program for fourth-year college students that featured supervised employment as part of one's options for graduation.[69]

While in college in 1923, Conrad became a member of U.S. Army's Quartermaster Corps. This move undoubtedly was influenced by his uncle, Colonel William L. Conrad, a consulting engineer, who was to become president of the Quartermaster Association of the United States.[70] There can be no doubt that William Conrad's military experience and advice later resulted in his nephew's sensitive and well-informed approach to events surrounding World War II. Then too, it also is evident from James Conrad's 35 years in Army reserve service that he enjoyed his time in the military.

Conrad arrived at the New Hampton School in 1926 with new wife, Annette Bourassa, also of Fitchburg.[71] He would be with Headmaster Smith until 1931 as a teacher of business courses and eventually Director of Physical Recreation.[72] Consistent with his original intentions, he began a period of coaching that eventually included three varsity sports each year. His football, basketball and baseball teams at New Hampton established a remarkable record winning nine out of a possible thirteen state championships between 1926 and 1931. This deep interest in athletics and desire to coach were permanent parts of his makeup. He also developed a lasting interest in horseback riding at New Hampton.

When at the New Hampton School, he was recognized by the school yearbook, the *Belfry*, for "his untiring efforts to promote a high standard of sportsmanship and scholarship. . . ."[73] He became Director of the New Hampton Junior College of Business Administration program and Head Coach of Varsity Sports by 1929.[74] After working with a dynamic and successful headmaster, Conrad was ready to take on other challenges. At some point in his New Hampshire years, his primary interest shifted from coaching to educational administration. And, as this change was occurring, he was beginning to demonstrate superior oratorical talents. Not surprisingly, the relationship between the New Hampton headmaster and his assistant that evolved between 1926 and 1931 was to be long and enduring. During his time in New Hampshire, Conrad carefully rebuilt the New Hampton School college-level business program.

A Junior College Program in New Hampshire

Under Conrad's leadership, the New Hampton program developed a fundamental curriculum for "the student who wished to transfer to a four-year course of business administration at a city university." According to the New Hampton catalog, full transfer credit, or credit for two year's equivalence of college work, was given to graduates of the New Hampton Junior College program by "leading colleges of business administration." This two-year college program was offered to high school or preparatory school graduates and said to provide "a broad grounding in business principles and in many diversified businesses."[75] It featured a "modernized" curriculum that included two years each of accounting, business law, economics, psychology, business administration, and English. To this, its director added one year of finance with a list of electives consisting of salesmanship, advertising, credits and collections, along with an optional typewriting course.[76] (For a comparison of the New Hampton School curricula in 1930–1931, with Nichols Junior College in 1933–1934, and in 1942–1943, see Appendix A.)

New Hampton School's junior college program of business administration combined the earlier work of its commercial college with new thinking regarding business education. These were brought to the school by its present director from schools in business administration at Villanova and Boston University. New courses designed by Director Conrad featured small group discussions, trips to business houses, and talks by business men intended to bring about a careful "correlation of the theoretical and the practical through textbooks, notebooks, theses, and reference books. . . ."[77] Conrad's program emphasized "real training for executive responsibility" in which students worked from small private offices, managed a staff, directed a venture, and assumed full responsibility for its operation and performance, as well as completing their specified academic subjects. This New Hampton educational experience was said to have been enhanced and stimulated by its central New Hampshire setting which featured a healthy environment, the influence of school traditions, a lack of distractions, and the availability of athletic, recreational and social activities.[78]

When the business emphasis reemerged at New Hampton in the late 1920s as a department, it was termed a junior college. According to one study of American education, the junior college movement was "one of the most interesting developments in the field of higher education at the end of the nineteenth and beginning of the twentieth centuries." Some educators saw this as an intellectual "renaissance" and a "fundamental reorganization of American education."[79]

However, as they first appeared, junior colleges were vaguely and variously described. A newly formed American Association of Junior Colleges defined the junior college as an institution offering "two years of instruction of strictly collegiate grade."[80] Some of these schools began with the twelfth grade, others offered courses typically placed in the first two years of college. Still others, such as Nichols Junior College, with its narrow professional focus, introduced courses generally appearing in the second two years of a standard university program.[81]

More specifically, some two-year colleges featured accounting and secretarial courses. Some focused on business management or general business. Others included fields such as banking, real estate, or insurance, while still others had a socio-business focus.[82] However, the program that appeared at Nichols Junior College was different. It focused on training its students to work in the business world on the executive level with many of its courses usually found on the third and fourth levels of universities such as the Wharton School. (A notation on Map 1 of the Nichols Junior College campus, drawn in 1931, refers to the new college's curriculum as featuring "The fundamental subjects of a university course in business administration [generally found in the university's third and fourth years] in two years of college work [at Nichols])."[83]

In the early spring of 1931, the following announcement was added to the New Hampton School *Catalogue*:

> The New Hampton Junior College of Business Administration has been transferred to Dudley, Massachusetts, where it is part of the Nichols Junior College of Business Administration. A catalogue of this school may be obtained by writing to President James L. Conrad, Nichols Junior College, Dudley, Mass.[84]

Quite logically, the institutional infrastructure introduced at Nichols Junior College mirrored what existed at the New Hampton School. At the same time, a number of interesting similarities existed in the backgrounds of the two founding institutions. Both had histories dating back to the pre-1827 era: New Hampton to 1821, Nichols Academy to 1815. When they experienced beginnings in 1926 and 1931, respectively; both had old buildings, little financial support, and few students. Then too, both institutions were started and led by individuals introduced to New England preparatory school administration in 1926. Five years later, Conrad, in Dudley, repeated the earlier rebuilding process that successfully worked at New Hampton. He and Frederick Smith briefly joined together in the new venture: Nichols Junior College of Business Administration and Executive Training.

When the New Hampton School educators brought a two-year college of business administration program to Dudley, they also introduced an approach to school administration and student development that had descended from headmasters such as Harlan Page Amen at Exeter Academy and the

"Headmaster" of them all, Frank L. Boyden, who was at Deerfield Academy from 1902 to 1968.[85] Conrad's initial approach, based on the models established by headmasters Amen, Boyden, and Frederick Smith, also is notable since he was involved in an additional game of small college building.

But the difference between the schools and their programs is important. The New Hampton program evolved in a functioning and supportive preparatory school environment whereas Nichols Junior College was to operate independently in its own formal college setting. The question regarding the potential for success of this program was answered positively in New Hampshire. The larger and present question, however, was whether similar success was achievable in Massachusetts on a campus the new College did not own.

CHAPTER 2

BUILDING THE COLLEGE, 1931~1943

Nichols Junior College Seal, 1932.
A Nichols Junior College seal was introduced in the *Tower 1932*, the first College yearbook. Years later, at the time of President Conrad's death in 1974, it was stated that he "exemplified every symbol of the College seal which he designed. . . ."[1] This seal was circular and somewhat rudimentary, with a scalloped edge on a border that was inscribed with *"Collegium, Juniorium, and Curriculum."* Probably it was sketched by President Conrad as well. In the center of the seal is an image of the Tower of the Nichols Academy building constructed in 1881. This building, the oldest and most venerable on the campus, became part of the College emblem and appeared on the cover of the first college catalog published in May 1931. Its presence here correctly suggests the strong connection between the young college and the old academy including a mutually acceptable campus symbol. Similar depictions are often found on small, country college campuses.[2] Placed around the tower are references to the virtues selected by President Conrad to comprise the school's principles: "Loyalty, Service and Culture." Above this motto is "Nichols."
Source for seal (1932): Nichols Yearbook, *The Tower 1932*, 1, NCA.

It took ten years for Nichols Junior College of Business Administration and Executive Training to gain control of its own destiny. The Dudley junior college could not present any traditional degrees until 1938, when it became the first junior college to receive the authority from the Commonwealth of Massachusetts to award the degree of Associate of Business Administration (ABA). Even then, Nichols Junior College did not own its campus; this was not to happen until 1942. This chapter chronicles a truly difficult, but eventually successful first decade for the new institution on Dudley Hill.

Upper Budleigh Gates.
Source: Nichols Yearbook, *1939 Ledger*, n.p.

Nichols Junior College's initial emergence was in large part the result of a gradually increasing demand for business education. America's rise toward world industrial leadership by the 1920s required that Americans obtain the educational backgrounds capable of understanding the new commercial and business worlds. What was necessary, many believed, was a higher level of business education.[3] The traditional industrial entrepreneur was about to be replaced by lieutenants; instinct was to be supplanted by knowledge.[4]

The Academy's search for another educational institution to occupy its Dudley Hill property ended in 1931 with the arrival of the junior college program formerly operating at a New Hampshire preparatory school. The character, courses, and direction of Nichols Junior College of Business Administration and Executive Training were set by James L. Conrad and Frederick Smith from The New Hampton School for Boys. Conrad, then 30, was Nichols Junior College's first and only president. He served in this position for 27 years during which time he energetically pursued his first goal: to offer a two-year, college-level business education in a rural setting at an all-male institution committed to providing extensive extracurricular and recreational programs, including intercollegiate athletics. Nichols students then either could transfer to a four-year college of business administration with two-years credit or enter the business world. And, at its foundation was a student-centric philosophy intended to promote individual achievement. This was his "new plan" for the new college.

Dudley is located in south central Massachusetts. In the middle of the 1930s, it was a small community of 4,570 bordered by the Quinebaug River on the west and the French River on the east with their scenic river valleys. Two mill

James L. Conrad, B.B.A.
President, Nichols Junior
College, 1931–1958;
Nichols College of Business
Administration, 1958–1966.

Quincy H. Merrill, M.D.
Chairman, Nichols Boards
of Trustees, 1942–1966.

towns of substantial note – Southbridge (population, 15,790) on the west and Webster (population, 13,850) on the east – existed on these rivers.[5] Dudley also featured a small industrial section adjacent to Webster. The Dudley community was one hour from Boston, Providence in Rhode Island, and Hartford in Connecticut.

A close look at the College's years between 1931 and 1942 reveals numerous challenging barriers. Even limited hindsight suggests that 1931 was not a good year to begin an educational institution. World War I had left Americans disillusioned and seeking isolation. The still-young nation also was entering the first years of its Great Depression with another world war on the horizon. At its beginning, Nichols Junior College was a small, unique, promising, but highly vulnerable institution that encountered more than its share of crises over its first ten years. This was both a severe testing time as well as a period of unparalleled opportunity.

Before the Start, April to September, 1931

Tentative approval of the agreement between the Nichols Academy trustees and the educators from New Hampshire was reached on March 24, 1931. Additional formal approval by the Academy trustees occurred the next month.[6] Smith and Conrad were considered by the Nichols Academy trustees to be "satisfactory parties" to lease the Academy property.[7] Conrad was named president of Nichols Junior College on April 1, 1931, and immediately left New Hampshire for Dudley. Headmaster Smith remained at the New Hampton

School, but stayed in frequent contact with his former assistant. When the Nichols Academy trustees acquired the former Conant estate from the Dudley (or Bethel) Bible Institute in the summer of 1931, the agreement to lease all the Academy properties to Nichols Junior College was finalized.[8]

This five-year lease for the Conant-built Academy buildings and campus included the Academy's just-acquired former Conant estate. The Conant estate consisted of three tracts: land east of Center (or County or Dudley Hill) Road including Budleigh Hall; the "Casino Lot" on the west side of Center Road; and land north of Healy Road, around the Conant-built buildings on Academy Row.[9] Final terms were set on September 15, 1931, establishing a yearly rental fee of $1,500 for five years, with an option for an additional term of 25 years, at a cost not to exceed $2,500 a year.[10] The leasing arrangement with Conrad and Smith required that the Academy trustees settle all boundary disputes with the Town of Dudley and provide insurance for up to $66,000 on the property leased to the junior college.[11] This seemingly minor part of the agreement had a great impact later on.

Much had to be accomplished between April and September, 1931, when Nichols Junior College students were scheduled to register. An initial announcement of the new college's existence immediately was placed in the New Hampton School Catalog in April noting that the New Hampton Junior College of Business Administration program was moving to Dudley, Massachusetts.[12] Further announcements, along with a catalog for Nichols Junior College of Business Administration and Executive Training, were prepared by late May.[13]

Without question, the new school's administration first had to oversee the upgrading of the physical plant by the Academy trustees. While the Dudley property was quaint and extremely attractive, it was not ready to support what Conrad and Smith hoped would be nearly one hundred students. Buildings had to be remodeled and modernized; athletic fields had to be constructed.

These were not simple tasks. The stables of the Conant estate (a three-story structure with two stories below the main floor) and an adjacent outbuilding, located between the stables and Budleigh Hall, were originally deemed "unfit for use." Nonetheless these structures then became a gymnasium and a dining hall, respectively. In addition, the brick, Conant-built Academy buildings – the Academy building and Hall, Conant Library and Observatory, and Roger Conant Hall – had to be readied for students since they experienced only occasional use after the Academy closed its doors in 1909. Some of Dudley's junior high school students used the Academy building until 1923 when the Dudley Bible Institute leased Academy properties for three years. Conant Hall – the inn – also was open in the summer for guests.

Steam heat now had to be installed by the Academy in all buildings. New plumbing, sanitary equipment and lighting were needed throughout the campus. Further, all buildings on the Hill experienced low water pressure.

And, finally, to provide for the Junior College's athletic program, playing fields had to be constructed on a spacious meadow on the west side of Center (or Dudley Hill) Road across from Budleigh "Towers" (formerly Budleigh Hall) and just south of the "Club House." Plans for this project included a football field, a one-fifth mile cinder track, a baseball field, hockey rink, and four new tennis courts.[14] The Academy trustees indicated they were ready to spend $15,000 to renovate their campus for the new college.[15] It probably cost more. (See Map 1, the First Map of the Nichols Junior College Campus, 1931. This map appears to have been drawn just before the campus was ready.)

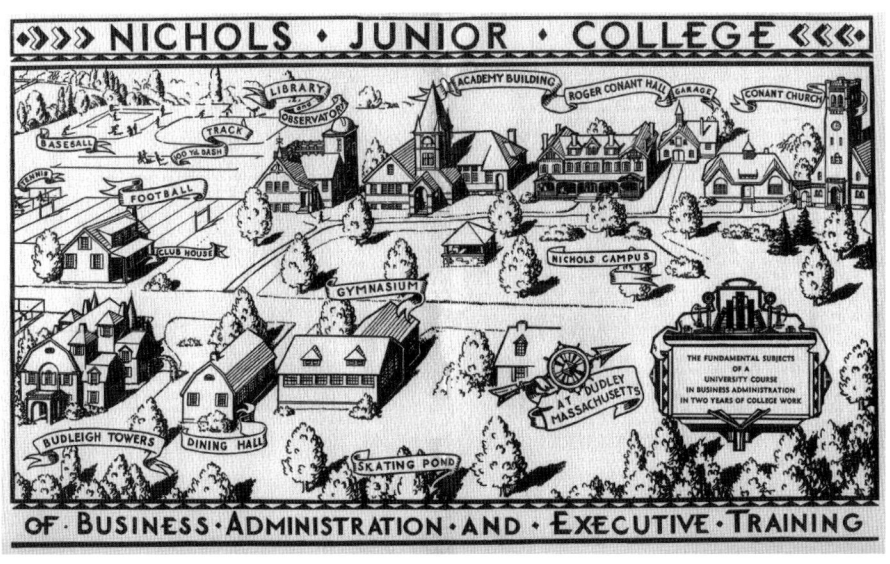

Map 1. First Map of the Nichols Junior College Campus, 1931.
Source: Nichols Junior College Catalog 1931–1932, 12–13, NCA.

These summer efforts generally were successful. All buildings were ready for full use and occupancy on opening day – September 21, 1931. Unfortunately, this was not the case with the new athletic fields which took a month more to complete. Observers as early as April 1st guessed that athletics would receive "much attention" at the new college because of President Conrad's previous experiences in intercollegiate athletics.[16] Two or three steam shovels were working daily on the new fields by the end of July.[17] The local newspaper predicted that "sports lovers are scheduled to see some great contests in football and basketball this year. . . ."[18] The College catalog also noted that the Dudley-Webster Country Club and golf course were adjacent to its property.[19]

One area that needed little immediate development was the new institution's academic program. (See Appendix A.) Nonetheless, and although it had been refined at the New Hampton School over the previous several years, the program still had to be promoted at its new location. Nichols Junior College catalogs and announcements contributed some information toward this end; the rest was the responsibility of the new president. In his role as advocate for Nichols Junior College, President Conrad said in August 1931:

> Our college is somewhat revolutionary in design and was declared impossible at the start [when in New Hampshire]. It has, however, been proven to my satisfaction that the idea [of business education on the small college level] was justified and we have already turned out some splendid young men [at New Hampton] well equipped for the business world.[20]

Always the promoter, he also stated that "the opportunities [for its graduates in business] were unlike those of any other school in operation." He added that his new two-year college "would be second to none in the United States." Its curriculum design was unmatched, he claimed. As for its athletic program, he remarked that the College's football field would be "as good as any college's."[21]

Frequent speeches by the Nichols president promoting the new Junior College provide an interesting view of Conrad's early educational philosophy. First, he firmly believed that a specialization in business education required training in ethics and should include an understanding of the value of culture in the human experience.[22] Much of this background undoubtedly resulted from his earlier experiences at Villanova College, a Catholic institution, which introduced him to a moral and ethical foundation for his approach to business education. Boston University's College of Business Administration then offered a more practical dimension including the incorporation of business experience or internship-like activities into its college program.

Second, he strongly believed in the inherent values and abilities of his students. He stressed the need for his students to "think out" problems for themselves. The new college president felt that it was wrong to criticize a boy for incorrect reasoning. Errors had to be pointed out, he said, but the use of one's reasoning powers always had to be commended.[23]

Initially, a student body had to be recruited while the campus and buildings were being readied. Eleven students, then completing their first years in the junior college program at the New Hampton School, came to Dudley for their second or final years. President Conrad reported traveling 63,000 miles during the summer to recruit 58 additional students; they were hoping for 70.[24] It was not unusual for headmasters or presidents of small colleges to recruit students by visiting their homes. Conrad, as college president, did this frequently. Occasionally that summer, prospective students spent a night or two in Roger Conant Hall (the Dudley Inn), while seeing the College and the area.[25]

It also was recognized that local support and confidence was a vital factor in building the Junior College. The President aggressively sought to create this support by meeting with numerous nearby organizations such as the Webster Rotary Club. There he worked to establish a "Rotary Scholarship" to be awarded each year to a resident of Webster and Dudley.[26] President Conrad saw one such scholarship to Nichols each year as a way of giving a worthy local student the "opportunity to make good thru this training in business administration." The first Nichols-Rotary scholarship went to James J. Morway in 1931.[27]

Aside from facilities and students, Conrad had to assemble a faculty and supporting staff. Logically, he recruited three faculty members from his staff at New Hampton who, like himself, graduated from Boston University.[28] Others were added during the summer to complete a faculty that numbered six full-time members when Nichols Junior College opened its doors. Their responsibilities aside from teaching assignments, included advising student activities, coaching, and living in college buildings as dormitory masters. This was similar to the resident-faculty model typically found in New England boarding schools. (See Chart 2.1 for 1940 institutional responsibilities.)

Nichols Junior College's administration was tiny, typical of many small private schools and colleges. It included its president, his secretary who was his sister, Margaret M. Conrad, and his wife, Annette, who acted as hostess. His uncle, Henry Booth, was in charge of the facilities. Quincy H. Merrill, M.D., of the Academy trustees, was school physician. Listed as trustees were the 17 Nichols Academy trustees, although they had no direct control of the College's academic program. A majority of these Academy trustees were from the Dudley and Webster area as had been the case for over 100 years. Their responsibilities were to oversee the now-leased Academy-owned buildings and campus and to manage Academy Trust funds.

Conrad and Smith then created a separate set of advisors to assist in developing the Nichols Junior College educational plan. A similar advising group was used at the New Hampton commercial college in the 1880s. Its role in 1931 was to work with the administration and faculty in establishing links between classroom activities and the world of business.[29] Of the first twelve Nichols Junior College advisors, generally well-known business men and educators from New England and New York, six were parents of students who were in the business administration program at New Hampton School. Frederick Smith, the New Hampton School headmaster, was an adviser; so was

Chart 2.1. Operating Philosophies and Responsibilities at Nichols in 1940

Classification	- Junior college
Guiding Philosophy	- *in loco parentis* (acting in place of parent)
General Attitude	- Focus on welfare of student
President	- Responsibility to parents
	- Chairs all committees
	- Meets all committees weekly
Presidential	- President's house on campus
President teaching	- Yes
Faculty	
Instructional	- Teaching - 15 hours a week
Required:	- Advising (student organizations)
	- Coaching
	- Dormitory Master
	- Attend campus events
	- Live on campus
	- Classes Saturday A.M.
Faculty Number	- 9, with 5 part-time
Students	- Attend all meals (sit-down meals)
	- Attend weekly convocations
	- Attend all classes
	- Follow all rules including grooming and dress codes
Curriculum	- Most courses required
	- Business education concentration
Staff – PR & Fund raising	- None
Automobile Policy	- None stated
Yearly Costs	- Board, room, and tuition (year) $985.00
Enrollment	- 163

Sources: *Nichols Junior College Bulletin, 1940–1941* (1940); Refer also to Clark Kerr, in association with Marian Gade and Maureen Lawaoka, *Higher Education Cannot Escape History: Issues for the Twenty-first Century* (Albany, N.Y.: State University of New York Press, 1994), 234–239.

Fred E. Corbin, then superintendent of schools in nearby Southbridge and president of the Nichols Academy Board of Trustees, as well as a former Academy student.

The Academy-College agreement made it possible for Nichols Junior College to begin with little investment. Smith and Conrad only had to acquire household furnishings, school supplies, dormitory and athletic equipment and fixtures, bedding, dishes, linen, as well as automobiles and other property to be used in connection with the "work of said school."[30] These modest costs were covered by anticipated institutional income.

Conrad and Smith had valuable assistance. Dr. Quincy H. Merrill of the Academy trustees was crucial to helping to keep the new school's initial development on track. A long-time inhabitant of Dudley Hill and prominent area physician, he had championed the efforts of the New Hampshire educators to become tenants on the Hill. It was possible for the new college to locate in Dudley due to his ability and willingness to work with both the Academy trustees and the junior college administrators. He acted as a liaison between the Trustees and the new college president, as well as becoming his close friend and long-time confidant. One observer correctly determined that James L. Conrad was able to establish Nichols Junior College "largely through Dr. Merrill's efforts."[31] Between 1931 and 1966, Dr. Merrill chaired the trustee boards of Nichols Academy, Nichols Junior College, and Nichols College of Business Administration. For a brief period during World War II, he also was acting president of Nichols Junior College.

To show their appreciation, Nichols students dedicated the 1937 yearbook to Dr. Merrill for "unselfish devotion to the welfare of Nichols both as physician and Chairman of the Board of Trustees. . . His willingness to help and his geniality have won for him the respect and admiration of the entire student body."[32] Student J. Manuel Calvo correctly noted that Dr. Merrill occupied a "unique place in the history of Nichols."[33] A memorial plaque placed on Alumni Hall dedicated to Dr. Quincy H. Merrill at the time of his death in 1969 states that his "long service to Nichols College [1931–1966] merits the highest honor which the College can bestow." Former President Conrad later referred to him as "the finest man I have ever known – Doctor – Man – Human Being."[34] This was a heartfelt and well-deserved tribute from probably the only person who truly understood Dr. Merrill's full contribution to Nichols College.

But just how new was this plan for Nichols Junior College? Certainly its roots can be identified. The two-year college movement had begun in the mid and far west, but it had not reached Massachusetts. Business administration programs usually were found in large, urban universities, not in rural, south central Massachusetts communities such as Dudley. And, while a student-centered approach was then favored in small, established preparatory schools, it generally was not found in city colleges of business administration.

It was quite remarkable that an old, rural, former Massachusetts academy considered leasing its facilities and entrusting the vision of its founder to a relatively untested plan of another educational operation. Nonetheless, the new junior college of business administration was relying initially on long-accepted operational approaches frequently part of an *in loco parentis* role that featured close student contact between the College and the student and a structured curriculum with few electives. From an institutional perspective, President Conrad noted that the Academy trustees had "reorganized" the institution as a junior college of business administration and executive training. This in itself was unique. But it was not so much that the roots of the educational plan were old; the question in 1931 was about the future.

September 21, 1931

The day was fair with some cloudiness and slowly rising temperatures when the new two-year college opened on Dudley Hill. For the rest of the world, however, September 21, 1931, was not as serene or promising. Newspaper headlines announced European stock exchanges closed that day, Great Britain went off the gold standard, and Japanese troops landed again in China. Closer to home, the crowd at the American Legion convention, where President Herbert Hoover was speaking, loudly chanted: "We want beer."[35] But, while international challenges and everyday frustrations may have greatly bothered most Americans, they were somewhat distant for those on Dudley Hill that day.

Nichols Junior College of Business Administration and Executive Training began under conditions termed by a local newspaper as "auspicious and promising."[36] Sixty-five students from nine states and one foreign country moved into Conant Hall and Budleigh Towers (the new name for Budleigh Hall), the college's two dormitories.[37] These remodeled facilities were referred to by the administration as "second to none," although this may have stretched the point.[38] Of the first Nichols Junior College students, 27 came from Massachusetts, nine from New Hampshire, eight from New York, six from Connecticut, and four from Rhode Island.[39]

Nichols Dining Hall, 1933–1934, said to be "spacious and attractive."
Source: Nichols Junior College, *Catalog*, 1933–34, n.p.

Dudley Hill and the new Junior College had much scenic beauty and superb 19th century architecture to offer visitors and new students. The College's setting was carefully described by the new college administrators as having a "desirable remoteness."[40] The scene itself was truly picturesque when one approached Dudley Hill on Center Road from the north. First to come into view on the west or right was a vista created by a series of towers extending south along Center Road. At the top of the Hill was the magnificent Gothic tower of the First Congregational Church – the Conant Memorial Church – built by architect Charles Francis Wilcox and Dudley-born industrialist Hezekiah Conant. The church was to serve as the College's chapel on special occasions, including baccalaureate and graduation services, although it was not part of the junior college or the Academy. Several hundred feet to the South was the tower of the Academy building designed by Worcester architect Elbridge Boyden & Son and also financed by Conant. This structure was said to be seventy-six feet high, four feet shorter than the Church tower. The Conant Library and Observatory building, located next to the Academy, also designed and financed by Boyden and Conant, had a domed tower for its observatory and telescopes.

A hundred yards or so to the south of the Conant-built Academy buildings, but on the east or left side of Center Road, were buildings of the former Conant estate. They also had their towers. The larger structure was the College's main administration building, now called "Budleigh Towers," with several tower-like chimneys and roof peaks reflecting its Queen Anne design. Finally, the new gymnasium, formerly the Conant stables, facing Budleigh Towers, easily belonged in this group with its impressive cupola. Not surprisingly, the Junior College's first seal featured the image of the Academy Tower; the College's yearbook was named "The Tower."[41] Unfortunately this image logically disappeared after the damage done to the Academy building and its tower by the Hurricane of 1938.

Second, a new arrival to the Hill could not fail to notice that the roads of the former Conant estate were lined with magnificent elm and copper beech trees. They formed the backdrop for college graduation ceremonies later to be held on the south side of the new Budleigh Hall, when weather permitted. With time, their stately presence became part of the new institution's developing traditions. Fortunately a number of trees remained even after the 1938 Hurricane. Their importance to the early college is suggested by the Nichols "Alma Mater," in place by 1942, which contains the phrase: ". . . neath copper beeches. . . "[42]

On June 4, 1932, nine months after the Junior College's first registration day, eleven students – the Class of 1932 – received certificates for completing the two-year program.[43] They had taken their first year at New Hampton. Quite fittingly, the Baccalaureate Sermon for the Class of 1932 was given by the Reverend Dr. Charles L. Goodell of New York and Dudley Hill, formerly president and long-time member of the Nichols Academy Board of Trustees and resident of Dudley's Black Tavern.[44]

The Class of 1932.
Source: *The Tower*, 1932 n.p.

"From an Absolute Beginning"[45]

Enrollment at the Junior College increased gradually from 65 to 163 students between 1931 and 1940. (See Chart 2.2.) This number was achieved despite the fact that total college enrollment at New England colleges generally declined during the depression years of the 1930s. The new institution was able to enroll 152 students after the completion of a new dormitory, Merrill Hall, in 1937. This group, 91 Juniors (first year students) and 61 Seniors (second year students), comprised one of the young college's larger pre-war student bodies.[46]

A notable feature of this student body between 1931 and 1936 was its wide-ranging geographic nature. This aspect of institutional growth was formally recognized in 1936 by President Conrad at a College convocation when he brought together the flags of the 20 states and ten foreign countries represented on the campus by Nichols students since 1931. Thereafter, a flag from each newly represented state or nation was added to this gallery of flags located in the Club House.[47] In 1942, the College reported that students from 28 states and 14 foreign countries had enrolled at Nichols over the previous eleven years.[48] In 1964, these flags, then 91 in number, were hung from the ceiling of the new field house (later named Chalmers Field House).

Much had to be done to face the challenges of the 1930s. It was one thing to formally announce institutional goals, it was quite another to achieve them. Newness dictated the need for extensive missionary work; a new idea had to

Chart 2.2. Nichols Junior College, Enrollment, 1931–1943

September	Enrollment	Source
1931	65	*Southbridge News*, Sept. 22, 1931.
1932	91	*Webster Evening Times*, Sept. 22, 1932.
1933	70	*Webster Evening Times*, Sept. 18, 1933.
1934	80	*Webster Evening Times*, Sept. 18, 1934.
1935	83	*Webster Evening Times*, Sept. 17, 1935.
1936	105	*Webster Times*, Sept. 21, 1936.
1937	111	*Webster Times*, Sept. 27, 1937.
1938	138	*Webster Times*, Sept. 19, 1938.
1939	152	*Nichols Budget*, Oct. 6, 1939.
1940	163	Nichols Newsclip, 1940–1941.
1941	145	*Nichols Budget*, Oct. 15, 1941.
1942	No record available.	
1943	College closed in summer for duration.	

be explained and promoted. New programs had to be described and then accepted. The focus of the new Nichols curriculum – business education – had not appeared before in central New England. In effect, the new institution had to combine an academic program developed elsewhere with a somewhat non-receptive educational environment in Massachusetts that was more accepting of four-year liberal arts colleges.

To add to the potential complications, the new junior college was the product of two partnerships. Each had to function properly for it to succeed. The first, Nichols, Inc., was formed by the two New Hampton administrators, Frederick Smith and James L. Conrad, and was responsible for the educational conduct and academic substance of Nichols Junior College. While Smith and Conrad had successfully worked together at New Hampton, they now had to function at separate locations in different states and in different institutional surroundings.

Furthermore, leasing the campus from the Nichols Academy trustees created yet another quasi-partnership. A similar arrangement between the Nichols Academy trustees and the Bethel Bible Institute from 1923 to 1926 had not been successful and Smith and Conrad knew this.[49] The future of their junior college was hardly assured. And, while the leased Conant-built Academy buildings and those on the former Conant estate offered examples of rural New England splendor and attractiveness, their ages, designs, and construction materials made them vulnerable to time, fire, and storm – as well as additional generations of students. During the first decade, two buildings on the former Conant estate (Budleigh Towers and the Dining Hall) were destroyed by fire while the Academy building was seriously damaged by the "Hurricane of 1938."

The school that began in September 1931 was designated a junior college of business administration and executive training for a specific reason. Clearly the title was intended to attract young men, as well as their parents, who desired their entry into the upper levels of American business management. Many were already there by virtue of their family connections; now they had to understand their roles and responsibilities. Of note is the fact that the mention of "executive training" came before "business administration" in all Nichols advertisements. An early charter granted to Conrad and Smith stated that Nichols, Inc. was to offer college "courses for business and executive training."[50] This distinction was intended to separate Nichols from institutions offering business programs concentrating on areas such as secretarial science.[51] The Dudley institution was established to provide a formal educational background for future leaders in business.

But much had not been anticipated. Conrad and Smith had not understood the difficulties of operating an institution of higher learning in Massachusetts. Soon after students had registered at Nichols in 1931, President Conrad learned that Massachusetts educational institutions were prohibited from using the title of "junior college" (or "community college" or "institute") without full legislative approval.[52] Apparently unaware of this regulation, the writers of the first Nichols catalog in 1931 referred to the Dudley school as "Nichols Junior College of Business Administration and Executive Training."[53] The next year, however, the college catalog changed its title page and page headings to read: "Nichols, a Junior College, Dudley, Massachusetts."[54] Formal permission from the state to use "Junior College" in its title was received two years later, but only after a certain amount of anguish and confusion including two years of observation by the Massachusetts State Department of Education.[55]

THE TWO-YEAR COLLEGE EMERGES

A degree-granting privilege was next. This, too, was a difficult challenge in Massachusetts where the educational environment tended to favor four-year liberal arts colleges. Nonetheless, after an advisory inspection by the State Department of Education and an appearance by President Conrad before the Educational Commission of the State Legislature, a bill was introduced, passed by the Massachusetts House and Senate, and signed by the Governor on April 14, 1938, authorizing Nichols Junior College to award the Associate of Business Administration degree (ABA).[56] This was the first degree of its type to be authorized by the state. It automatically entitled Nichols graduates to receive third-year status at a state four-year college of business administration. It was first awarded at Nichols in 1938. Local State Representatives Wilfred P. Bazinet and Joseph O'Kane correctly received credit for assisting President Conrad in what was a legislative and educational achievement at that time. While this had taken five additional years and much effort, it was one of the high points of the institution's first decade as it provided Nichols graduates with a greater ability to transfer without losing academic credit. This was a purpose of the school.

Clearly, much of the new college's success during its first ten years was based on its curriculum. Four, year-long, required courses – accounting, economics, English, and business law – some covering a two-year period, made up the Nichols curriculum first introduced in the New Hampton program. (Refer to Appendix A for a comparison of the curricular of New Hampton and Nichols.) After 1931, courses such as public speaking and ethics were added to a now somewhat crowded Nichols student schedule. Taken altogether, these courses were considered by the College administration as "fundamental to business and life amid cultural surroundings."[57] Business courses at Nichols were required in the student's first year of college, unlike the traditional university approach to business education which did not offer its professional courses until the student's third year. This was a basic and significant distinction as well as an important attraction for incoming students.

One important Nichols curriculum innovation occurred in 1938 when what was then a unique elective course in psychology became a required course. This was in line with President Conrad's earlier thinking regarding the preparation of students for careers in business. This new course featured required testing for students, work on the selection of a career, understanding one's personality, recognizing personal needs, and learning the "art of effective living," among others. It also included collateral readings for developmental areas such as studying, learning, and thinking. Another feature of what came to be a two-year course was the requirement that each student meet individually two or three times a year with the course leaders, generally from the Psychology Department, to discuss the results of testing and the need to identify individual learning weaknesses. This course added a significant yet sometime overlooked dimension to the new Dudley school's academic program by focusing directly on the personal and intellectual development of each individual. One Nichols instructor concluded that Nichols was "one of the few schools in the country that was in a position to offer such advantages. . . ."[58]

During these early years, President Conrad made his first attempt to develop a four-year program. This probably was a goal from the beginning. Originally he had formed the two-year business program by including a number of courses normally found in the third and fourth years of traditional four-year university business programs. According to its catalog of 1932–1933, "Nichols offers its students the required courses of the ordinary four-year college of business administration, with enough electives and cultural courses to give the student a well-balanced education, either of a terminal or a preparatory nature, in two years."[59] This was a new approach in 1931.

But he did not stop there. At a convocation on January 20, 1939, the Nichols president announced what he saw as "an entirely new plan in the field of education."[60] This included a proposed Nichols four-year program being designed with Psychologist Arthur Miller mentioned as one of the "main cogs" in its development.[61] The third year of this proposed program had the Nichols student working away from Dudley in his field of interest while maintaining frequent contact with his Nichols advisors. The fourth year saw students returning to Dudley for courses and discussions directly related to their work experience.

Not surprisingly, the new "Four-Year" program attracted a number of interested students in 1939. The first candidates were selected by the faculty on the basis of attitude, academic standing, and personality.[62] Four were scheduled to begin their third years of the new program working away from Dudley, but administrative indecision and the threat of war apparently interfered with its implementation.[63] Nevertheless, as late as 1942, the College was still seeking to establish a third year for students who had been selected to be members of a "Nichols Executive Training Group" based on a comprehensive psychological analysis and a "Personalized Executive Analysis Chart" developed by the Nichols Psychology Department. Wartime demands halted further development.[64] While this program was not revived in its entirety, parts of it would go forward after 1945.[65]

Plans for further expansion of Nichols programs also can be identified. A move was considered in 1933 to offer business courses to students from baccalaureate or university programs.[66] In this case, the President indicated that a one-year program was being designed for graduates of liberal arts colleges, although there is no record of any enrollees. Such a program was not new, but it would have been a challenging step for a school that had just begun as a two-year college. This program eventually materialized in 1975 when the first MBA student was admitted to Nichols College nearly twenty years after Nichols became a four-year college.

Curriculum development at the Dudley college during the 1930s clearly reflected current thinking regarding business education. Results of just-completed surveys of college business programs across the country offer important comparisons. For instance, these wide-ranging studies found that English was considered of primary importance by business students in most of the country. These same business students logically favored courses involving business activities or analysis, as well as courses examining the social setting of business and economic life. Then too, there was general agreement regarding the need for an instructional focus that was organized around seminars, research, field and laboratory work as well as the use of business cases and current business problems. Foreign languages fell into the least favorable category for business students.[67]

These findings were mirrored by a poll of Nichols students in 1939. Seniors (or second year Nichols students) considered their most valuable courses to be English, then finance and accounting. Juniors (or first year Nichols students) selected accounting as their most valuable course, followed by English, and then economics.[68]

The Nichols administration also focused on promoting the development of an "executive" attitude throughout its entire program. Toward that end, "modern" classrooms and equipment were designed to accommodate classes of no more than twelve to allow the student "twice the attention" since he was in a class one-half the usual size.[69] One Nichols classroom was set aside as a "director's room" where problems in the field of business were discussed by students acting as "directors." Instructors then pointed out the "errors of reason" at the end of these directors' meetings.[70]

In the process of clarifying institutional goals, a sharper picture of the College's formal role emerged. Six years after its beginning, Nichols Junior College dedicated itself to the following goals:

- to educate young men to a conception of executive requirements and problems;
- to provide the tools necessary for a successful foundation in business;
- to prepare young men to be of service to their community through a broad understanding of social, economic and political problems;
- to inculcate an appreciation of the finer things of life by study and association;
- to strive to contribute to the advancement of ethical and moral standards in business.[71]

Institutional development required the creation of an administration and faculty capable of contributing to desired goals and purposes. Generally accepted junior college standards specified that faculty had to have at least one year of graduate study and should not be required to teach more than 18 hours per week. A maximum class was not to have more than 30 students in programs composed of either terminal courses or courses providing transfer credits.[72] In fact, Nichols faculty members were expected to do more. Student-faculty interaction beyond the classroom was important and required. Additional faculty responsibilities included advising student activities, attending college events, having Saturday classes, coaching Nichols athletic teams, and functioning as dormitory supervisors. After beginning with a faculty of six, Nichols Junior College had the equivalent of ten full-time faculty members by 1940.[73] (See Chart 2.1.)

Reference to the activities of two Nichols faculty members will help to understand their roles. Robert H. Eaton, with degrees from Dartmouth College and the University of Connecticut, began at Nichols in 1936. He offered courses in economics, advertising, and accounting. According to a Nichols yearbook, "His pleasing personality made him a campus favorite." He was referred to as the "Beau Brummel" of the campus as well as being voted the "best teacher" by the 1939 Senior Class. He also coached soccer. Further, he was the dormitory master in Conant Hall where he lived with his wife. When World War II began, he became dean of the college until the Nichols Junior College trustees "recessed" the school in 1943. After a number of years in industry during and after the war, he returned to Nichols as a part-time instructor and then became dean of men/registrar in 1962 until his retirement in 1979.[74]

Another, Karl A. Hill, came to Nichols in 1940 with the degree of master of commercial science (MCS) from the Amos Tuck School at Dartmouth College. Aside from his academic specialties of finance and marketing, he spent a considerable amount of time as the faculty advisor to the social committee, as athletic director, and as an assistant coach in football and baseball. He and his family lived in Budleigh Hall where he was dormitory director. His career after Nichols included a number of years as dean of the Amos Tuck School at Dartmouth College.[75]

Over the first decade, President Conrad also added necessary administrative assistance by appointing Bradford Kingman as dean of students in 1933. Dean Kingman, who had been at the New Hampton School with the Nichols President, was an extremely well-qualified leader and strong student adviser as well as a successful director of an active Nichols Dramatic Club and coach of the golf team. When he left Nichols, he became headmaster of preparatory schools in Worcester, Massachusetts, and Kansas City, Missouri.

Wesley Spencer, with degrees in physical education and education and also a former assistant headmaster at New Hampton, was appointed dean at Nichols when Kingman left. He assisted the Psychology program and directed the Glee Club while remaining at the College until 1942.[76]

While internal adjustments in curriculum and basic institutional directions are relatively easy to follow, the actual place of Nichols among pre-war New England junior colleges needs clarification. Fortunately some contemporary studies make this task easier. In one, Nichols was found to be one of two New England junior colleges for men (Tilton Junior College in New Hampshire was the other) and one of two specifically committed to offering two years of transferable course work.[77] Nichols, however, was the only New England junior college that focused on business education. Another study completed in 1939 identifies 22 junior colleges in New England, with ten in Massachusetts.[78] Again, Nichols was the only junior college in Massachusetts to enroll men and

Bradford M. Kingman,
A.B., A.M., Dean,
Nichols Junior College,
1933–1938.

Wesley G. Spencer,
BPE, Ed.M., Dean,
Nichols Junior College,
1938–1942.

the one New England junior college preparing its students to transfer to a business program.[79] Most of the courses taken at Nichols were transferable to the third and fourth years of the traditional university business program.

In 1936, the Nichols administration reported that nineteen different colleges and universities had granted Nichols graduates the opportunity to transfer to their baccalaureate degree programs.[80] When Nichols received the authority to grant the ABA degree from the Commonwealth of Massachusetts in 1938, students could expect an even simpler transfer process. Within a short period, the Central Association of Colleges also recognized Nichols Junior College thereby expanding the opportunity for Nichols graduates to transfer credits to a still greater number of colleges and universities.[81] A significant number of Nichols Junior College graduates eventually received their bachelor's degrees elsewhere.

Nichols may have been alone on Dudley Hill in 1931, but it was not the only junior college in the area. Two others existed in nearby Thompson, Connecticut: Marot Junior College and St. Mary's College, later renamed Marianapolis. Marot was established originally in 1913 as a private women's college with programs on the high school and junior college levels. It was closed in September 1942.[82] St. Mary's College, begun by the Order of the Marian Fathers of the Immaculate Conception on the former Norman B. Ream estate in Thompson, Connecticut, as a college for young men of Lithuanian descent, opened just a few days before Nichols registered its first students. Two years later it became Marianapolis College established to preserve the Lithuanian language and culture through high school and junior college courses. Marianapolis eventually awarded several baccalaureate degrees.

Both Thompson colleges were actively involved in early Nichols student activities. Marianapolis was considered a "traditional" Nichols football opponent by 1933. In a different role, Marot's women students held numerous social events such as tea dances and combined glee club concerts that regularly included Nichols students. Neither Marot nor Marianapolis College opened after World War II, although Marianapolis Preparatory School did continue.[83]

How, in 1941, did Nichols Junior College measure up to goals set ten years earlier? In what is essentially an end-of-the-decade summary, the College catalog of 1942 presents some important highlights. While college catalogs are self-serving and promotional by design, the following points seem supportable. For one, theoretical instruction at Nichols had been balanced by contacts with business and industry through Advisory Council meetings as originally intended. Further, the student remained central to the program. For instance, remedial courses were being offered, a reading program had been introduced, student class standing was evaluated every three weeks, and students were required to attend all conferences regarding individual academic performances. In the process, a firmer instructional philosophy emerged that was supported by its new program in psychology focusing on the "growth and development of the entire individual." And, aside from its academic goals, a Nichols education was intended to promote "principles of gentlemanliness and culture."[84]

College and Campus Become One

Without question, the Junior College's successful start would not have been possible without the original leasing agreement between Conrad and Smith and the Nichols Academy Board of Trustees. The first decade, however, did see some subtle but meaningful changes in the Nichols campus. Most, if not all, were in response to obvious needs such as rebuilding due to two devastating fires destroying Budleigh Towers and the Dining Hall in 1931 and 1937 and the significant damage to the Academy building caused by the hurricane of 1938. Increasing enrollments required some expansion. Other renovations were necessary to create a more collegiate-like appearance and to counter a long-existing preparatory school or academy image. And, ironically, it was the success of Nichols Junior College that made the leasing agreement with the Academy Trustees virtually unworkable by 1941.

Problems for the school began several months after students arrived on the Hill. Budleigh Towers, the magnificent former summer home of Hezekiah Conant, was completely destroyed by a devastating fire less than three months after the first students registered. Fortunately, no one was injured on December 2, 1931, in a fire that started during morning classes in a defective chimney and quickly leveled the wooden building. The student body was notified by telephone in their classes in the Academy building and responded immediately. Nonetheless, some students lost everything. Several days later, the *Nichols Budget*, the College newspaper, reflected on the fire and its effect on the students noting: "We are all more closely united than we were before. . . . we know, and the world knows that Nichols can, does, and shall go on in the face of misfortune."[85]

Support for the College quickly appeared. Classes resumed the following day with many displaced students offered rooms by townspeople.[86] This was in the tradition of the Academy. Others moved in with friends in Conant Hall as plans soon were announced by Academy trustees regarding the construction of a new building for nearly 80 students. This new structure was named Budleigh Hall and designed as a traditional college dormitory with running water and wash basins in every room – a luxury in 1932. Importantly, the new dormitory was to be ready for the following September. Its student capacity was more than twice that of old Budleigh Towers.

And, if this were not enough for the young school, another fire hit the College community several years later when its dining hall burned to the ground. This had been an original outbuilding on the Conant estate. Remodeled in 1931 and enlarged in 1933 to handle increased enrollment, the small wooden building was destroyed on March 30, 1937, by a fire that started in a chimney. The gym next door was utilized as a dining hall with a new building scheduled for construction that summer.[87] This new dining hall, a larger building, also contained rooms for students and a dormitory master at a total cost of about $15,000. It was constructed a few feet from where the original dining hall had stood.[88]

Discussions between President Conrad and the Academy trustees regarding the rebuilding of these two structures became contentious when the Nichols president insisted on adding rooms to each new building. While enabling the College to increase its student body, this also raised the values of the Academy's buildings and resulted in higher insurance rates. The issue of replacing smaller buildings with larger ones was to emerge again after the hurricane in 1938.

Then too, there were other factors influencing the Junior College's use and development of Academy properties. This included a desire to give a more collegiate look to the campus, the need to better utilize available space, and a need to increase enrollment. Combined, they put in motion the first construction spurt in the young College's history. The first decade of the College's existence saw several buildings being redesigned to look toward Center Road. A new entrance for the gym saw it facing west consistent with the placement of the main entrance of newly built Budleigh Hall, also constructed to face westward and overlook the College's athletic fields. Through the cooperation of the Class of 1936, four large pillars were purchased for the College with two being placed on the new front of the Gym.[89] The other two went on the front of Conant Hall. A face-lifting for this building was approved by the Nichols Academy trustees who agreed to remove the Conant porch and replace it with a "dignified entrance."[90] Later the student newspaper, while bemoaning the loss of a comfortable porch, conceded that the building's appearance was now "modern looking."[91]

These and other moves were accomplished just as President Conrad was taking another step to deal with a projected increase in enrollment. In 1935, with his wife, Annette Conrad, he purchased a 2.7 acre tract of land southeast of Budleigh Hall from the Academy trustees for one dollar.[92] He then constructed a small two-story wooden dormitory in 1937 on this land and named it Merrill Hall for Dr. Quincy H. Merrill. This building was quickly filled with students.[93]

Merrill Hall, completed in 1937,
was the first new dormitory constructed
for Nichols students. Source: The *1941 Ledger*, n.p.

Just as Merrill Hall was first being utilized by students, the Hurricane of 1938 hit Dudley Hill. Winds of 120 mph severely damaged the Academy building on September 21, 1938. Several classes were being held at the time and a few students received minor cuts and bruises.[94] College officials immediately evacuated the upper floors of Budleigh and Conant Halls fearing the storm's force might damage these buildings as well.[95] Fortunately, except for the loss of a number of large elms and copper beech trees, there was no further damage

Damage on Dudley Hill caused by the Hurricane of 1938. Pictured are the Academy building after the hurricane and views of the destruction looking north on Center Road from Merrill Hall. The writer is a participant-observer. Source: Pictures of Hurricane damage in Nichols Archives and Conrad family photographs.

to the campus and its inhabitants. Not surprisingly, the College was closed for a week because of widespread damage in the area. During this period, a small group of students accepted the assignment of protecting the College from possible looting. (For a first-hand account of the hurricane hitting Dudley Hill, see Appendix B.)

Work began almost immediately on the reconstruction of the hurricane-damaged Academy building. This renovation was planned by President Conrad who again sought additional space pending the approval of the Academy trustees. The remodeled building was to have nine classrooms, or four more than before, as well as extra office space. The first phase of this rebuilding was accomplished by the Academy trustees within a year. The second and final phase, involving an addition to the northeast front section of the building, was not to be completed until 1958, long after it was acquired by the Junior College. Unfortunately, the magnificent Academy tower had to be torn down because the hurricane damaged its supporting structure.

And, again, the Academy Board of Trustees had to deal with the problems resulting from the destruction of its long-held property and the desire of the young College's administration to expand its facilities. The 1938 hurricane was the final straw. It was to lead to a redefining moment in the young College's history.

But change had already begun for the Dudley Hill College. During the institution's first decade, the increased growth of Nichols Junior College had been paralleled by adjustments in its own organizational structure. Initially, in 1931, the Nichols Academy Board of Trustees had leased all its property to Frederick Smith and James L. Conrad who then assigned the lease to Nichols, Inc., the corporation which they formed.[96] For a brief period, its corporate name was Nichols Junior College, Inc., but was changed back to Nichols, Inc., in 1933. Its incorporators were listed as Frederick Smith, James L. Conrad, and George R. Stobbs, Attorney.[97]

Originally, the Academy trustees agreed to carry insurance on all its campus properties up to $66,000. However, it was not possible to predict the extent of campus destruction to occur between 1931 and 1938 or to recognize the determination of the young College's president to expand this campus. In 1936, Nichols, Inc., received a scheduled lease renewal from the Academy trustees for 25 years. Concurrently, President Conrad purchased all the assets of Nichols, Inc., including those of Frederick Smith.[98] At that point, the Academy trustees considered offering James L. Conrad employment for twenty-five years, although no agreement was finalized.[99] By 1937, the president's sister, Margaret M. Conrad, became a stockholder in Nichols, Inc.[100] Most income, if there was some, went into enlarging campus facilities and purchasing several nearby homes.

Not surprisingly, a number of general disagreements occurred between the Academy trustees and the President of Nichols Junior College between 1931 to 1938. On one occasion, the Academy trustees notified President Conrad that there could be no plant expansion until all accounts the College had with Academy trustees were paid, including "rent, taxes, boiler, etc."[101] In several cases, the Junior College used its monies to refurbish Academy-owned buildings; in another, the College president constructed his own dormitory – Merrill Hall.

With few options, the Academy trustees on these occasions generally appointed committees to meet with the energetic president. Arguments simply increased when the Academy building was badly damaged by the hurricane in 1938. At this point, yet another trustee committee went to work carefully examining the terms of its lease with the Junior College. This committee then worked for a year "to evolve a plan which would amicably adjust all the elements at issue in a manner designed to establish the whole situation [Academy-Junior College relationship] on a sounder and more permanent and equitable basis."[102]

An Academy Decision

According to the Academy committee's report completed in June 1941, the Academy trustees were responsible for Academy property (the Junior College buildings and campus) leased for 20 more years, or until 1961. Conrad's rebuilding and upgrading had raised the assessed value of this property from $15,000 in 1931 to $39,300 by 1941. The Academy committee concluded that invested Academy funds and rent income now was barely adequate to pay increasing insurance costs and taxes, to complete repairs, and to fulfill additional responsibilities related to a long-held fund – the Hancock Trust Fund. The Academy trustee committee concluded that the trustees could not assume further liabilities other than those of "a very minor nature."

At the same time, the committee raised the possibility that the Junior College might leave the Dudley Hill property if it were not allowed to expand. Probably this option had been mentioned by President Conrad in their discussions. Extending this thinking further, the trustee committee determined that without the benefits of a going concern, such as the present institution, Academy trustees' assets "would be extinguished by taxes, repairs and other expenses within a relatively short time." In short, because of the Junior College's success and obvious need to expand, the Academy could no longer afford the arrangement made in 1931.[103]

To complete its report, the Academy trustee committee also examined the Junior College's position. In a careful description of the school's success, Conrad was seen by the Academy trustee committee as operating his venture for 10 years achieving steady development and goodwill, with "splendid" future possibilities. The Academy trustee committee determined that the degree granting privilege authorized by the Commonwealth was a vital and distinguishing asset and should be "indissolubly identified with the property of the Academy." This was a significant and transforming moment for both the Academy and the Junior College. The Academy trustee committee reasoned that the value of the property, having more than doubled under President Conrad, now was "contingent upon occupation by the College." It believed that the value would disappear if "the college were not there."[104]

This report also considered the need for future institutional development on the part of the Junior College. The Academy committee concluded that potential donors to the Junior College, and even the lessee himself, would be reluctant to contribute to future construction or improvements on leased land. The Academy report also noted that the expansion and continued growth of the Junior College were important to Dudley and adjacent towns. The subsequent recommendation of the Academy committee then went to the point: "Only by the sale of the physical property can the Academy be relieved of its burden and at the same time protect its Trust [the Hancock Trust]." Its conclusion was that the sale of Academy property to Nichols Junior College would release the Academy of all obligations and provide the Junior College with growth opportunities resulting in "an organization which would merit the enthusiastic support of all persons interested."[105] Indeed, this Academy committee report was farseeing.

A brief period of correspondence and debate followed. A newly formed Nichols Junior College of Business Administration Board of Trustees made an offer to purchase the Academy property in December 1941. The Junior College's charter incorporated some of the original commitments made by Conrad and Smith. According to this Junior College Charter, the College was to open Conant Library for Dudley citizens, promote the "ethical, social and intellectual culture" of the community, and "maintain" free tuition for worthy students from Dudley. These had been Academy responsibilities. The new Junior College charter was approved just as the Nichols Academy Board of Trustees was considering the sale of its campus. This timing was not accidental. (See a section of the "Charter of Nichols Junior College, December 23, 1941," Appendix C.)

After an exchange of correspondence and debate in Academy trustee meetings, a motion was made and seconded on December 23, 1941, "that the Trustees accept the offer of Nichols Junior College to buy the real estate and buildings of the Academy located in Dudley, Massachusetts, for $33,200."[106] In addition, several Academy mortgages were to be transferred to the Junior College and claims by the Junior College against the Academy were to be dropped. This set the value of the transaction at $62,428 with the sale recorded on April 6, 1942.[107] The terms of the agreement required that the Junior College

New Budleigh Hall, 1933.
Source: Nichols Junior College, *Catalog*, 1933–34, 6.

pay $1,000 per year for 20 years. In the meantime, President Conrad assigned his lease for the campus to the newly organized Board of Trustees of Nichols Junior College, now preparing to become a non-profit organization.[108] Nichols, Inc. was dissolved in May 1942.[109] The transfer of the Academy property ended formal interaction between the Academy and the College in 1942. This was a pivotal point in the history of the College that was determined by the hurricane of 1938.

Unfortunately, whatever elation might have been felt at that moment was greatly dampened by the fact that Japan attacked Pearl Harbor on December 7, 1941, and the United States was now at war. Eight months before that, in April 1941, President Conrad had been called to active duty with the U.S. Army Quartermaster Corps. And, probably because of the war, the first formal announcement of this purchase of the Academy property was not made by the Junior College until 1947, five years after the actual event.

An important although delayed statement eventually made in the *Nichols Alumnus* offered additional reasons for the transfer of the Academy's property. According to this publication, there were some concerns during the 1930s on the part of Junior College administrators and Academy trustees that the College's plan and policies had been inconsistent with the original Charter of Nichols Academy.

Two such instances were mentioned in the *Nichols Alumnus*: coeducation and curriculum. For one, the Academy had been co-educational while the Junior College was all-male.[110] Second, the Junior College curriculum did not include specified subjects such as foreign languages and liberal arts courses referred to in the original Academy Charter.[111] These inconsistencies apparently had been intentionally overlooked by the trustees of the Academy and by College administrations during the 1930s. Regardless, this justification of the 1942 property transaction states that "... for the purposes of simplification and coordination, it would serve all interests to have the Trustees of the College take complete jurisdiction of the Dudley Hill campus and its buildings."[112]

This ended the existence of the Junior College originally formed by the partnership between the Academy trustees and the Junior College administrators. It also ended a remarkable and unparalleled 123-year leadership effort made by the Academy trustees as they sought to carry forward the visions of Amasa Nichols and Hezekiah Conant. This task was now the responsibility of the College.

Nichols Junior College gained control of its campus and now became a college within itself. This was a significant moment greatly blurred by the arrival of war. The future, which had been hopeful, but somewhat murky in 1931, was still in doubt in 1942 and would remain so until 1946, if not beyond.

CHAPTER 3

Nichols Junior College Seal, 1937.
A second version of the College seal appearing in the College yearbook, The *1937 Ledger*, was professionally designed with no perceivable changes otherwise.
Source for seal (1937): The *1937 Ledger*, 2.

"Ye Strong Sons of Nichols," 1931~1946

> Ye strong sons of Nichols, join in the chorus
> Neath copper beeches
> Raise your song.
> Thy sons Alma Mater, rally around thee
> Pledging their service
> Eternally.
> Bound by a loyalty still undivided
> Giving allegiance
> Nichols to thee.
>
> Unknown writer, *Nichols Alma Mater*, circa 1942.
> Source: The *1942 Ledger*, 2.

In his classic *Tale of Two Cities*, Charles Dickens writes of "the spring of hope . . . the winter of despair."[1] For the Dudley junior college, the period between 1931 and 1941 surely had been the "the best of times."[2] Nichols had received the authority to grant the Associate of Business Administration degree (ABA), more than doubled its enrollment during a depression period, applauded its student newspaper as it achieved national awards, secured a nickname and mascot (Bisons), adopted the lyrics and music for an Alma Mater, experienced

59

Nichols Student Body, 1931–1932.
Source: *The Tower, 1932,* n.p.

undefeated teams in soccer and football (unbeaten, but tied), and acquired an established campus with a history to go with its academic program. For all involved – students, faculty, alumni and administrators – this had been a challenging, but successful time of growth. Nonetheless, Nichols Junior College students, like college students elsewhere, experienced a gamut of human conditions and events during this period. These ranged from carefree college days, the impact of the Great Depression, prohibition's end, the threat of war, and the horrors of battle.

This era offers evidence of remarkable contrasts in the lives of young men at Nichols. They went from being successful pioneers in a new educational venture to students scrambling to take advantage of programs established by the Junior College and the United States military services to allow them to finish their college programs. These efforts failed when America entered a period of all-out war. The Junior College and its students who, before 1941, experienced hope and success, then gradually slid into their "winters of despair." Without a student body in 1943, the Nichols Junior College Board of Trustees had no choice but to "recess" the College.

Students enrolling at Nichols Junior College from 1931 to 1943 fall into three specific periods: a pioneer era to 1938; the pre-war time from 1939 to 1941; and the years from 1941 to 1943 when war influenced all decisions and most outcomes. The College itself then experienced yet a fourth period – a "recess" from 1943 to 1946 – when only the barren grounds and empty buildings of a very quiet institution graced the top of Dudley Hill. That it reemerged again in 1946 testifies to the commitment of those involved and to their abilities to endure both the best and worst of these early years.

THE PIONEERS

Student commitment to Nichols during the 1930s was a necessary and vibrant part of the institutional fabric. Members of the first group of students were the pioneers. Their activities swirled around four main themes: academics; athletics, intercollegiate and intramural; college-sponsored non-athletic activities; and, finally, a category best labeled as miscellany and hi-jinks. At the very beginning in 1931, Nichols students were confronted by a new academic plan, a new administration, a partially remodeled campus set on a frequently cold and windy hill, as well as the usual individual and personal challenges of a first-time college experience. They encountered newness, smallness, different ideas (in business education) and leadership styles from administrators and faculty blessed with far more enthusiasm than experience. And this was not all. Over its first decade, the Nichols campus endured two disastrous fires and suffered much damage from a once-in-a-hundred-years hurricane. Throughout, those at Nichols managed remarkably well.

Nichols students were immediately aware of the institution's newness and uniqueness. They also understood their roles as pioneers. This too challenged them. An editor of the student-run college newspaper, the Nichols *Budget*, wrote in 1933 that they realized Nichols was "a new educational idea" and that it was the "first college of its kind in the east."[3] Nichols students also were reminded that they "were pioneers seeking preparation for a better and more productive life [as leaders in business]."[4] It was suggested to fellow students that there was much to be done ". . . before the business school can place its guaranty upon its products so that the world will be sure that the graduate is fit for the practice of his profession. . . ."[5] They were challenged to become professionals in business and most understood this.

Easily recognized, however, was the nature of their institution and they quickly acknowledged its size. William O. Kohnke, a first-year student, was on the Nichols football team when it played the Holy Cross College Freshmen in 1931. Later, Kohnke remembered: "They [the Holy Cross Freshmen] had more players on their team than we had students."[6] Not quite, but he was close. The final score of this game played on the new Nichols field: Holy Cross Freshmen 46, Nichols 0.[7]

Other factors became important for the first Nichols students. They were quickly made aware of the College's commitment to continually improving academic standards. The "quality of undergraduate learning" was a dominating goal for everyone connected with higher education.[8] This was a definite challenge for the new institution. Visits by state legislative review boards and others re-emphasized this point. So did President Conrad, and often. Virtually all Nichols students knew what was involved in the College's beginning.

61

Not surprisingly, however, appreciation from the student body for raising academic standards was not always forthcoming. For instance, the Nichols student body was greatly upset when a 10,000 word theme became part of a second-year English requirement.[9] Later a thesis was added to graduation requirements with little applause from the senior class.[10] On at least one occasion, an editorial in the college newspaper complained about the College's crusade for higher standards.[11] In another instance, harsher study hall rules brought out a student vote not to attend classes. And, when students received word in 1938 that the Massachusetts legislature had granted Nichols the authority to award the ABA degree, the student newspaper, after dutifully noting the student body's appreciation, bemoaned the possibility that this might mean higher standards and an increase in weekly class hours from 15 to 18.[12] But the College was going to be judged by others on the level of the academic performance of its students and most understood this.

Quite logically, Nichols students of the 1930s generally reflected the backgrounds and interests of their families, many were connected to the business world. This conservatism was evidenced by their choices at election time. For instance, just before the 1932 presidential election, a poll of the Nichols student body and faculty gave the incumbent president, Republican Herbert Hoover, 70 votes, while the challenger and eventual winner, Democrat Franklin D. Roosevelt, received only nine.[13] This strong conservative position also was present in the next poll four years later at the depths of the depression which showed 83 Nichols votes for Republican presidential candidate, Alf (Alfred) M. Landon, while only 25 supported President Franklin D. Roosevelt. Nonetheless, he was easily re-elected to his second term.[14] F.D.R. apparently had picked up some additional supporters on Dudley Hill – but not many.

Similar statistics also emerged from a different source. In 1936, the Junior College reported that its student body included the sons of 50 corporation presidents, vice presidents, and company treasurers (out of about 105 students). Six years later, 45 private schools and 17 colleges were represented in the Nichols student body suggesting student and family backgrounds, academic preparation, as well as the ability to afford a college education.[15]

In other aspects, however, the first Nichols students were little different from students elsewhere. It almost goes without saying that they also coveted the right to complain. One editor of the Nichols *Budget* pointed out there was an important maturity underlying much of what was being said by fellow Nichols students. In an article with a seemingly uncomplimentary title of "Nichols Guinea Pigs," he evidenced an underlying pride in his college:

> This experimentation [at Nichols] will go on forever. The heads of the college are too interested in betterment to stop at five years. The older Nichols gets, the prouder Alumni and the prouder we present students

will be. We are sacrificing our own pleasure for the future of Nichols. But at this time we are satisfying one of human nature's greatest pleasures, that of kicking about things. . . . Deep down, we all have to admit we are proud to be members of a promising institution.[16]

Students reported positive results when they headed for jobs before doing further academic work. As war came closer, the College newspaper announced that Nichols was a "Recognized Leader" in the category of job development. The College was described in a student editorial as committed to finding the "right job for the right student" and complimented for following up after graduation.[17]

ATHLETICS

Other phases of college life also were most important for these first Nichols students. As with academics, the Nichols athletics program contributed directly to college life on Dudley Hill. According to one of the first College catalogs:

> A part of the educational scheme of Nichols Junior College is to provide a recreational program that will give to every young man ample opportunity for wholesome, competitive sports. Athletics should be made to contribute to the health and character of the individual, it is felt at Nichols, and should contribute to college spirit and college life.[18]

Such an institutional commitment by the College required an active athletics program and a careful scheduling of events and competition. Understandably, the school initially found it difficult to locate logical competitors because of the lack of similar two-year or junior colleges in the northeast. Consequently, the first Nichols teams competed primarily against college freshmen and junior varsity teams, preparatory schools with large numbers of post-graduates, and nearby high schools willing to play a junior college team.

In its first year with a total enrollment of only 65 students, Nichols fielded athletic teams in football, basketball, hockey, baseball, tennis, and golf – a substantial initial commitment to intercollegiate athletic competition. The first football schedule in 1931 that began one month after the College opened, included: Keene (N.H.) Normal School; freshmen teams from New Hampshire State (now University), Boston University, Holy Cross College, Amherst, and Springfield; and one secondary school – Worcester Trade School. Nichols defeated the Boston University Freshmen and Worcester Trade School. (It should be noted that freshmen at four-year colleges were not allowed to play on varsity teams; they had only three years of eligibility.) The Nichols basketball team that year played two college freshmen teams, four teams from small colleges, and fourteen from preparatory or high schools. Soccer was added in 1932.

Hal Chalmers '36.
Coach: Football, Basketball, Baseball, Cross Country;
Athletic Director; Alumni Secretary; Assistant to the President, 1936–1975.
Source: The *1939 Ledger*, n.p.

Interestingly, this Nichols athletics program eventually expanded to include the Nichols Yacht Club. By 1939, using the Brown University Yacht Club in Providence, Rhode Island, the Nichols club was listed by the College as an extracurricular activity. Two years later the Nichols sailors defeated the visiting Princeton University Freshmen on Webster Lake.[19] Other races were scheduled with clubs from MIT, Tufts, Coast Guard Academy, Brown, and UNH. Occasionally, additional sports such as wrestling and boxing were considered for recognition by the College; intramural competition was introduced in 1933.[20]

While not a priority at first, it soon became necessary to provide Nichols athletic teams with a "traditional emblem" and a nickname. Initially, Nichols teams were called the "Hurricanes," and then "Hilltoppers," at least for several months in 1931 and early 1932.[21] Nichols teams also went by their school colors: the "Black and Green," or "Green and Black." The first Nichols basketball team was referred to as the "Green and Black Hurricanes" by the College yearbook.[22] Probably, at the urging of the administration to end confusion and establish greater institutional cohesiveness and spirit, the student body voted in February 1937 on a nickname for Nichols teams.[23] This was part of building the College.

After much campus discussion, the vote favored "Buffaloes." It is not clear exactly why the "buffalo" was nominated for this distinction. The fact that the buffalo image was on the back of the nickel (commonly called the "Buffalo Nickel") then scheduled to be replaced in 1938 probably gave the "beast" of the plains greater public recognition. Perhaps the Nichols-buffalo combination just made more sense to Nichols students. The image of the American Bison on the buffalo nickel is widely believed to have come from a portrait by James Earl Fraser of "Black Diamond," a bison at the New York Bronx Zoo.[24] This 1500 pound bison originally came from the Barnum and Bailey circus.[25] The American buffalo or bison also was featured in Walter Prescott Webb's classic, *The Great Plains*, written in 1931.

Buffalo Nickel, 1936.
Source: *Nichols Alumnus*, November 1973, front cover.

The "Buffalo" nickname was in use at Nichols for a year or so when it quietly evolved into "Bison."[26] The specific reason for this adjustment is not clear, although discussions regarding the new five-cent coin then being prepared to replace the buffalo/bison coin probably alerted students and others at Nichols of the need to correctly identify its "buffalo." This occurred by 1939.

Not surprisingly, small college athletic competition in the 1930s featured a series of frustrations and challenges. For instance, President Conrad was determined that the hockey competition he had observed in wintery New Hampshire was going to be duplicated in Dudley. Unfortunately, nothing seemed to work very well during the early years of Nichols hockey despite extensive efforts to build a rink on the Dudley campus on Conant Pond. Practices for the hockey team, never mind games, were difficult to schedule without proper ice. Results were predictable. For instance, the Nichols hockey team in 1932 lost 33 to 0 to the Yale Freshmen.[27] And, when the Nichols team lost several years later to the Boston College Freshmen hockey team 15–1, it too seems to have been a game to forget. Not so, however, for Nichols goalie, Tom Gross. The key statistic here is that Gross made over 150 saves in this game.[28] Goalie Gross, an experienced goal keeper who played most of the game, recalled that this was one of the "best games" he ever played.[29] Seldom do hockey goalies get the opportunity to stop that many shots in one game. For goalie Gross, it was the chance to play and compete that counted.

Hockey on Conant Pond, Tom Gross in Goal.
Source: Nichols Junior College, *1938 Ledger*, n.p.

These extreme cases aside, this first decade emphatically established intercollegiate athletics as a part of the Nichols educational scheme. Further, and to add to the competitive picture, by 1941 a New England Junior College Conference was formed in football, basketball, track, and baseball with Nichols Junior College a leading participant.[30] The Nichols Junior College football team won the New England Junior College Conference football championship in 1940 beating Green Mountain Junior College and then the Nichols basketball team beat Vermont Junior College in 1941 to win the Conference's Invitational Basketball Tournament.

View of Nichols athletic fields and campus in mid-1930s looking northeastward from the southwest corner of what is now Shamie Hall.

But reasons for the success of Nichols athletics program cannot be identified through won-loss records during the 1930s. Generally the first Nichols teams lost more than they won. Small enrollments produced squads barely sufficient to field a full team. For instance, the backfield of the 1933 football team with a record of no wins and five losses averaged 151 pounds with the heaviest player weighing in at 158 pounds. Three in the backfield were 20 years of age, the fourth was 21.[31] With student enrollments from 65 to 163 during this period, the school nonetheless sponsored teams in at least seven different sports each year, not including junior varsities. In 1937, a 16-man Nichols football team, possibly the smallest Nichols football squad ever, beat Hyannis State Teachers College, previously undefeated over three years.

To later honor their efforts and those of other Nichols athletes, the Nichols Athletic Hall of Fame was created by the College in 1972. Thirteen athletes representing five major sports from the years 1931 to 1942 eventually were elected to the College's Athletic Hall of Fame. (See Appendix D.)

Another occurrence of great importance for Nichols athletics and for the College was the arrival of Hal Chalmers on Dudley Hill in 1934. A former athlete at New Hampton School, a 1936 Nichols Junior College graduate, and a multiple letter winner as well as the leading scorer on the basketball team for two years, he served as coach of the junior varsity basketball team in 1937. In his first years at the College, he also was an instructor in mathematics and typewriting and served as a dormitory master. Chalmers was named head coach of football and baseball in 1938. After his selection, the Nichols student newspaper noted prophetically that "It is expected that he will coach many victorious Nichols teams. . . ."[32] Within two years, Chalmers became athletic

Campus buildings are listed along the top margin.
Source: Nichols Junior College, *Pictorial*, insert, circa 1936.

director, an important position in the Conrad administrative model. He was to serve as a flexible anchor in the ongoing structuring of the Nichols administration. In 1939, he married President Conrad's sister and secretary, Margaret M. Conrad. He coached, served as Nichols athletic director, alumni director, assistant to the president, and much more, until his death in 1975.

Behind the institution's commitment to athletics was its president, its foremost rooter, and occasional coach. President Conrad missed few games. Furthermore, he coached football for at least one year and basketball in 1935 and 1936. This was in the image of the all-involved small college president. Also, it was what he liked to do.

OTHER EXTRA-CURRICULAR ACTIVITIES

All other college-sponsored activities were intended to be equally contributive. In fact, non-athletic school-sponsored activities involved as many, if not more students, than the athletic teams. President Conrad and deans Kingman and Spencer accepted the thinking that a commitment to extracurricular activities was crucial for a successful college experience. It was understood to be a means of developing executive leadership skills and other crucial factors necessary in creating a stronger student-faculty bond in the small college.

As a consequence, a large number of school-sponsored student activities were extremely active by 1936. They included the Justinian Society (intended to motivate and recognize students involved in extracurricular activities), a debating society, the Thalians (dramatic club), Glee Club, college newspaper (*Budget*), yearbook (the *Tower*, as named by the first Nichols students, later the *Ledger*), the Hilltoppers (a dance orchestra), the Social Committee, and the Outing Club. One of the most active early Nichols students was Ferdinand Wachenheimer (Fred Friendly), later president of CBS News.[33] The Nichols Fire Department manned by students was active as early as 1932. The College was committed to supporting and training many members of its fire department thereafter. By the end of the decade, these groups were joined by the International Relations Club, the Camera Club, the Yacht Club, the "N" Club, and the Athletic Council, all with assigned faculty advisors. Some, like the *Budget*, received national awards; dramatic club productions were invited to perform off-campus for local groups, as was the College Glee Club.

Several student-run radio stations emerged including WNJC, WVOW (Menacing Voice of Webster) – essentially a Dictaphone hookup with a range of two floors in Budleigh – and MUCK, a later station. Occasionally Greek letter fraternities appeared on Dudley Hill. Phi Sigma Nu (a national fraternity) and Phi Delta Chi were the first; Phi Kappa Epsilon and Beta Cella Rata came later; all made brief but important contributions to school spirit.

For its part, and in an effort to "balance" academic, cultural, and technical courses, the early College sponsored special convocations at least twice a month; eventually they became weekly. These occasions brought prominent speakers to campus and allowed the administration to address important institutional issues. Sometimes held in the "Village Chapel" (Conant Memorial Church), programs might include organ music and a short reflective period. The College catalog made it clear that these convocations were non-denominational in nature and that all students were required to attend.[34]

When possible, some activities were designed to extend the College's presence beyond the Dudley Hill community. Foreign students at Nichols spoke frequently at Rotary Club meetings in Webster, dances often were held on campus after football games, and Nichols students were invited to tea dances by young women from nearby Morat Junior College in Thompson, Connecticut. Furthermore, on weekends a large number of Nichols men traveled to such institutions as Smith College in Northampton, Massachusetts, a favorite women's college. Freshmen frequently paraded through Webster (usually, but not always, with police permission), yearly Advisory Council meetings brought different programs and speakers to campus, as did smokers before football games, and, on at least one occasion, a Nichols spelling team competed against a Webster women's team – and lost. And, when possible, Nichols student leaders attended conferences with their New England junior college counterparts from Marot, Mt. Ida, Larson, Portland, Colby, Stoneleigh, Bradford and Green Mountain.[35]

Another significant dimension of life on the Hill had to do with rules pertaining to student activity and conduct. To begin with, the College administration believed that "high-school and preparatory-school graduates should be made to feel responsible for their own conduct."[36] Students and their faculty advisors were asked to develop regulations for the college community that were in the best interests of the group and the individual. However, this did not mean that unlimited freedom was the rule. The regulations that existed, as it turned out, hardly seem draconian, even judged by the standards of that time, although some might disagree with this assessment.

During this first decade and beyond, attendance in proper attire (sport coats and ties) was required at lunch and dinner as well as other College events, including classes. Quiet periods in dormitories were maintained from 8:00 P.M. to 10:00 P.M., radios were to be turned off after 11:15 P.M., lights were to be out in rooms at 11:15 P.M. (by 12:00 midnight on Saturdays), and rooms had to be cleaned and checked by instructors before students left for weekends. On the academic side, classes were held throughout the week and on Saturday mornings, with cuts carefully tabulated by the Dean's Office. One over-cut led to "bounds" or "campus," two such occurrences resulted in "suspension." Meetings on individual cut situations were held with erring students once a week.[37] This oversight and regulatory process was labeled by the Nichols administration as "College life under sane control."[38] Not surprisingly, debates on the nature of the "sane" controls occurred frequently throughout the decade.

Some of these restrictions achieved the purposes intended, some probably did not. And not all activities were sanctioned by a watchful administration. Complaints and opposing reactions to regulations were quite common. The bell clapper, necessary to establish the rhythm of the school day, occasionally went missing and disrupted a day's schedule.[39] Sometimes students did strange things that earned them recognition in the College newspaper and elsewhere. There was the case of a young man who tried to win a prize offered to anyone who could drink two gallons of water in one hour. He failed, downing only one gallon in a half hour before he had to quit.[40] Freshmen initiations sometimes were boisterous as evidenced on one occasion when a march through Webster resulted in 57 students being arrested and jailed, although this event had been planned and sanctioned by college administrators – including the arrests.[41]

Students did challenge rules on occasion; sometimes quite vigorously. In 1932, the relatively conservative college newspaper, the *Budget*, logically concluded that the "surest way to have abolished all rulings in time was by cooperating with the few that were in existence."[42] Not all students accepted this thinking. Protests were not unusual. Students complained about having to turn lights off, to attend meals, and the need to get weekend permissions. Also there were additional concerns about too many tests each week (they were required to have three) and simply having to comply with too many rules.[43]

On occasion, it was necessary for the administration to react and it did. Apparently after a few trying months in 1934, the entire school was assembled to consider subjects that the President believed were affecting the welfare of the school and the student body. He focused on three: firearms on campus, the use of intoxicating beverages, and general attitude of students towards their studies.[44] There was no wavering on any of these subjects. On the first, President Conrad stated simply that firearms were the cause of numerous accidents, regardless of how carefully they were handled. They were to be turned over to resident faculty for safe keeping. He added that pistols and revolvers were to be removed immediately from school property.

Next, he considered a subject of "utmost" importance – the use of intoxicating beverages. The President emphatically stated that "anyone detected and determined to have been partaking of anything in this form would immediately be expelled." It should be noted that in 1933 the United States had just repealed the Prohibition Amendment with the 21st Amendment.[45] As a consequence, it was necessary to establish the administration's position on the use of alcohol.

And, finally, the student body was told that it had not been performing well and had not achieved adequate grades the previous month. As a result, everyone reported by their faculty for failing grades had to attend a special study hall. To add to the penalties, Monday morning permissions as well as late lights on Sunday nights were abolished. This was intended to be a wake-up call for those who assumed that they had no responsibilities to the institution for their academic performance or personal conduct.[46] In response, the *Budget* predictably criticized the administration for crusading for higher standards.

In another interesting case in 1937, every student signed a petition challenging the College's rule that students had to be in their rooms at 12:00 midnight on weekends. The specific problem Nichols men faced occurred because women's colleges generally allowed visitors to stay until midnight. Unfortunately, Nichols students had to be back in Dudley at that time. As a result, they had to leave somewhat distant colleges such as Smith College in Northampton, Massachusetts, long before midnight – and too soon for everyone. This made them less desirable dates. Nichols students also argued that this requirement to return to Dudley by midnight (for those who did get dates) might result in speeding and reckless driving to make it back in time. In this instance, the plea worked; this privilege was extended to 2:00 A.M. by the College Administrative Committee.[47]

Clearly young president Conrad was challenged by some of what occurred during the first decade. In one instance, when a class president called off the participation of his class in a rope pull, President Conrad criticized the class for withdrawing. When the withdrawing class was defended by its elected leader, the president said "It is the group in which I am disappointed, not the individuals."[48] On another occasion, President Conrad suggested that members of the senior class make a list of the virtues a person should strive to achieve. Seemingly commendable advice, it was questioned by one student in the *Budget* who advised his classmates that they should not be "too honest when you put them [virtues] down."[49]

Food protests had to be dealt with on other occasions. One of these protests involved the writer, who was then only five years old. During a period when I was required to attend daily lunches at the College (a family commitment), I learned that institutional food in the 1930s could be less than enjoyable. Fortunately, a sympathetic Nichols cook offered me a hot dog before each lunch. Consequently, I ate very little of the food on the table. When the students demanded more and better food, they used the argument that even the President's son would not eat what was being served. The solution, as I understood it, was to offer the students more milk and additional helpings. At the same time, and apparently part of the solution, I no longer was required to have lunch in the Dining Hall. Nothing happened to the cook involved; he eventually retired from the College in the 1990s.

Throughout, adversity pulled the college community together and then pushed it forward. In his "Farewell Message" to Nichols students in 1938, Dean Kingman, wrote:

> To me one of the most attractive features of a small college such as this is that it makes possible something more than the traditional student-teacher relationship. It provides an opportunity for better understanding and, therefore, a more intelligent solution to many problems. The College is well aware of these unusual opportunities and is developing its educational program accordingly.[50]

With War on the Horizon, 1938~1941

In 1938 the young college pushed forward on two fronts. As the college newspaper, the *Budget*, put it on April 26, 1938: "Two great honors have been recently conferred on Nichols which should make every student proud of himself...."[51] The *Budget* added: "Let it be said that Nichols Junior College is the nucleus of high standards and the incubator of leaders and not followers."[52]

There was reason to be proud. First, came the Commonwealth's approval for the College to grant the degree of Associate of Business Administration (ABA) to graduates that year. This degree requirement also included "everyday conduct and gentlemanly behavior." As the *Budget* reported: "Nichols graduates will not only be men ready for the complicated business world of today, but, even far better, they will be weighed in those qualities which are always admirable and will prove a real tribute and source of satisfaction."[53] At a different time and in a later context, a Nichols faculty would have to deal directly with the precise meaning of this degree requirement.

Recognition by the Commonwealth was not the only achievement earned by the young junior college that spring. In March, 1938, Nichols Junior College became the first educational institution in the country to become affiliated with the Quartermaster Corps of the United States Army. The mission of the Quartermaster Corps was to feed, clothe, and transport the Army. The relationship between Nichols students and the Quartermaster Corps was established through one course each semester. This was sufficient to prepare students to become reserve officers in the Corps when they became 21 and completed all requirements.[54]

From the College's perspective, this program offered yet another opportunity for a leadership experience that would benefit Nichols students in times of peace and national emergency. After meeting for the first time in May that year, students also were informed they could qualify for a commission in the Quartermaster Corps in fewer than four years.[55] Some years later the

College learned that every man who followed through with Quartermaster course requirements under the Nichols program received a commission.[56]

There can be little question that President Conrad's long-time association with the Quartermaster Corps played a major role in bringing this program to Nichols. Colonel William L. Conrad, the president's uncle, was president of the Quartermaster Association of the United States and also a director at Nichols Junior College from 1931 to 1937. Beyond this, the Nichols president had been a reserve officer in the Quartermaster Corps since 1923 making him sensitive to the benefits of military training and the possibility of a coming war. Regardless, most of American society remained in an isolationist mode throughout the 1930s apparently believing that the country was separated from problems in both Europe and Asia. This attitude changed quickly in December 1941.

Not surprisingly, Nichols students were not bothered by the early warnings of trouble abroad. Events on the Nichols campus between 1939 and 1940 generally followed experiences of previous years. Extra-curricular activities continued without disruption although issues related to possible war occasionally were discussed in the college community. For instance, a student poll conducted on the campus in 1937 questioned Nichols students regarding war and summarized their opinions. But, like their parents and so many others in America in 1937, they believed war was a long way off.

This isolationist mind set was about to change. By the late 1930s, advancing totalitarianism throughout the world forced the United States, led by President Franklin D. Roosevelt, to move slowly away from neutrality and into a position of involvement. A series of moves and military strikes by Germany and Italy in 1938 in much of Europe coupled with parallel Japanese aggression in Asia culminating in an attack on Pearl Harbor on December 7, 1941, turned America away from isolation and directly into war.

War's early rumblings did have some impact on life on Dudley Hill. In September 1940, the U.S. Congress passed legislation requiring the registration of men 21 to 35 years of age that could lead to one year of military training. Even then, most Americans were not concerned and continued to support non-involvement.[57] By the next year, however, a threatened gas shortage caused eight New England college campuses to ban cars. Apparently not too concerned, Nichols students agreed to use less gas, but only after extensive discussions involving students and faculty and a decision not to use their cars for errands on the Hill and to the Dudley Hill Post Office. This voluntary agreement, however, did not apply to use of cars on visits to Webster or elsewhere. The Nichols *Budget*, perhaps sarcastically, referred to this decision as a "noble action."[58]

Quite appropriately, the immediate pre-war period presented a significant challenge for the still young Nichols President and his school. James L. Conrad had been drafted in 1917 and prepared to enter military service in WWI.[59] This war ended before he was called into service, but he had not forgotten his experience.

Furthermore, the College could not exist if everyone had to serve in the military – as eventually was the case. Somewhat ironically, President Conrad was one of the first reservists to be called to active duty in April 1941 as a captain in the U.S. Army reserves. Initially assigned to Fort H.G. Wright, Fishers Island, New York, he was in Dudley on many weekends for consultations.

The College Faces War, December 1941~June 1943

Nine days prior to the Japanese bombing of Pearl Harbor on December 7, 1941, the November 28th issue of the Nichols *Budget* presented a picture of life at Nichols College. It discussed numerous school activities including scheduled events for the Dramatic Club, the Yacht Club, a football loss and basketball practice. The *Budget's* editorial page featured topics such as "Trying"as in "do better" and the comparative merits of kissing and nose rubbing. It also included an interview with a faculty member and a reference to an increase of school spirit on campus. One lengthy article dealt with a presentation at the College given by major league baseball player, Dudley's Gene Desautels, who was then with the Boston Red Sox. He was an excellent fielding catcher who frequently caught Bob Feller when with Cleveland.[60]

There was little mention of an approaching war. The closest the *Budget* came to discussing American foreign policy or world affairs was a few lines regarding the spirit of good fellowship developed between the Nichols International Relations Club and the Smith College Club at their joint November meeting. How much was actually discussed about United States foreign policy was not reported. Nothing in the *Budget* referred directly to world conditions.[61] This changed after the attack on Pearl Harbor.

In fact, however, the College had somewhat prepared for what was to come. Nichols had two small programs available for students interested in military careers. The Quartermaster Course, begun at Nichols in 1938, was now offering professional and semi-professional courses for military-bound students in order for them to qualify for appointments as reserve officers. Rapidly advancing wartime conditions, however, meant that the College could not give assurances to students who hoped to complete their college education before entering military service.[62]

Nichols CPT students at North Grafton Airport, 1941.
Source: "Civilian Pilot Training Corps," Nichols Junior College *Pictorial*, 1942–1943.

In 1940, Nichols also had been selected to participate in the Civilian Pilot Training Program (CPT) sponsored by the Civilian Aeronautics Administration. Ten Nichols Junior College students at a time were accepted into this program designed to qualify them for a private pilot's license. All expenses were paid by the government. Students agreed to enter the government's military aviation service, either through the army or the navy, after successfully finishing the course and meeting all requirements.[63] Pilot training was completed at the North Grafton airport in central Massachusetts.

Everything changed after December 7, 1941. College administrators reacted immediately to the Pearl Harbor attack. At a special convocation, Dean Spencer spoke to Nichols students and then reported to their parents. He was most concerned about the immediate reaction of members of the student body to the reality of war. As he saw it:

1. No decision involving enlistment or defense work should be made hastily;
2. The nation's leadership was in the best position to decide when college students can best serve their country by forsaking their studies;
3. The College will not sanction any action which does not have parental approval.[64]

During the holiday period, President (then Captain) Conrad stationed on Long Island Sound sent a message to all parents and students. His letter read: "'your college is prepared to make its adjustments and carry on. . . . It has been, and will continue to lead its students, intelligently, to that end which we have dedicated ourselves, the best interests of our men.'"[65] At the same time, others complimented the College for having the "foresight and vision" to have established its army course in 1938 seeing it as a "real trait of leadership."[66]

Yet, the school could continue only if it had an adequate number of students. Its very existence was at stake. Within several weeks after December 7, 1941, plans were finalized to have Nichols remain open all-year-round. Under this plan, a student graduating high school in June 1942 could immediately enroll at Nichols and complete the two-year program in fifteen months by not taking traditional vacation periods, including summers. Courses added for the Civilian Pilots Training Corps and the Quartermaster Corps also became part of the Nichols academic program.[67]

Captain Conrad, traveling from his Army post on Fishers Island, Long Island Sound, in March 1942, made some careful observations at an important convocation regarding the future of the Nichols student. He believed that students, with a few possible exceptions, were going to serve in the armed forces. Consequently, it followed that they should prepare "rationally" and "thoughtfully" for this experience. He concluded that both students and country then would be better off. If Nichols students were to advance in the military, he said, they would have to compete against the best. He followed with two observations. First, "The task here at school is the easiest you shall have to face in many years to come." And, second, "After this war the upsurge of demand for consumer goods shall be advantageous to you [as business men], with the possibilities of a military career not too remote [either]."[68]

War's impact on the Junior College was unavoidable despite efforts to have it otherwise. Many students did not return to Nichols after the 1941 Christmas holiday. In mid-January 1942, Conant "House" was closed due to the shortage of fuel as well as a lack of students. Unofficial estimates suggested that the Class of 1942 was diminished by 50% in number during its second year due to enlistments, reservists being called to active duty, and involvement in war-related work. In 1942, the College dropped a week from Spring vacation to allow an earlier graduation, the Spring dance was cancelled, and nationwide gas rationing was imposed by May 15, 1942. Moreover, those who were associated with the Nichols CPT program in either the Army or Navy Air Corps were soon called into military service.[69]

Further changes came during the next academic year. The College administration now was led briefly by Acting President, H. Jack Hunter, of Montclair, New Jersey, and new Dean, Robert H. Eaton. Courses, including physics and mathematics, were added to the Nichols curriculum to better prepare Nichols students for military reserve assignments. The College also required compulsory physical education. In September, 1942, Nichols listed eleven faculty, including part-time members.[70]

But these adjustments did not delay the inevitability of total war. The College administration hoped that its students could complete Nichols' two-year degree requirements by enlisting in reserve programs. The institution then could remain open. Nonetheless, events at Nichols that fall had to be limited because of a shortage of gasoline. Where possible, the use of local transportation systems was encouraged. As a result, only four football games could be scheduled, and these had to be with nearby schools.[71] Gas usage restrictions in October 1942 threatened to end the Junior College Athletic Conference; Coach Chalmers went into the Navy that fall.

Throughout the year, the nation's need for additional qualified recruits became more obvious. Prior to 1942, college students had been deferred by the Selective Service Administration for being in an activity – attendance at college – deemed essential to the nation's welfare. Shortly thereafter, however, this deferment status was changed and students were no longer included in a deferred group.[72] By mid-November 1942, everyone assumed that the draft age would soon be lowered to include 18- and 19-year olds.[73] Ninety-five percent of the just-graduated Nichols Class of 1942 quickly became members of armed forces reserves.[74] Dean Eaton pointed out six months later that all but ten Nichols students were members of the military reserves.[75]

At the same time, the need for additional recruits resulted in more aggressive efforts by the various military services to convince young men to join their respective reserve programs. By January 1943, a total of 53 Nichols students had enlisted in the reserve programs of the Army, Navy, Army Air Force, and Marine Corps. Many were given some assurance that they could complete their college programs although this did not happen. In 1942, the College expanded the nature of its relationship with military authorities by agreeing to house a 22-man army glider pilots group in Merrill Hall. This group ate with Nichols students while flying at the North Grafton Airport. This program lasted eight weeks and was followed by a group of army liaison pilots that had a similar arrangement with the College.

Nichols Junior College's twelfth graduation was held on January 17, 1943. It was the first Nichols class to graduate under the guidelines of the war-time, continual study (no vacations) program. This graduation ceremony was in the Conant Memorial Chapel where graduation exercises had been held for Nichols students (Academy and College) since 1897. Nineteen students received the degree of Associate of Business Administration. At that time, it was determined that over 100 Nichols students and former students were serving in the American armed forces.[76]

As draft quotas increased and more reservists were called into active duty, the Nichols student body significantly decreased in numbers. One way to illustrate this decline is through the experience of the basketball squad that year. By January 21, 1943 (graduation had been on the 17th), the team had lost three players to graduation and four to enlistment.[77] Although unbeaten in early February, the basketball team was down to seven players; it was expected that when the next calls for reservists were made, the entire squad would be in military service. One game eventually had to be cancelled because only four players were available.[78]

Nichols Junior College was not the only nearby college affected by the course of the war in 1943. In March, Marianapolis Junior College in Thompson, Connecticut, closed due to lack of students.[79] Other colleges, along with Nichols, had arrived at this point. Classes ended at Nichols for remaining students in April and May 1943. The few students at Nichols either transferred or enlisted.[80] With no students available, the Nichols Junior College trustees were forced to close the College in the summer of 1943 for the duration.[81]

When the usual September registration date for Nichols students arrived that year, the *Webster Times* acknowledged the closing of the College with an insightful and appropriate editorial piece.

Nichols College

> The fact that Nichols Junior College will not open this fall is a casualty of the war. The situation, both as to faculty and students, is such that it would not be possible to continue with the junior college until the war is over.
>
> . . . .
>
> Nichols has made a real name in its field of education. The closing is a recess, not for all time. Nichols will return.[82]

"THE WINTER OF DESPAIR," 1943~1946

The period from 1943 to 1946 was a period of "despair" for Nichols Junior College. Its buildings were not being used. Its president had been in active military service since early in 1941. He was in England and then France when Allied forces invaded the mainland. He would not be available again until 1946. A care-taker administration was in place led by another new acting president, Quincy H. Merrill, M.D.

Some wondered if the Dudley Hill institution was going to close again as had been the case in the late 1920s. There were factors that suggested this might be the case. For instance, the Nichols Junior College Board of Trustees found that "war conditions" made it impossible to make its scheduled yearly payments to the Academy trustees due on the Dudley campus. Herbert L. Plummer, College Treasurer, instead offered to pay an interest rate of five percent per annum on the amount owed on the Academy buildings and campus.[83] The Nichols Academy trustees apparently accepted this arrangement rather than invoke an acceleration clause that might have forced payment of the entire sum. The College simply could not have paid even if required.

That the College reopened at war's end was in itself an achievement. Nonetheless, much was lost during these years. Clearly, the Junior College was without the full services of its founding president for more than five years. This occurred at a critical time in the institution's history just as it was about to reach for further institutional recognition, possibly a three- or four-year bachelor degree granting program. Whatever could have been achieved by immediate action had to be delayed. And the campus itself simply had to wait for improvements and avoid problems frequently experienced by unused buildings. That it survived was due to the careful oversight of acting President, Dr. Merrill.[84]

Then too, the educational context for higher education in Massachusetts changed significantly during the war period. For one, in 1943, the Massachusetts legislature created a state board to oversee higher education in general and junior colleges, specifically.[85] This meant much less legislative involvement, a political system that President Conrad had come to understand and even appreciate. Individuals with liberal arts backgrounds logically were put in control of review processes. At the same time the need for an improved process of institutional review saw the New England Association of Colleges and Secondary Schools become involved in the accreditation process.[86] World War II probably cost Nichols the opportunity to become a four-year college in 1943, long before this eventually was to happen in 1958.

Once the war ended, it was possible to see some benefits that assisted in the College's re-emergence. The two people most critical to the College's first 40 years of operation, Athletic Director Hal Chalmers and President James Conrad (now a Colonel, a title he decided to retain once his active duty ended) had gained much during their war experiences. Both returned to Dudley in 1946.

Chalmers, Nichols coach and athletic director, as well as a graduate in the Nichols Class of 1936, originally enlisted in the Navy program for physical fitness instructors set up by Gene Tunney, former world heavyweight champion. He entered a nine-week training program in Norfolk, Virginia, that began in October 1942. There he became acquainted with many prominent players and coaches in the athletic world. After completing the program in the top tenth of his group of 150 athletes, Chief Specialist Physical Instructor Chalmers was assigned to Bainbridge, Maryland, Naval Training Station, in December 1942.[87]

Seven months later he was sent to Dartmouth College, Hanover, N.H., as a physical instructor for Navy students and named to the Dartmouth football coaching staff where he first worked under coach Earl Brown helping to coach the Dartmouth backfield.[88] He also was an assistant to Dartmouth's baseball coach, Jeff Tesreau. Both Dartmouth coaches were extremely well-known in

Colonel James L. Conrad, circa 1945.

Hal Chalmers, Chief Specialist Physical Instructor, circa 1945.

the athletic world. With war's end, he spent the fall of 1945 coaching the football team at New Hampton School in New Hampshire, before returning to Dudley to assist in reopening Nichols Junior College. This included painting floors and replacing windows.

But this war time experience introduced Coach Chalmers to a wide range of significant contacts, especially in New England collegiate athletic circles, and was essential in upgrading his skills as a coach. And, through his work in athletics during the war, he made Nichols known to others as well. Amiable, sensitive, hardworking, and enthusiastic, he later was referred to as "probably the most outstanding man to enter our college" by Colonel Conrad.[89] Chalmers was back in Dudley by December 1945 and directed Nichols athletics until his death in 1975.

Colonel Conrad had a parallel experience in the U.S. Army. Originally appointed as a second lieutenant in the Quartermaster Corps in 1923, he was called into active service in April 1941 as a captain. Stationed at Fort H.C. Wright on Fishers Island in Long Island Sound, he became Quartermaster Head of Harbor Defenses for the Sound, including New London, Connecticut. He was promoted to Major in May 1942 and to Lieutenant Colonel in December 1942. In June 1943, Conrad was named Commanding Officer of the Willimantic Distribution Center in Connecticut where he was promoted to Colonel. While on duty on Long Island Sound and in Willimantic, he occasionally traveled to Dudley on weekends to oversee activities at the College. His rapid military promotions and assignment responsibilities were indicative of his abilities as a soldier and leader.[90]

In early 1944, Colonel Conrad left for England to be part of the build-up for the invasion of Europe. After landing in France, he served as Quartermaster of the Port of Rouen and was awarded the Bronze Star. Like Hal Chalmers, he brought sharpened skills back to Dudley. His experience in a leadership capacity contributed to his ability to lead an all-male college. Nonetheless, significant time had been lost in a critical period in the College's history.

The return of President Conrad and Athletic Director Chalmers in 1946 was preceded by the Servicemen's Readjustment Act of 1944, or the so-called GI Bill of Rights. Initially, it was intended to relieve anticipated peace-time pressures and crises, including an expected post-war depression caused by large numbers of returning servicemen. In fact, it essentially made a new America.[91] The financial benefits of this bill meant that many more veterans could enter higher education thus affecting both the size and character of American educational institutions. Its impact on American higher education, including institutions such as Nichols, went beyond every projection by its initial promoters.

Nichols Junior College reopened on February 4, 1946. To what extent this college was to differ from the pre-war school remained to be seen. The world, however, had changed greatly since 1941.

Other Notable Events, People, Items, and Pictures 1931~1946

1931   Board, room and instruction, for two semesters (1931–1932): day, $900; non-resident, $425.
First football win over B.U. freshmen, 7–6.
First basketball team win was over Tourtellote High School, Putnam, Ct., 46–37.
Students released from class to attend Springfield Fair (Eastern States Exposition), reports required.

1932   Student Newspaper, the *Nichols Budget*, features a Bridge game problem.
College President buys fire truck for College, first one in Dudley.

1933   *Tower* (yearbook) wants to know "Who was the Conant Ghost?
Student Norman Woolford, runner extra ordinaire.
Bell clapper disappears.
First national frat at Nichols – Phi Sigma Nu – installed 12.

1934   Graduation speaker, Nason Arnold (of Holden, Mass.). His great grandfather said to have founded Nichols.

1935   Outing Club dedicated Wadsworth Cabin in Charlton.
President's new home (later the Justinian House) occupied by President and his family.
Graduation speaker, famous war correspondent, Floyd Gibbons, was first honorary member of U.S. Marine Corps.
Malcolm MacLeod, Canadian W.W.I. ace said to have shot down seven enemy planes, is operating Club House.

1936   President's Council started.
Fred Wachenheimer (Friendly) seen as "the Father of Nichols Dramatics."
Flood hits Webster; with no gas or electricity available, students go home three days early.

1937   Roberto Mercade led soccer team with 20 goals (out of 47 scored by team).

1938   Merrill Hall first new dorm for junior college.

1939   President Conrad runs for position on Dudley School Committee – and loses.
Frequent police raids on the Forest Club in Webster of great concern for some Nichols students.
Tom Sweet, elected mayor of the Hill.
Ken Dorman, German student at Nichols, spoke to Webster Rotary club on Hitler's impact on the German people.

Listing continues on page 88

1931–1946 College Buildings or Renovated Structures not Pictured in these Chapters (and as they appeared during this period).

Academy building and Hall
1938–1959

Conant Hall
1936–

Apartments
1941–

Conant Library and Observatory
1883–1935

Club House
1890–1972

Conant Library in Academy Hall
1935–1955

~ OTHER NOTABLE EVENTS, PEOPLE, ITEMS, AND PICTURES 1931~1946

Dean's House
1934–1964

Gym
1931–1965

Dining Hall
Above: 1931–1937
Below: 1938–1947

President's Home
Above: 1935–1939
Below: 1939–2004

First Congregational Church (Chapel)
1931–1962

Student Life, 1931–1946.

~ OTHER NOTABLE EVENTS, PEOPLE, ITEMS, AND PICTURES 1931~1946

1. Soccer on the first soccer field; **2.** Academy classroom; **3.** Academy Hall with debating club practice; **4.** Sailing Club members on Webster Lake; **5.** Football, 1936; **6.** Small Class in Academy; **7.** A pool game in the Club; **8.** Baseball team, circa 1939; **9.** Basketball Court, original College gym; **10.** Glee Club, 1941; **11.** Dramatic Club presentation, "Ceiling Zero," 1936; **12.** Conant Library in action, 1934; **13.** Reception Line, Winter Carnival, 1941; **14.** Members of Nichols Track team; **15.** An early graduation on Budleigh south lawn, 1938; **16.** "Pop" in the "Club House;" **17.** Lounge area in Budleigh Hall; **18.** Interior, Conant Memorial Church, with Roger Conant Memorial Window.

Listing continued from page 83

1940   Football team back early for fall practice for first time.
       Soccer team (10–0) first undefeated and untied team in Nichols history. Headline in *Worcester Evening Daily*: "Nichols boys get gold [soccer] balls" for athletic awards.
       Football team (6–0–1) undisputed holder of first New England Junior College Conference title, only junior college team in northeast to be undefeated.
       George Munce leading scorer of football team, best freshman athlete, enlists in U.S. military.
       Oscar, the dummy, comes to Nichols (from Green Mountain Junior College) when Nichols wins annual football game; goes back next year.
       Justinians move into President's former home, President's new home is at the four corners on Dudley Hill.
       Ten Nichols students (and more) accepted for pilot training (CPT).
       Largest graduating class with 58 graduates; George Gromelski (to be College Bursar) is Valedictorian.

1941   President Conrad leaves for active duty with U.S. Army Quartermaster Corps, April 2, 1941.
       New England Junior College Conference formed (football, basketball, track, baseball); Nichols basketball team wins conference tourney.
       Conference of Junior College student governments included Nichols, Mount Ida, Larson, Portland, Colby, Stoneleigh, Bradford, Green Mountain.
       Robert H. Eaton named Assistant Dean.
       Board, Room, and Tuition for year (1941–1942): $985. Day student fees arranged on application.
       Most popular course for Class of 1941: Ethics

1942   First Summer Session opens at Nichols.
       Gas rationing hits.
       Those in CPT program called into Army or Navy Air Corps.

1943   Last student departs in May. Without students, college cannot open in fall.

CHAPTER 4

REDESIGNING THE HISTORIC CAMPUS, 1946~1958

Nichols Junior College Seal, 1942.
When the tower on the Academy building was damaged beyond repair by the Hurricane of 1938, it had to be taken down. As a result, the tower design was removed from the interior of the College seal. The center then was redesigned as shown in the 1942 yearbook, The *Ledger*. The result was a shield-like internal image which added symbols to "loyalty" (an open book), "service" (a gear implying readiness), and "culture" (a lamp frequently used to depict knowledge). Also added was a sharper reference to Nichols ("Nichols Junior College"). One other important new feature within the shield was a pair of fasces with inward-facing axes. Ancient Roman fasces symbolized power and jurisdiction generally with outward-facing axes. However, the fasces on the Nichols shield have their axe blades facing inward. In a few locations in the United States, the axe blades are pointed inward suggesting a protective rather than a provocative stance. Aside from Nichols, two good examples of inward-pointing axe blades in the United States are on the Great Seal of Harvard University and on the rostrum of the United States House of Representatives. In the latter case, they appear to be so placed to protect the flag of the United States.
Source for seal (1942): The *1942 Ledger*, 2.

Virtually all Americans stood to benefit from the growth and development that occurred in American higher education after World War II. Conditions resulting from population increase, the expansion and blossoming of American democracy, and the emergence of the United States as the world's leading industrial and military power touched everyone. As for higher education, what came forward in the post-war period, according to sociologist Martin Trow, stemmed from a transition in American society whereby a once-elite higher education system had to absorb greater numbers of Americans now able to afford its costs due to the Serviceman's Readjustment Act of 1944, or the GI Bill.[1] While Trow's assessment generally is accurate, reactions to this legislative action could differ due to varying past experiences and unique, long-existing conditions or designs.

Significant features of both continuity and change in higher education generally can be identified in the immediate post-war period from 1946 to 1950. Basic forms of institutional classification, such as two-year colleges, four-year colleges, and universities, continued to exist. So too did self-images and traditions including curriculum patterns and institutional missions.[2] Nichols may have been a junior college in classification but it was more accurately described as a two-year business college. The two years of business education at Nichols were based on the third and fourth years in the university model.

Nonetheless, as formidable as tradition appeared to be, change also became a reality. It could be no other way since veterans made up almost 50 percent of the total college enrollment by 1948. As serious students, they saw higher education as an opportunity for greater success and not merely a rite of passage to adulthood.[3] Increased faculty professionalism occurred on all levels of higher education as well. Serious students began to gain control over their elective courses and sought more flexible programs. Then too, more attention was paid to business and industry-related professional courses while the roles of federal and state governments expanded exponentially.[4] The resulting admixture formed the future.

Post World War II America was fertile ground for a new era in higher education. Nichols Junior College is a case in point. In the twelve years that followed its February 4, 1946 post-war reopening, the Dudley junior college sought to achieve one of its president's long-time goals: to become a four-year college. Much, however, remained to be done before this event could occur. First, the Junior College had to reestablish itself in the increasingly dynamic and competitive post-war educational environment. Second, Nichols Junior College had to prepare to meet standards required for further development. This applied both to institutional potential and student performance. It then would be possible to apply for four-year college status.

Resetting the Plan

It was one challenge to reopen an institution that had been closed for nearly three years, it was quite another to put it back on track. Not surprisingly, the Nichols "Special Catalog" published in 1946 differed little from pre-war catalogs. As before, its educational program was said to be an "answer to the demand for an institution which offers a program of studies fundamental to business and life amid cultural surroundings."[5] A direct emphasis on competitive sports was absent from these first post-war announcements,

Campus Signs, 1957.
Source: *1958 Ledger*, 17.

although later statements reminded readers that "athletics contribute to the health and character of the individual and to college spirit and college life."[6]

While it was possible to point to the still existing goals and achievements of the pre-war Junior College, much was different in 1946. The students were new. So too was the faculty; few newcomers were aware of Nichols ways that had evolved over its first decade. The President, too, had the opportunity to develop a new agenda, although he was most anxious to regain the school's 1941 pre-war level, its character, and to continue to work toward becoming a four-year college. After returning from active duty he married his second wife, Beulah M. Bruce; his first marriage ended in divorce. And, importantly, President Conrad now functioned with a board of trustees committed only to the growth of the Junior College, not the preservation of the Academy. This was a dramatic difference between the pre-war and post-war years at Nichols.

There was much to be done in 1946. First, President Conrad quickly dealt with the physical reality of a campus that had two distinct parts: the first was the upper campus and former 19th century home of Nichols Academy next to the town common and to the west of Center Road at the top of Dudley Hill; the second, or the lower campus, included the former Hezekiah Conant estate to the south of Healy Road and on both sides of Center Road. (Refer to Map 1.)

President Conrad addressed the tasks or challenges faced by this first-back class. He believed in 1946 that it would be difficult to reestablish the "college procedures and customs [at Nichols] with no association or precedent available and largely with a faculty also making a similar adjustment."[7] He called the eventual success of this class, as individuals and as a group, "a milestone."[8] In fact, however, he should not have been concerned. Attending college was an unexpected opportunity for many of these students. As ex-servicemen, they were not going to waste time reestablishing new guidelines and rules for student governance that had worked before.[9]

Gilbert C. Garland,
B.S., M.Ed. Dean, 1946–1948.

Editors of the *Budget*, saw this period as a "new beginning . . . for recreational and social foundations. . . ." They expected that it would be just a short time before they matured. Opportunities and goals were clear to them: "It is the advantage of every man in college today," the college newspaper, the *Budget* explained, "to obtain as much information as he can concerning various phases of basic business administration, and to maintain the material for later reference."[10] The Nichols president once said that the first academic year at Nichols was more demanding in total academic hours than the average first year in an ordinary college.[11] He also stressed the need for continuing education "in order to adequately fulfill the obligations and responsibilities expected of him [the business man] in his respective positions."[12] Most understood this charge. Not surprisingly, the rhythms of the pre-war college quickly returned. For instance, the annual faculty reception for members of the entering Freshman class resumed almost immediately when Nichols reopened. In September 1946, the *Budget* reported that activities such as the Advisory Council were being "constantly renamed and reactivated."[13]

Most of the College's buildings were ready for use in February 1946. Hal Chalmers returned to Nichols as assistant to the president and athletic director. Gilbert Garland, with undergraduate and graduate degrees from Springfield College and a former head of the English Department at Vermont Junior College, was named dean of students. A Nichols graduate and valedictorian of the Class of 1938, George Gromelski, completed the rather slim administration as bursar. Some taught a class as well. A faculty of 13, including the President and his administrators, was in place with the same responsibilities as their pre-war predecessors.[14]

Success for the post-war college was clearly dependent on enrollment numbers as in the past. Although much suggested that an increasing demand for higher education was about to take place when the war ended, this was not a certainty. Fortunately, the first post-war Nichols class entering in February 1946 numbered 112 men; more than half, possibly as many as 90 percent, were war veterans.[15] This "GI Bill" class was to attend summer school, as would classes in 1947 and 1948, under the College's so-called "accelerated wartime" schedule. In June 1947, the first Nichols graduating class since 1943 numbered 56 men. Another graduation followed in January 1948 with 40 graduates.[16] Within three years, enrollment stood at a record high of 280 students, including 132 freshmen from 14 states and Cuba, Venezuela, Turkey, Iceland, Ecuador, and the Hawaiian Islands.[17] The enrollment high in the pre-war years was 163 in 1940.[18]

THE ALUMNI MEMORIAL HALL

Rapid growth in numbers quickly exposed weak links in the Junior College's ability to provide adequate student services. By the first fall class in 1946, the Nichols dining facility, situated between Budleigh and the gymnasium, and then 10 years old, no longer could serve the entire student body in one sitting.[19] As a result, the need for a new dining facility combined with the President's desire to bring together the upper and lower sections of the campus, led the Nichols Board of Trustees to approve the Junior College's first campaign to raise money for a new building. This was one and one-half years after the post-war era began. The relocation of the dining hall was the beginning of a series of moves to reset the design of the post-1946 college.

The campaign to construct the Alumni Memorial building on Center Road on Dudley Hill just to the north of the Club House began on March 22, 1947.[20] This building was dedicated to the eighteen Nichols men who died or were killed during World War II as well as to their colleagues in this war. The memorial building was the first to be financed and built by Nichols Junior College. Ground was broken for Alumni Hall on September 13, 1948. Because of a post-war lack of building materials, beams and floor joists for the building had to come from a large nearby barn off West Main Street in Dudley.[21]

Fund raising efforts for Alumni Hall included alumni of both Nichols Academy and Nichols Junior College. Nichols Junior College alumnus, Sterns Smalley '34, served as General Chairman; Dr. George J. Searle and Charles L. Robinson of the Nichols Academy Class of 1884 were listed as honorary chairmen.[22] Dr. Searle helped to complete the tower of Alumni Memorial Hall by adding the former Academy bell. This was a Meneely bell cast in West Troy, N.Y., in 1883 and originally located in the Academy building's tower until this structure was partially destroyed by the 1938 hurricane. The bell initially had been a gift of Dr. Searle's Nichols Academy Class of 1884. The Tower of Alumni Hall was dedicated on October 25, 1952.[23] In presenting this gift, Dr. Searle wrote: "May the bell that rings again in the tower of Nichols College inspire the same love and devotion I have had for my school for 68 years...."[24]

This bell, a gift to the Academy by the Class of 1884 was made in West Troy, N.Y. It was originally placed in the tower of the Academy building in 1884, then located in the Alumni Hall tower.
Photograph, Justin Dolan '09.

This building was to serve as a dining hall for 23 years, while also initially providing rooms on its bottom floor for ten boarding students. The previous dining hall became a student dormitory (T-Hall) allowing for additional enrollment.[25]

Once plans for this building were underway, the Junior College made several other important adjustments. The gymnasium, or the former Burnett barn, had been used as a dining area while Alumni Hall was being completed. Its floor also was lengthened to provide a standard basketball court of 84' x 44' (the exact size of the Boston Garden floor). An extended stage area was also added. This multipurpose building with a seating capacity of 750 soon was being used, as in the past, for weekly convocations, examinations, glee club concerts, dramatic club presentations, dances, baccalaureate services, and for an occasional commencement.[26]

In 1946, the Nichols Junior College Board of Trustees purchased the historic Black Tavern on Dudley Hill from Mary D. Goodell. This building, with a nearby shed and carriage house or barn, was the summer home of the Reverend Dr. Charles L. Goodell. He was a nationally known minister, who reached millions of Americans with his radio program, "Sabbath Reveries." Reverend Goodell had been a member of the Nichols Academy Board of Trustees serving for a number of years as its president. The Black Tavern then was used by the College as a guest house and provided living quarters for students as did its renovated barn, later referred to by the College as the Tavern Annex.

Alumni Hall and its tower intended to be the center of the campus. It contained the dining hall capable of seating 300, a faculty dining room, stewards office, trustee room, and other facilities.
Source: Nichols College *Pictorial*, circa 1955.

The Black Tavern was given to the Black Tavern Historical Society of Dudley to be preserved and properly utilized as a historic structure in 1983. During this period the Nichols Board of Trustees also obtained the right to purchase all property then owned by President Conrad including the Justinian house, President's house, Dean's house, and the faculty house or apartments.[27] Further additions to the College campus included nearby land and properties owned by Roger Durkee and Robert Towne. The College trustees also agreed to assume full responsibility from the Webster-Dudley Golf Course's Board of Governors for operating the challenging nine-hole, 3,125 yard course next to the College.

Colonel Conrad then sought to reestablish the College's commitment to a four-year program. No one should have been surprised when he re-introduced this topic soon after the College reopened. In March 1947, the Nichols Junior College Board of Trustees petitioned the Board of Collegiate Authority of the Commonwealth of Massachusetts to change the name of the corporation from Nichols Junior College to Nichols College and to change its purpose to allow Nichols to grant the degree of Bachelor of Business Administration.[28] This was its first formal application. It was not successful. The Nichols Board filed another request the following year as well.[29]

Perhaps it was too much to expect prompt approval by a new Board of Collegiate Authority just created in 1943 by the Massachusetts legislature. No longer was the Massachusetts legislature going to directly grant the right to confer degrees to Massachusetts institutions. The Commonwealth now had a board of collegiate authority to determine standards. Logically this board was staffed by educators from the Massachusetts educational establishment. Nonetheless, Nichols Junior College was preparing to be the first Massachusetts junior college to be authorized to become a senior college.

THE POST-WAR NICHOLS STUDENT

The continued development of student life on campus also was critical to post-war institutional growth. Post-war college students generally differed from a pre-war enrollment that had been predominantly male, white, middle to upper class in orientation, attending school on a full-time basis, and living on a residential campus with most courses required.[30] The post-war college was heavily populated by veterans supported by the GI Bill who were serious students and welcomed their educational opportunities.[31] Recent high school graduates who were matriculating with them at Nichols and elsewhere also benefited from their maturity. Students without military experience who later followed them into college had to endure repeated questions from frustrated faculty members who wondered why they could not do as well as students who had been in military service. On one occasion, Colonel Conrad explained simply that "The veteran seemed more eager to study and accept responsibilities."[32]

An examination of the post-war student body is helpful in understanding this group of students although this view is less precise than ten years before. As in the past, home locations continued to demonstrate the widespread geographical appeal of the Dudley college. Most at the immediate post-war college also came from families with business connections living in metropolitan areas while a surprisingly large percentage came from foreign countries for an American business education. (See Chart 4.1. Geographical Distribution of Nichols Student Body in 1957. . . .)

Fortunately, there are many indications as to how these students looked at their world after the war. One column in the *Nichols Budget*, rather unremarkably titled, "Campus Quiz," brought out student attitudes from the 1946–1950 period. In response to a question about how to make Nichols better, most student answers were predictable. They recommended that the College's athletic equipment be improved, Saturday classes should be given on weekday afternoons, students should join organizations outside the jurisdiction of the College, Nichols should become coeducational, and parking had to be improved.[33] When a small group of students were asked directly: "Should Nichols become a four-year college?" – three out of six approved (one on the condition that it also became a co-ed school); two others believed that the college should remain a two-year school; while one said either was fine with him.[34] Apparently this was not an important question for Nichols students in the late 1940s.

Chart 4.1. Geographical Distribution of Nichols Student Body in 1957, 1960, 1963, 1974

United States and Territories	1957	1960	1963	1974	Foreign Countries	1957	1960	1963	1974
Canal Zone			1		Argentina	1			
Connecticut	45	75	99	127	Brazil		1		
Delaware	2				Canada		1		1
D.C.	6	2			Colombia	1	1		
Florida		2	1	4	Cuba	5	4		
Georgia	1				Ecuador				1
Hawaii		2	2		France	1			
Iowa		1			Haiti				1
Kentucky	1		1		Indonesia		1		
Maine	7	17	16	5	Iran		1		
Maryland	1	1	4	4	Japan			1	
Massachusetts	79	167	239	369	Mexico	2			
Michigan	3	2	1	1	Nicaragua	1			
Missouri				2	Pakistan		1		
New Hampshire	4	3	4	4	Panama		1	3	
New Jersey	38	67	69	49	Peru				2
New York	122	128	108	55	San Salvador		1		
North Carolina		1			Singapore		1		
Ohio	5	3	3	4	South Africa			1	
Pennsylvania	10	13	20	14	Spain				1
Puerto Rico			1	2	Tanganyika		1		
Rhode Island	9	6	15	6	Thailand		2		
Tennessee					Venezuela		1	1	3
Vermont	6	12	10	5	TOTALS	352	531	603	650
Virginia		1							
Wisconsin	2	2		1					

Sources: *The Bison*, October 28, 1957, 4; *Nichols Alumnus*, XI, November 1960, 6; Nichols College of Business Administration, *Bulletin*, Catalog Issue, 1964–1965, 87; *Nichols College Catalog*, 1974–75, 87.

Responses of students to other questions also are interesting. On school spirit, Nichols had some, one said, "but not enough."[35] On fall weekends, according to one comment, "the Hill is as quiet as a boiler room in the middle of July . . . ."[36] In response to a question regarding "the greatest gain during your stay at Nichols," one student gave a rather puzzling, although interesting response. He claimed his greatest accomplishment at Nichols had been: "the inspiring thought I have had during the moment of silence at weekly Thursday morning convocations. . . . "[37]

Another set of examples of student thinking, perhaps even more revealing, is identified by the topics of an all-college public speaking contest. Each year a competition was held for the Eldon C. Grover Cup for Public Speaking with the top finishers addressing the entire College. The winners and their topics in 1949 suggest what some Nichols students then were thinking. The first prize that year went to Donald Hobson for his paper on "Our Current Trend toward Socialism." Student Hobson stressed the growing significance (or threat) of socialism as he saw it. Second prize was given to Stanford Renaud for his "Cruising Down the River," a rather insightful and realistic treatment of student attitudes regarding their college experience as suggested by his title. The third paper in the competition, "Has Free Enterprise been Overlooked?" resulted in Richard Hartman also winning a prize. His concern in 1949 about the apparent disappearance of free enterprise in the United States suggests what some Nichols students then perceived to be a changing economic climate.[38]

In a wider sense, the College's student newspaper, the *Nichols Budget*, focused mostly on extra-curricular activities and athletics during the period 1946 to 1950. And, as club activities expanded, there was more to cover. Yearly concert series, numerous and appreciated glee club appearances, the development of unique singing groups such as the Metronomes and Nicholodians, the appearance of a 25-member band, weekly convocations for the entire college, the existence of radio station WNJC on the second floor of the Academy building, campus building projects, and new faculty members all were featured in the college newspaper. But the principal *Budget* focus was on Nichols athletics. Additional successes by Bison teams as well as the appearance of new teams such as lacrosse occupied more than half the available news space. Surprisingly, even in the context of a post-war world, the *Nichols Budget* reported little on national events, political issues, and foreign affairs.

If this post-war era was destined to reset the Junior College's educational plan, it appears to have accomplished its goal by 1949 or 1950. Colonel Conrad's message to the Class of 1949 graduating that June summed up his feelings regarding the place of this class in the history of the College. As he saw it, "The Class of 1949 has left an indelible impression on the college in achievement, in contribution to athletics and other campus activities, and in the acceptance of responsibilities individually, and as a class, towards the ideals of the College."[39] This had been the high point of a brief era when the future of Nichols was still in doubt. With its 154 graduates, the Class of 1949 was the largest Nichols graduating class to that time and a fitting conclusion to an era that in many ways paralleled the first four years of the Junior College's existence in the 1930s.[40]

It also was easier for the College to spell out its educational plan with greater clarity after this period of "resetting." The College president explained it this way:

> Nichols is quite different in its outlook, its methods and its goal, and for nearly a quarter century it has occupied a unique place in the educational world.

> Nichols outlook is quite different because we believe the individual, not the material he studies, is the controlling factor in college life. The academic program, however, is a sound major in a business administration program balanced technically, socially and culturally. Mental ability and academic achievement no matter how highly developed, can be completely nullified by emotional instability or personality deficiencies which count more proportionately in social and economic life than in college. Nichols is attempting to contribute to the development of the whole individual.
>
> Our methods are unusual because we make comprehensive tests of each individual at the beginning of his first year and base our counsel and assistance on the results of our analyses. We examine his personality, his leadership characteristics, his vocational interests and general development and endowment in order to determine what he is best fitted for. We then employ all our human and educational resources in his individual growth and development.
>
> Our goal is unique too, since we require not simply that a student pass certain courses as such, but also that he develop his inherent abilities and capabilities to the fullest extent, and direct them into fields and levels where the greatest opportunity for his personal success exits.[41]

This new educational plan reemphasized close and frequent contact with individual students including counseling and comprehensive testing, numerous conferences with the Director of Guidance, and meetings with members of the Advisory Council.[42]

Perhaps one of the most obvious testimonies to the success of this "resetting" is found in the College's athletics program. By the end of 1949, Nichols, with its student body of 285 students, fielded teams in football, soccer, basketball, lacrosse, track, cross country, baseball, tennis, golf, and sponsored a Yacht Club. The most notable accomplishment in 1949 was the first and only undefeated and untied football team in the College's history. The team's 7–0 record qualified it for participation in the Junior Rose Bowl in Pasadena, California, a game intended to pit the best junior college football team in California against the best junior college eleven from the rest of the nation. Unfortunately, Little Rock Junior College from Little Rock, Arkansas, was chosen over Nichols Junior College to play in California.[43]

Then too, in another act of formal recognition, Ray Walcott of the 1947 Bison football squad and a 1949 graduate, was selected as a center on the All-American Junior College Football squad.[44] In another sport, the schedule of the 1949 Nichols soccer team included games against freshmen teams from three Ivy League schools and MIT. Not to be overlooked either is the fact that Nichols played its first home night football game in October 1947 at Webster's Memorial Field against the Stockbridge Aggies (a 0–0 tie) before 2,000 people.[45] This dimension of the College's educational plan was on its way to even greater success.

James L. Conrad at Mid-Point

In his brief history of Nichols, Darcy C. Coyle, third president of Nichols College, said of Colonel Conrad: "For thirty-five years beginning in 1931, the story of Nichols is, for the most part, the story of one man, James Lawson Conrad, the founder and first president of the College."[46] He generally was correct, although President Coyle does not go into specifics. In another instance, George Chisholm, professor emeritus of art at Nichols, who painted the official College portrait of its first president and only president of Nichols Junior College, presented him as a builder. Clearly he had been that, but there is still much more to be said.

In a general sense, the small college president has an awesome responsibility. Out of need and inclination, the president must be a leader, catalyst, administrator, teacher, confessor, and disciplinarian. The small college president is responsible for getting his or her students the best education, the best educational guidance, and the most rational physical and nutritional direction all in a healthy and complete educational climate and generally with the least amount of resources. The president also has to employ creative ability, give evidence of a broad educational philosophy to increase the value of the college and its students, and to understand the details of institutional operation.[47] If further illustration of this point is necessary, it can be said that the small college president needs to have both the "vision of a seer and the voice of a prophet."[48] Over time, President Conrad performed all of these tasks.

Without question, the first Nichols president always savored his relationships with his students and faculty. His leadership style and authority set the purpose and goals of his institution.[49] Furthermore, like so many of his presidential colleagues in these years, he also taught a course required of his senior class. Some presidents in liberal arts colleges offered capstone courses in "moral or natural philosophy."[50] In President Conrad's case, it was ethics or business law.

As to President Conrad's nature and leadership style, a number of people have spoken directly to this point. One yearbook recollection put it this way: "We will always remember him as a man who never let us down. His cheery smile and willingness to help made life easier for many of us. The graduating class [of 1939] can never give sufficient recognition to this man who has put the college on the map."[51] On a different note, one football player recalled President Conrad's words at the end of the school's first season in 1931 with a 2–5 won-lost record. According to this player, "The president's speech was delivered from man-to-man and not from president to students. President Conrad's address will be remembered for a long time as the highest tribute anyone can pay a team."[52]

He was a most effective communicator, even a splendid orator. Everyone at Nichols was a member of his team and he was able to make most understand this. He was always the coach, and a winning one at that. He understood that the game was won by the success of the players or, in an educational environment, the performance of the students.

Alumni from the 1932–1950 classes made a number of pertinent comments regarding President Conrad's nature, character and contributions in response to a question on a recent College "Historical Questionnaire." This asked for specific events or people to be included in the College's history. Some remembered his personal touch: he knew everyone by name as well as their GPA (grade point average), others recalled his "wonderful talks" at convocations. He was complimented for his "visionary leadership," his understanding of people and his emphasis on high ethical management. One concluded by noting that "the education at Nichols is so important, but it was the personal touch of Colonel Conrad that set the standards others followed."[53] Another added, "I thank him from the bottom of my heart for his steadfast faith in God, for his belief in the individual valor and dignity of every man, for the fostering of talent and ability in all whose lives he touched; the enthusiasm and understanding and a paternal affection that embraced us all."[54]

There also is much to say about the endurance of a college president who essentially began the same institution three times – in 1931, 1946, and 1958. Perhaps the earliest formal assessment of President Conrad's work came from members of the Nichols Academy Board of Trustees' Committee in 1941 that debated selling their campus and buildings to Nichols Junior College. As they saw it, in the first ten year period of his presidency, he doubled the value of the Nichols Academy property and obtained a "most vital" asset: a degree-granting privilege authorized by the Commonwealth. They concluded that "the College and Conrad. . . . would at once become an organization that would merit the enthusiastic support of all persons interested."[55]

But the task was not over in 1950. Nichols Junior College was just part of the way to his ultimate goal. At this point in the College's history, President Conrad had started and then restarted Nichols Junior College; he had adjusted his "new plan" and developed a program to fully focus on the talents of the individual students and their abilities. He created an institution that offered its students the opportunity to develop the skills and abilities necessary to be successful in a business environment that was becoming more difficult to understand.[56] His advice to a young man was to "strive for a balanced education."[57] And, perhaps most importantly, he taught them to accept and respect their responsibilities as professionals in the business world.

While the previous two decades had been devoted to preserving and building the institution, the next decades were to concentrate on changing it. This required the adjustment of all aspects of the still young college's administration, curriculum, academic standards, faculty, and campus – at the same time staying within the guidelines of initial educational plan and goals.

Recent studies have attempted to describe the leadership qualities necessary for complex tasks such as those faced by President Conrad throughout these early years. While these findings are intended to apply to today's business conditions, they conclude that the most effective leadership knows "how to blend technical competence, conceptual capacity, and interpersonal, even ethical dispositions."[58] For some, the type of mind set that seems to be best suited for dealing with these tasks is "integrative thinking." Leaders with this ability can put together patterns, connections, and relationships to make "integrative solutions."[59] This was the strength of the Nichols president.

Institutional success occurred at Nichols College in the 1950s because its trustees, president, and faculty worked to integrate the goals of the College (institutional acceptance and then regional accreditation) with the needs of its students (individual achievement and the desire to be part of a successful endeavor). This in turn led to the emergence of a successful and appreciated institution.[60] As to the results of his efforts, a recent analysis by generationalists Neil Howe and William Strauss commented that the people who built the widely acknowledged "GI Generation" came of age during the Great Depression and World War II. According to Howe and Strauss, the generations of Roosevelt and Truman "provided young people with principled leadership, challenges to character, ambitious national goals, and solid foundations for long term achievements."[61] This was Colonel Conrad's generation and these were his aims as well.

1950s – Adjustments for Growth

Colonel Conrad may have been a visionary but there was much to be done before Nichols could become a four-year college. For instance, the two-year college had to respond to a changing America and to the needs and opportunities stemming from the school's position and history as a successful innovator in business education. President Conrad now better understood that the educational context in which he was operating had become more complex. To be successful, extensive dialogue was necessary with groups representing state and regional accrediting agencies as well as the Nichols trustees, alumni, faculty, administration, and students. If a new school was to be constructed on the shoulders of the old, he had to be sure that the foundation was substantial.

This was a decade of immense achievement for the College and its president. The 1950s saw Nichols striving to become a four-year college of business administration. This required careful planning, patience, and commitment.

Over time Colonel Conrad created an administration with the experience and background capable of establishing a four-year institution. As had been

Colonel and Mrs. James L. Conrad.

the case since 1938, he was ably assisted by Hal Chalmers, now director of publicity and alumni relations, as well as athletic director, coach of three major sports, and assistant to the president, and George Gromelski, Class of 1938, who had joined the administration as bursar in 1946.

Dean Edward C. Leech, who replaced Dean Gilbert Garland in 1948, also became central to the process of expansion. He provided Nichols with an administrator of broad and active business experience as well as an important background in business education with a Master of Commercial Science degree (MCS) from the Amos Tuck School of Business Administration at Dartmouth College. His understanding of the nature of a complex business education was vital in making adjustments to the College's curriculum structure and faculty design. Dean Leech remained in this position for 11 years. In 1959 he resigned as Dean to head the College's marketing department.[62] He was assisted for a year by the appointment of a former instructor and Nichols coach, Everett Nordstrom, a Clark University graduate, to a newly created position of dean of men.

Dean Leech and Colonel Conrad were aided in curriculum matters by an active advisory council that met each semester with students and members of the faculty regarding current developments in their respective fields. After the Junior College reopened in 1946, the council reestablished its role in giving students all possible information regarding employment in any given field through an Advisory Council Day. This all-day event, which required the participation of all students, featured visiting speakers, including Nichols graduates. Students were offered "a concept of the scope and importance of business from a broad viewpoint, and in the panel discussions to provide an opportunity to explore the various fields, discuss potentialities and

Charles E. Leech,
B.S., M.C.S.
Dean, 1948–1959.

Everett R. Nordstrom,
B.B.A.
Dean of Men, 1956–1957.

requirements of the future, and to listen to or participate in case problems under consideration."[63] On more than one occasion, the student newspaper referred to an Advisory Council Day as "the most beneficial event of the school year," noting that it gave students the opportunity to get better acquainted with the business world.[64]

Second, a relatively new force was about to become increasingly active by 1950. Although a Nichols Alumni Association existed since the earliest days of the College, its strength, due to small enrollments and the war era, did not increase quickly, at least until 1950. In the meantime, Hal Chalmers served as alumni secretary and helped to produce the *Nichols Alumni Bulletin* several times each year. This moderately active pattern was to change significantly in late 1949 with the first unbeaten and untied Nichols football team.

While impressive athletic accomplishments occasionally occur at most colleges, the emergence of the 1949 unbeaten and untied football team was an energizing event for Nichols alumni. This team's record and consideration for an invitation to the Junior Rose Bowl in Pasadena, California, attested to the caliber of the team. For a small alumni group from a tiny school, this became an awakening moment. The 1949 team was "a big help for greater institutional recognition," as Nichols alumni saw it. Coach Chalmers became an "institutional hero" for a now generally excited alumni that concluded more was "needed to improve the public acceptance of the active college."[65]

Yet another move was made in 1950 to prepare for the new decade. That year, the College significantly expanded and strengthened its board of trustees. Originally composed of seven members, four new trustees were added that year. It had been President Conrad's original intention to bring together a "balanced" group of trustees including representatives from business, the public sector, and education. Perhaps one of the most important developments of the decade occurred in 1950 when three well-known educators with national reputations joined the board. They included Herluf V. Olsen, dean of the Amos Tuck School at Dartmouth College from 1937 to 1951; Dr. Frank L. Boyden, the highly respected headmaster of Deerfield Academy, Deerfield, Mass.; and Professor Leo D. O'Neil of the College of Business Administration at Boston University. A fourth new Nichols trustee, successful industrialist F. Harold Daniels, from Worcester, Massachusetts, also became a vital and contributing member of this reconstituted Nichols Board. Already in place as Nichols Junior College trustees were: Dr. Quincy H. Merrill who was chairman, Arthur J. C. Underhill, Joseph A. Smith, Nelson Conant, Earl Goodell, James L. Conrad, and Harry W. Wallis. Shortly thereafter, the Board was restructured into three committees focusing on finance, building and scholarship.[66]

Immediately this new trustees group reviewed the previous efforts of President Conrad to develop a four-year program in business administration. At the same time the College also considered an affiliation with the F. Harold Daniels School of Conservation and Forestry in Rutland, Massachusetts.[67] Trustee discussions during the early 1950s touched on wider topics as well including the restructuring of the Nichols campus, allowing the campus to be used by outside groups for educational and business purposes, considering a system of rank and tenure for faculty, and the expansion of the curriculum.

No one, however, understood the needs of the Junior College better than its president. In an interview with editors of the college yearbook in 1954, he said that Nichols, like many other private, non-profit institutions, was facing a critical period. He also felt that the demands for a college education due to population increase and generally improved economic conditions would necessitate physical plant and staff developments that were going to pose serious challenges.

A New Campus Emerges from the Old

In these discussions about expansion, President Conrad listed what was important to the future of Nichols. In the category of "essential construction projects" for the College, he included an addition to the infirmary, an architectural facelifting and addition to the Academy building, making the library adequate, adding a new dormitory, and construction of a new administration building. He also believed that alumni participation and contribution were critical to accomplish these goals.[68] In planning sessions between 1954 and 1965, he continually emphasized the need to balance residential needs with service facilities such as provided by the dining hall, recreational buildings and fields, and additional classroom space. It was concluded then that optimum student registrations would fall best for Nichols at the 700–1100–1500 enrollment levels. The Junior College with 345 students was going to aim for 700 immediately after becoming a four-year institution.

Based on these conclusions, the planning scheme for the redesigning and rebuilding of the campus was soon being implemented. (See Chart 4.2.)

Chart 4.2. Major Acquisition and Construction Projects, 1950–1958

1952	– Alumni Tower completed, bell installed.
1954	– Dormitory constructed for 68 students, named for F. Harold Daniels.
	– Ridings Memorial attached to Club House for visiting team locker rooms.
1956	– Conrad Hall administrative building to include four classrooms, library, and President's Office to be constructed over a Federal Reserve Bank vault.
1957	– Red Village School leased from Town of Dudley, originally built in 1893, later (1962) to be acquired.
1958	– Academy building front completed. (Project first begun after 1938 hurricane.)
	– Food service in Alumni Hall expanded to lower level.
	– Acquisition of 15 acre "bowl-shaped" area off Tanyard Road for new athletic fields.

Each of the three larger construction projects of the 1950s had a uniqueness that is worth noting. Daniels Hall, a dormitory intended to allow a 20 percent enrollment increase, was carefully constructed using former military barracks available as government surplus. Commercial building materials were difficult to obtain in a rapidly expanding American society.

Conrad Hall, named after President Conrad and intended to be the primary administrative building, was constructed on Academy Row with a base or lower level designed and built for the Federal Reserve Bank of Boston as a depository for its documents. Whether or not it was bomb-proof, as some claimed, is arguable, but it was considered to be a safe distance from a possible nuclear attack. By November 1955, records of the Federal Reserve Bank of Boston were being sent to Dudley Hill. When the lower level of Conrad Hall was no longer needed by the bank, it was to be turned over to the College. This occurred in 1963.[69]

And, third, an addition to the front of the Academy building was begun 20 years after its partial destruction by the 1938 hurricane. A five ton bell donated by the Federal Reserve Bank of Boston helped to complete a 44' x 24' addition to the Academy building. This bell was cast in 1877 by W. Blake of Boston, said to have been an apprentice of Paul Revere. It was set in place on the roof just

James L. Conrad Hall, the new administrative building
and library, also provides classrooms and individual
faculty offices. Completed in 1956.
Source: *Nichols Junior College Pictorial*, circa 1958.

over the main doorway.[70] These and other projects were funded by the College through individual donations, gifts, and the Surplus Property Act of 1944, in the case of Daniels Hall.

Construction and remodeling of Conrad Hall and the Academy building was intended to be consistent with the architecture originally put in place by Hezekiah Conant and Elbridge Boyden, the Worcester architect, in the 1880s. These buildings also fully established the academic nature of the upper campus. The President's office moved from Budleigh Hall on the lower campus, now a primary student residential area, to the upper campus and to Conrad Hall, with its new classrooms and the library, thus reestablishing this

**Construction underway for new athletic fields
off Tanyard Road, begun 1958.**
Source: Photograph in College Archives.

area as the campus academic center. To further expand and complete the upper campus, the College leased (and later acquired in 1962) the so-called Red School or town school (now Currier Center) originally constructed in 1893 by the Town of Dudley.[71] The latter completed an architecturally unmatchable row of Conant-built structures on the top of Dudley Hill.

And, in another significant and redesigning move, the College began to shift its long-established athletic fields from the west side of Center Road to a newly acquired area on the east side of Dudley Hill. This move required draining swamp lands and the construction of an athletic building on a steep hillside. The potential success of these construction projects was questioned by many skeptical local observers. In the process, the campus map of the Junior College was greatly altered.

Without question, the 1950s was a busy decade for the little school on the Hill. As the character and appearance of the College began to change, its educational program experienced adjustments as well. College officials had little choice but to deal with conditions simply not present before World War II. For instance, the administration's awareness of its vulnerability to losing students through military call-ups, its need to react to societal issues, and a desire to continually improve the College's academic standards all contributed to an already busy period for a small institution on its way to becoming a four-year college.

THE ENLISTED RESERVE CORPS

Seemingly apart from the business curriculum, Nichols became involved with the U.S. Army's Organized or Enlisted Reserve Corps in 1950. In fact, this partnership was closely associated with the College's historic vulnerability, as an all-male, two-year institution, to losing its student body during wartime. It also was consistent with its long-existing responsibility of providing leadership opportunities for its students. A lesson had been learned when Nichols Junior College was unable to function during World War II and all potential students either were in military service, enrolled in four-year colleges

Nichols Own Third Battalion. "Present Arms," on Nichols football field.
Source: *1954 Ledger*, 129.

The Colors, with the Ridings Memorial and the Club House (Bazzie's) in the background.
Source: *1957 Ledger*, 110.

where they might receive draft deferments, or involved in necessary war work. To improve the College's position after World War II, President Conrad requested that the Army award Nichols with an ROTC unit, but was refused because Nichols was only a two-year college.[72]

During the Cold War that followed World War II, many Americans believed that military action in the near future was probable. This, according to the college newspaper, raised the question of whether college students were going to be deferred.[73] As a result, in 1950 Nichols Junior College requested and received permission from the Department of Army to establish the first college-based unit of the Army Organized Reserve Corps: the 3rd Battalion of the 376th Infantry Regiment of the 94th Infantry Division.[74] This new program had the combined purposes of providing students with an opportunity to prepare for military service by completing military service requirements while in college and offering the chance for additional leadership experience all while establishing a stable enrollment for the College.

The new program, termed the Enlisted Reserve Corps (ERC, sometimes ORC), was later adopted at other colleges. It made it possible for some students to complete their academic programs without interruptions, although military deferment was not guaranteed by an ERC enlistment. Those involved in satisfying military reserve requirements through the ERC received elective college credits and were paid for duty time, all on the Nichols campus. A summer 15-day training period at an Army reserve camp completed the requirement.[75]

Foresters demonstrate their skills.
Source: *1967 Ledger*, 46.

Six companies of Army reservists were in place on the Nichols campus by 1952. This program began at Nichols in September 1950 with 34 enlisted men; 130 were enlisted by 1952.[76] Some came from outside the college community. After it began, the *Ledger* recalled that "Colonel Conrad had become recruiting sergeant and C.O." although this was not actually the case.[77] Seven years after the program had begun, the College received the Department of Defense Reserve Award and Citation for outstanding cooperation with the Reserve Program of the Armed Forces. The program eventually ended at Nichols in 1963 when military reserve requirements were changed.

A Conservation and Forestry Program

Importantly, the ERC was not the only new program of some consequence introduced at Nichols in the first half of the 1950s. When Worcester industrialist, F. Harold Daniels, joined the Nichols Junior College Board of Trustees in 1950, he brought a long-held interest in education. Aside from former associations with several Worcester colleges as a trustee, Daniels also was responsible for the F. Harold Daniels School of Conservation and Forestry at the Daniels Forest in Rutland, Massachusetts. He was assisted there by the Worcester Museum of Natural History directed by Richard Potter. After some discussions, the Nichols Junior College Board of Trustees agreed to create an academic specialization in the field of conservation and forestry with its graduates receiving the College's ABA degree.

This arguably was the only program of its type in the East. Courses were first offered on the Nichols campus by Museum Director Potter. A five-week summer session was held at the 1,500 acre Daniels Forest, later at a state park in nearby Douglas, Massachusetts. After a slow beginning with seven students in 1954, 30 were admitted in 1956.[78] These new students took the College's required courses in business, as well as their own specialized courses. This made it possible to educate men for the business of protecting our natural resources. Much more would be heard from the Nichols foresters during the 1960s.

To a Four-Year Program in Business

In this active growth period during the 1950s, the Nichols Board of Trustees also approved adult education courses, a foundation and refresher program especially for foreign students and former servicemen, a freshman program for improvement in English, the development of an integrative approach to senior year classes (the beginnings of specializations), and a larger number of electives along with a two-year concentration in conservation and forestry. Integrated classes were made available for forestry students by instructors such as Professor John Katori who offered accounting courses to foresters. Nonetheless, in the larger picture as seen by the College, its "Educational Plan" remained constant – "a program of studies fundamental to business and life amid cultural surroundings" now included conservation and forestry.[79]

Of some help in evaluating general curriculum development at Nichols are the results of a questionnaire done in the mid-1950s by a large national company that provide a guide for courses most suitable for a program in business administration. "Most valuable," as in the past, was English followed by mathematics, economics, accounting, and specialized business. "Least valuable" included physics, chemistry, sciences, history and foreign languages. In another category labeled "most recommended for management responsibility," first came English, then economics, various business courses, mathematics and engineering. The same study found those who completed the questionnaire believed that subject matter rather than teaching personality (55.8% to 44.51%) was more important in their courses. It also revealed that 80% of those surveyed participated in extracurricular activities.[80] One suspects that similar results would have been obtained at Nichols.

While the busy course of the Junior College can be traced without difficulty during the early 1950s, the story of efforts to acquire the four-year college designation is less obvious. For one, College officials were concerned that a failure to receive state approval for the four-year program could result in a negative mark against the Junior College. President Conrad's desire to create a four-year college had been introduced during the 1930s and followed by requests for changes in name and purpose to the Massachusetts Board of Collegiate Authority in 1947 and 1948. These requests brought mixed signals. This Board's suggestions for curriculum changes led the Nichols president, after a brief trial, to reject its recommendations and Nichols trustees restored the former curriculum.[81]

The College trustees then formally reviewed the position of Nichols Junior College achieved prior to 1955. This review, conducted by new trustees with established educational backgrounds, verified that Nichols Junior College had been the first college of its kind to introduce required courses in psychology, obtain degree granting privileges, develop an operational plan for an advisory council, institute a full program of extra-curricular activities and athletics, offer a Quartermaster Training Corps program, and promote new courses in ethics, news analysis, production, and forestry and conservation as well as offering a business administration program.[82]

At the same time, Colonel Conrad began to take definite steps to put a four-year college in place. The *Bison* (formerly the *Budget*) pointed out the advantages of such a program from a student perspective.[83] According to the College newspaper, gains could include a wider selection of courses, stronger athletic teams, better student leadership, as well as the eventual acquisition of a four-year diploma. In March 1953, the College announced the establishment of a three-year program.[84] This was first seen as a post-graduate year with no degree to be awarded.[85] It was intended to be a step toward a bachelor degree for the College. In fact, however, only a small number of students took this additional year and it soon was discontinued.

In 1955, the Nichols Board of Trustees recommended that a trustee committee consider the advisability of Nichols becoming a four-year institution.[86] Over the next three years, the trustee committee examined this recommendation.[87] The Nichols Board then voted to accept a change of name and purpose including previous graduation requirements focusing on good character, citizenship, and gentlemanship.[88] Formal state approval was next.

The Nichols Man

As the Massachusetts Board of Collegiate Authority considered the Nichols proposal, students in Dudley had more immediate concerns. Nichols registered a total of 352 day students in 1957. (See Chart 4.1.) The student body that year hailed from 17 states with the largest representation from New York (122) followed by Massachusetts (79). Five students came from Cuba, two from Mexico, with one each from Costa Rica, Nicaragua, Argentina, and France.[89] Veterans no longer were in the majority.[90]

When registering in the 1950s, students received the customary advice from college administrators, faculty, and upper classmen. This "rule of thumb" for campus living focused on courtesy and consideration, personal satisfaction and development through intramural activities, training in working democracy, intellectual growth, decision making, and discharging responsibilities through student government. According to the *Bison*, incoming students also were informed that "The Colonel [Conrad] makes it a point to make close personal contacts with each boy here at Nichols."[91]

Student interests and preferences for this 1950s group can be determined by responses in the *Bison* "Question Box" and topics in the annual public speaking competition that reveal broadening student horizons. Topics and responses in the last years of the two-year college dealt with more expansive social issues such as "segregation," "Argentina," "Are you a Man?" and "Public Accounting as a Career." On weekends these students said they went in search of interesting people.[92] When asked why they did not seem to support activities on the Hill, their answers ranged from "laziness" to "Nichols is one of the few schools that prohibits any drinking. . . ."[93] One student who transferred to Nichols was able to compare the Dudley college's students with those of his previous college. His conclusion: Nichols men thought more about more things, other than studying. Nichols men preferred rock n' roll and jazz over classical music, beer and liquor over Coca-Cola, "bull sessions" over studying, and liked their weekends elsewhere.[94]

But this only begins to introduce the "Nichols Man." In the 1950s, most accepted that a Yale man or a Harvard man or a Dartmouth man existed as an identifiable male. To complete the Nichols picture, the editors of the 1955 Nichols yearbook, the *Ledger*, set out to describe "what kind of boy goes to Nichols."

"Vital Statistics" (and more) of The Nichols Man

The Nichols man seems to be slightly taller than the average for the American population. He is about nineteen or twenty and averages one hundred and fifty-five pounds. He is at ease and most comfortable in sport clothes with cordovans, a four-in-hand slim tie, over a button-down white shirt. More often than not you will find him in khaki pants, T-shirt and white bucks. He is not an early riser, and prefers coffee or milk with his breakfast. (In fact, milk seems to be his favorite beverage throughout the rest of the day.) If he smokes, (and the majority do) he prefers Chesterfield or Lucky Strikes. He finds Saturday classes unnecessary; his greatest interest is in Law with the straight business subjects following a close second (Marketing, Management, Accounting, etc.). This seems most appropriate since his goal is to plan to further his education after leaving the Hill and would stay if four years were offered, including fraternities and feminine companionship.

Like most Americans he is an ardent sport spectator and participator. Basketball, Baseball, Lacrosse and Soccer in that order appear to be most popular. His avocation and activities run the gamut from art appreciation to uke playing with photography and sailing outstanding. He prefers to dance to popular music in waltz or fox trot time to bandleaders as Miller, Elgart, Anthony, and Kenton. If he were to sit and listen to music in his dorm the popular or jazz records would be spinning on his phonograph. As for vocalists, he likes Doris Day and Eddie Fisher.

His ideal girl would have the classical 36-bust, 24-waist, 36-hips, with blond or brunette hair, he feels that Marilyn Monroe or Terry Moore excitingly fit this description. Paradoxically enough, when asked who he would like to be snowbound with, he answers very practically, his own girl, who more than likely does not fit the description of his own ideal. He goes steady and thinks that engagements should last between one and three years, without the customary ring. He does not approve of teen-age marriages or elopements. Before getting married he would like to be financially stable and after marriage he plans on being the head of the house, with three or four children, where the wife stays at home; he would rather have his home situated in a small town.

In his serious moments he would say that Lincoln was our greatest president, and believes that Churchill and Eisenhower are the greatest men of our times. In rapid succession he would approve of Universal Military Training, and tell you that eighteen years olds should not vote. Pessimistically enough, he believes that we will eventually have war with Russia. He would like to see segregation ended and believes the reinforcement of these laws are timely.

And as our picture of him fades he would be most happy if he could drive away from us in a brand new Ford.[95]

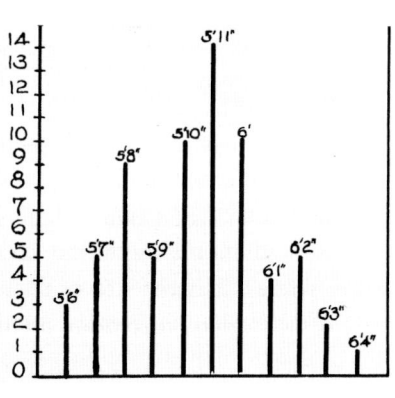

"Range" of heights for Nichols Students, Class of 1955.
Source: *1955 Yearbook*, 47.

Obvious growth and excitement on campus also strengthened the recreational program as it managed to keep its place in the "educational plan" of Nichols Junior College. In 1956, the institutional purpose remained to "give every young man an opportunity for wholesome competitive sports."

Athletics continued to be seen contributing to the health and character of the Nichols man as well as being necessary for college life and spirit.[96]

With this continued support and faculty involvement, the Nichols approach to athletic competition continued at the highest level. Chalmers-coached basketball teams represented New England in regional championships in 1952 and won the New England Junior College championship in 1957.[97] The College also briefly added swimming to its list of supported teams and developed a lacrosse squad that was successful beyond all expectations. In 1958, the Nichols soccer team saw seven of its members selected for the New England Junior College soccer team.[98]

Nonetheless, even in the best of times, the course of a competitive athletics program could not be guaranteed. After a difficult and unsuccessful football season in 1958, coach Chalmers approached the President about dropping football (other small colleges were doing this) and focusing on soccer which was attracting outstanding players to Nichols. After a quick discussion, President Conrad then bluntly informed Coach Chalmers that "the College always had football and always will."[99] The next year a new football coach was hired. Coach Chalmers then coached only two major sports along with his other numerous duties. In 1955 he also became a part time scout for the Detroit Tigers.[100]

As in the past, the generally successful experience of the athletics program was paralleled by an active intramural program and other extra-curricular activities. At one point, the college newspaper, the *Budget*, changed its name to the *Bison*.[101] The editors of the College's *Alumni Magazine* immediately complained. But apparently the new *Bison* editors felt the name "Budget" was too closely associated with business. In response, the alumni editors sarcastically responded that they thought Nichols was a business college.[102]

And, with time, "college regulations" were adjusted to the likes of more students although never far enough. Generally these "adjustments" focused on times of meals or other limitations in dormitories. The later dealt with quiet hours and limited the use of radios to 11:15 P.M. The possession and use of alcohol was strictly forbidden on the two-year college campus and a dress code still existed. Class attendance was being monitored by the Dean's office, but some cuts were allowed.[103]

One serious incident marred an otherwise impressive march toward four-year college status. In 1953, 60 Nichols students were involved in a panty raid at a Worcester junior college that drew the attention of the Worcester police and news services. One former student declared that the planning of this raid had been so skillful that they should have been complimented rather than punished. The administration saw it differently. A number of students were restricted to campus for three weeks.[104]

Few institutions experienced the tides of good fortune that affected Nichols Junior College between 1946 and 1958. Due to a committed board of trustees charged with supporting the still-young college, Nichols could rearrange its campus – and it did. Colonel Conrad could further develop his plan for a four-year college of business administration – and he did. More students could attend Nichols – and many did in part because of the GI Bill. An improved institutional academic performance was a result. By its efforts and commitment to the plan of 1931, Nichols Junior College and its students moved to a level of accomplishment necessary to become a four-year college.

Many students understood the significance of this time at Nichols. In an editorial in 1956 titled "Enthusiasm, Spirit, Determination," the *Bison* reminded freshmen:

> It is your spirit that will prove your worthiness as a group. Nichols needs a forceful and driving student body who will repay her for what they take from her. You paid $1500 to be able to call Nichols your college but that right is still not yours until you earn it. . . .She will thrive only if you inspire her. . . . be worthy of your heritage.[105]

These had been memorable years for those associated with Nichols. At the graduation of one of the last associate degree classes in June 1959, Dean Leech wished them well. In his words, "May you all develop that kind of leadership that others will gladly follow."[106]

Graduation 1959. ("Neath Copper Beeches")
Source: *1959 Ledger*, n.p.

CHAPTER 5

NICHOLS COLLEGE OF BUSINESS ADMINISTRATION, 1958~1966

Nichols College of Business Administration Seal, 1959.
A new College seal appeared after the two-year college became a four-year college in 1958. Its center shield, noting the virtues of loyalty, service and culture with fasces displaying inward-facing axes, was virtually unchanged. Altered, however, was the seal's border which now included two dates: "1815" for the school's founding as an academy and "1958" for the four-year College's beginning as "NICHOLS COLLEGE OF BUSINESS ADMINISTRATION." This becomes part of the border. (An unofficial, Latinized version of this seal appeared on several College yearbooks in the mid-1960s.)
Source for seal (1959): *Bison*, October 31, 1959, 1.

On Friday, June 9, 1961, the first graduate of Nichols College of Business Administration walked across the stage in the College auditorium to receive his degree of Bachelor of Business Administration (BBA). He was followed by 47 other graduates of the new four-year college. Forty-four members of this class began at Nichols Junior College in September, 1957; four transferred from other colleges. Nichols trustee, benefactor, and industrialist, F. Harold Daniels, added to the importance of the College's celebration by delivering the commencement address. President Conrad then congratulated the members of the class for being the first four-year graduates of Nichols College and thanked them and their parents most sincerely "for having confidence in the College's administration and faculty."[1] This was a memorable day carefully described in Hal Chalmers' five-page article in the *Nichols Alumnus*.[2]

Between 1958 and 1966, Nichols moved from a comfortable and long-established niche as an outstanding all-male, two-year, private college of

Academy Building with new frontage, 1958.
Source: *1959 Ledger*, 18.

business administration to become a four-year college of business administration. It was a notable achievement that led to the further development of an innovative curriculum and to additional institutional facilities and personnel capable of promoting and sustaining this change. This also included students carefully selected for admission to the two-year college in 1957 and then individually reviewed by the Nichols faculty before being accepted in 1959 as juniors and members of the College's first graduating class in 1961.

Transition from a two- to a four-year college entailed three development phases. The first or pre-1958 period was introduced in the previous chapter as the College prepared for a change in classification. This was achieved in December 1958 when the Board of Collegiate Authority of the Commonwealth of Massachusetts approved Nichols Junior College's request to become a four-year college. The second phase occurred during the years between 1958 and 1961 as the College worked to graduate its first students and achieve the internal status and structure of a four-year institution.

The third period was from 1961 to 1966 as Nichols sought to gain acceptance from the greater educational community through regional accreditation and approval of its athletics program. Each period had its own separate challenges. This led to a busy, exciting and unparalleled eight-year era as Nichols gained long-sought goals.

Not surprisingly, during this period of institutional emergence, initial and significant internal debate occurred regarding College standards and directions. How many students already preparing to leave Nichols Junior College in 1959 and 1960 would be interested in remaining for a third and fourth year? Another group of students looking for an established two-year school might go elsewhere. Nichols trustees, numerous visitation teams, members of various associations, faculty members, and students all became involved in the complex details of this institutional advancement. Yet, despite the numerous barriers, a number of additional institutional milestones were reached by 1966. This included a Sesquicentennial Celebration, regional accreditation, membership in the National Association of Intercollegiate Athletics (NAIA) and the National Collegiate Athletic Association (NCAA), as well as the retirement of its first and only president.

Business Education in 1958

Business education was much different in 1958 than it had been in 1931 when Nichols was firmly alone in New England as a two-year college of business administration. By the mid-1950s, however, a number of studies appeared that examined the quality, role, and direction of business programs in American higher education. This was to be one of the first occasions when educators focused on the nature of business education in America. Most accepted that the sudden and remarkable growth of business education had to be examined due to the increasing number of business students and the continued concerns of some educators about accepting professional courses in place of traditional liberal arts courses. Their studies were sponsored by the Carnegie and Ford Foundations along with various doctoral dissertations all seeking to determine the primary features of a successful business curriculum.[3] To these can be added a study done by a Nichols trustee committee as part of its consideration of the new four-year Nichols program.[4]

One frequent issue underlying their collective assessments in 1958 was the perceived need to create programs combining liberal arts and business or professional courses. Less certain, however, was the specific arrangement of these courses in a curriculum. There also was a growing concern regarding the quality of business education in the United States due to the increasing "impact of American business and industry on the world...."[5]

Nichols trustees, including former Dartmouth Tuck School Dean, Herluf Olsen, and former B.U. Professor Leo O'Neil, took note of much of this material.[6] With President Conrad and trustee Harry Wallis, they sought to focus on the relationship between business schools and their students. The Nichols trustees' subsequent report concluded that a student's educational preparation should be determined by intellectual qualities, to the extent needed in management positions, and to "relate more to habits of work, ways of going at problems, and capacities for analytical and imaginative reasoning rather than to specific bodies of knowledge or specific types of training."[7] And they determined that "... little will avail if the individual does not take up the task of self education."[8] It also asserted that "a major responsibility of any Business School ... is to do everything possible to get the student to think for himself, and develop the necessary habits of mind and basic intellectual equipment for doing so effectively."[9]

A special thirteen member committee initially was created to assist in the planning of the new Nichols curriculum. This group, consisting of trustees, Nichols Advisory Council members, alumni, and educators from outside the College, concluded there was a place for a small, select, four-year, country-campus college of business administration in New England and that Nichols had the potential to become this institution.[10]

The "Momentum of Growing"[11]

Not surprisingly, speculation on the Nichols campus about a new four-year program was high in the late 1950s. The editor of the *1958 Yearbook* wanted to know: "Will Nichols become a senior college?"[12] The Nichols *Bison* was carefully watching this development and reported in December 1957 that "a few gentlemen visited the college to see if Nichols could be converted into a four-year institution." The newspaper then added, "If this college is going to be turned into a four-year college there are numerous problems that will have to be solved." It also wondered if Nichols Junior College was going to be called "Nichols College."[13] Several months later, in the spring of 1958, after an interview with Nichols trustee and professor, Leo D. O'Neil, the *Bison* decided that Nichols eventually would go to four years, but considered it doubtful for the next year.[14] Few on campus thought that a decision was imminent.

At the Nichols Junior College Board of Trustees Spring meeting on May 10, 1958, it was voted to propose that Nichols Junior College of Business Administration and Executive Training become Nichols College of Business Administration. This included the request to change its purpose by granting the degree of bachelor of business administration to candidates judged by the administration and the faculty "as having successfully completed the required four-year academic program and having demonstrated qualities of good character, citizenship, and gentlemanliness."[15] Once the Nichols Junior College Board of Trustees voted to "recognize" Nichols as a four-year college, a dynamic process was set in motion.[16]

History was made in December 1958 when the Massachusetts Board of Collegiate Authority voted unanimously to permit Nichols Junior College, the state's first all-male junior college, to be the state's first junior college to become a four-year degree-granting college.[17] With this announcement by the Commonwealth, the next stage of institutional expansion began.[18]

Nichols, however, was not the only institution affected by the 1958 decision of the Massachusetts Board of Collegiate Authority. A number of private junior colleges in the state now gained the opportunity to change their classifications. Several other specialized institutions in New England could consider becoming four-year colleges of business administration and this happened – after 1958.

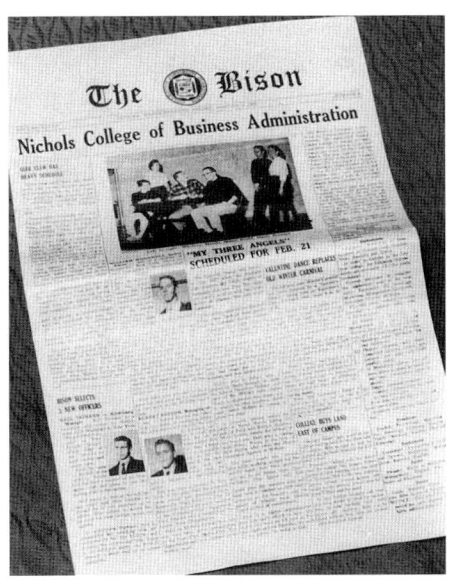

Photo of *Bison* issue announcing Nichols
College Business Administration.
Source: *1959 Ledger*, 77.

"4-YEAR PROGRAM OKED FOR NICHOLS"[19]

The years between 1958 and 1961 then became a most challenging period for Nichols College and its administrators. For instance, in September 1958, prior to the decision of the Board of Collegiate Authority, as director of admissions I had to deal with a number of issues. First, I was informed that two catalogs had to be ready for December: one for the junior college; the other for a new bachelor degree program yet to be described, announced, or approved. Once (and if) the bachelor degree program was approved by the Commonwealth, the admissions department then had four different assignments: first, admit two-year students for the next September (the last class for two-year business students to graduate with an ABA degree would be in 1961); second, develop an admission process for four-year students entering as freshmen in 1959 and graduating in 1963; and, third, to consider applications from members of the Nichols Junior College Classes of 1959 and 1960 applying to become members of Nichols College classes graduating with bachelor degrees in 1961 and 1962.[20] The fourth concerned the admission of forestry students to the ABA program.

This was a momentous occasion in a period of challenging developments. New academic programs had to be available for this increased enrollment, housing had to be constructed, and athletic director Hal Chalmers had to change virtually all athletic schedules within three years to reflect the College's change of classification.

The Commonwealth's decision in 1958 made it possible for Nichols Junior College of Business Administration and Executive Training to become Nichols College of Business Administration. For nearly a year the College's trustee-appointed committee worked to expand the two-year college curriculum essentially in place since 1931. According to President Conrad in 1958, the new four-year curriculum, then about to be introduced, had first-year students taking courses similar to those offered in a liberal arts college. Second- and third-year Nichols students were to take courses in basic business programs in marketing, management, finance, and accounting that had previously made up the two-year program. Nichols Junior College students found the move to the four-year school was easily accomplished since the new curriculum was built around the existing two-year program. (See Appendix E.)

In addition, new requirements had students working in approved summer jobs before both their third and fourth years. This, President Conrad said, would provide an excellent background for students about to enter the business world. Fourth-year students were to return to classes and analyze business problems in a scheduled business clinic. The problems discussed in this clinic were to be supplied by an active advisory council composed of Nichols graduates and outstanding businessmen. Seniors also had to write a thesis and take two semesters of logic and commercial law. Their various concentrations were supported by courses in art, literature, and science intended to enrich individual backgrounds.[21] (See Appendix E.)

As presented in 1958, the Nichols four-year program required a number of institutional adjustments. For one, total enrollment was expected to nearly double in a few years leading to the construction of new dormitory facilities along with additional service and recreational areas. Between 1958 and 1963, student enrollment increased from 362 to 603. Then too, the institution's administrative and faculty infrastructures had to be re-evaluated as they moved from a two-year to a four-year academic environment. The former dormitory master approach which had worked so well for so long was to be changed; faculty members were required to improve their academic credentials in order to teach in a program now granting baccalaureate degrees. More faculty had to be appointed as well to offer courses to an increasing enrollment. And, to add to this upgrading, accreditation as a four-year college had to be achieved. This was a significant challenge for a specialized school in the 1960s.

What followed over the next eight years was the most complete reconstruction of the institution since Hezekiah Conant rebuilt the Academy's entire campus in the early 1880s. A new campus area had to be created to the east and rear of Budleigh, Daniels and Merrill Halls and next to Conant Pond. To add necessary space to this area, a parcel of fifteen acres was acquired in 1958 for new athletic fields replacing those existing on the west side of Center

Chart 5.1. Major Plant Acquisitions and Construction Projects, 1958–1966

1958	Land with bowl-shaped terrain off Tanyard Road acquired for athletic facilities.
1959	Forestry Hall constructed as dormitory for 28 students, to be classroom building in 1961. Football field with quarter mile track under construction at "big bowl;" first used in 1960. T-Hall renovated. Underhill Hall, dormitory, constructed to house 42 students.
1960	Smith Hall, dormitory, constructed to house 42 students. Goodell Hall, dormitory, constructed to house 65 students.
1962	Library Building, four-stories, constructed to include Conant Library. Former Village School, constructed in 1893, purchased, renamed Dr. Quincy H. Merrill Infirmary.
1963	Former Conant Library and Observatory renovated to become an Interfaith Chapel. O'Neil Hall, dormitory, constructed to house 65 students. Senior Dining Room opened on the lower floor of Alumni Hall. Houlberg House acquired to assist in development of new athletic area.
1963–5	Physical Education Building, swimming pool (dedicated to Robert Hermann, Class of 1948) and field house (later named Chalmers Field House) completed.
1963	Federal Reserve Bank turned over lower floor of Conrad Hall to Nichols as per agreement.
1964	Forestry Hall expanded, laboratory added.
1965	Way House on Dudley Hill purchased. Former gymnasium renovated to become a permanent auditorium with seating for 725. Discussions with Town of Dudley begun on all-campus sewerage connection. New clubhouse constructed for the Nichols College Golf Course.

Sources: Minutes, Nichols College of Business Administration, Trustee Meetings, 1958–1966; *The Nichols Bison*, 1956–1966; Nichols *Yearbooks*, 1958–1966; Nichols College of Business Administration, *Bulletin*, Catalog Issues, 1958–1966.

Road. This included the construction of a field house. Some details were being discussed by college administrators prior to 1958, but all adjustments were contingent upon a change of classification to a four-year school. These plans immediately were activated in 1958 although this only began the process.

Specifically, during the period 1959 to 1966, the new four-year college erected four new dormitories (Underhill, Goodell, Smith and O'Neil), renovated another (T-Hall), and converted a sixth (Forest Hall, about to be Forestry Hall) into classrooms. New athletic facilities being built included a football field and track, a swimming pool, a physical education building and a field house. Additional structures included a four-story library building, remodeled older buildings, a general up-dating of the infirmary (now in the former Village School), the renovation of the former gym and auditorium, and the creation of a chapel in the former Conant Library. Planning for a new all-campus drainage and sewage system was begun as well. And Conant Hall, a long-time dormitory, was scheduled to become a faculty office building. (See Major Plant Acquisitions and Construction Projects, 1958–1966, Chart 5.1.)

These new buildings shifted the residential and recreational center of the Nichols campus to the eastern part of the lower campus. At the same time, the upper or northern section of the campus now featured a new library building thereby adding to the area's role as the College's academic center.

Library Building, 1962.
Source: *Nichols College of Business Administration Bulletin*, 1963–64, n.p.

Much of this construction was somewhat unique. While its buildings were practical and conservatively built, their construction had to be accomplished with scarce building materials. Parts of some new buildings were acquired from Otis Air Force Base on Cape Cod. Moreover, the dorms with capacities of 50 to 60 students were intended to last for no more than 30 to 40 years. President Conrad believed that student living styles changed with each generation. When he reviewed the need to renovate the former Conant Library and Observatory building, he determined that it could serve as an interfaith or non-denominational Chapel for the Newman, Hillel and Christian Clubs or organizations. Organ music as frequently heard in vesper services could be piped from the Chapel to the upper campus from 5:15 to 5:45 P.M. each afternoon.[22]

Interfaith Chapel, 1963.
Source: *Nichols College Bulletin, 1984–87*, 14.

A NEW ATHLETIC AND RECREATIONAL CENTER

Vastly improved athletic facilities by 1965 made it possible for the College to conduct more extensive sports and recreational programs. This expansion seems an easy decision. Nonetheless, some staff members had been concerned that an expansion of the athletic program could succeed only "if the new four-year program created additional interest in the College athletic set-up."[23] That this question was asked at all suggests the status of small college athletics in 1958 and the risks involved in the commitment regarding new athletic fields and a field house. Furthermore, as a microcosm of the greater changes that also were occurring, it identifies the nature of the much greater risk being taken by President Conrad and the College's board of trustees in 1958 with its institutional change to an unknown new four-year specialized college.

As for the new athletic complex itself, it was intended to be substantial. This structure or structures contained a then standard collegiate swimming pool – the "Robert Hermann Swimming Pool of Nichols" (dedicated to Robert Hermann '48) – a physical education area, a portable basketball court, a carefully prepared dirt floor (for baseball practice) and a batting cage. When needed, as was the case for graduation ceremonies, this building had a seating capacity of nearly 1500.[24] According to one report, in 1964 the College had the largest swimming pool and the only field house on a college campus in Central Massachusetts.[25] The field house was the ninth addition to the physical plant between 1958 and 1964.[26] This building's cost, along with its attached structure was given as $1,237,000 in 1965. ($8,870,921 in 2011 dollars.)[27] This had been made possible by gifts from Nichols trustees, Nichols alumni, the Academy trustees, and one alumni fund drive. Accumulated college surpluses and

View of field house from the east.
Source: *1966 Ledger*, 210.

New Auditorium (formerly old gym, now Daniels Auditorium), 1965.
Source: Nichols College of Business Administration, *Alumni Bulletin, 1969*, rear of back cover.

Merrill Infirmary, 1962–1997.
Source: *Nichols College Catalog, 1984–87*, 14.

instances of careful borrowing provided for the remainder. Partly as a result of the College's expanded athletic facilities, the College could become a member of the National Association of Intercollegiate Athletics (NAIA) in 1962 and the National Collegiate Athletic Association (NCAA) in 1965. This was a proper and appreciated recognition for the College's commitment to intercollegiate athletics since 1931.

Other institutional changes followed as well. New lecture halls, each seating 200 people, were built in both the new library building and Forestry Hall. The "old barn" originally used by the Conants as a stable in the 1880s, later a gymnasium, and occasionally a dining hall, was renovated to become an auditorium with seating for over 700 people. Forestry Hall initially was constructed to house 28 students to pay for construction costs. Within five years, and encouraged by the continued growth of the forestry enrollment, it was converted to a classroom building with laboratories and a lecture hall. (For a brief overview of these developments, see Chart 5.1.)

In a 1966 report, President Conrad said that he designed these new College buildings himself.[28] As for institutional debt when he left office, he reported: "As of July 1, 1966, the College was completely free of debt, except for current 30-day obligations, and has a very substantial surplus."[29]

Other Needs

Aside from substantially altering the campus footprint between 1958 and 1966, the essential nature of the school was being changed as well. Adding to the College's physical plant was only part of the adjustment necessary for Nichols to become a regionally accredited four-year college. The second step was to transform its administration and faculty to meet the projected needs of the College and the standards of an accrediting agency. Also necessary was the need to finalize its new curriculum. The College immediately began to make the necessary physical plant adjustments. Virtually everything was being reviewed and possibly changed to support the College's new classification.

Administrative leadership evolved from a tightly organized, administrative committee in the 1950s to a more formal group with several layers of administrators by the mid-1960s. A new Dean of Faculty, Charles M. Quinn, was added and the responsibilities of the new Registrar and Dean of Men, Robert H. Eaton, were increased. Both were to make significant contributions to the development of the new College. Dean Eaton replaced Dean George Chisholm in 1961 who succeeded Dean Leech in 1959. The trustees focused on strengthening the faculty structure by carefully identifying areas of development that included such benefits as salary structure, ranks, tenure, sabbaticals and other considerations. Many were made available for the first time. (See Appendix F.)

Charles M. Quinn,
B.S., M.B.A.
Dean of Faculty,
Executive Vice President,
1961–1976.

George F. Chisholm,
A.B., M.A.
Dean of Students,
1960–1961.

Robert H. Eaton,
A.B., M.A.
Dean of Men/Registrar,
1962–1979.

Perhaps most interesting and innovative was the manner in which the four-year curriculum was supported by several non-academic requirements. These included an organized summer work program – then described as "a type of business internship" – initially conceived and supervised by Dr. Lawrence Nath, and a business clinic and thesis requirement scheduled for the senior year. All had one basic goal for the Nichols student: to create "close ties between the practical world of business and the classroom."[30] As such, they reflected President Conrad's best effort to bring the two together. Professor Nath also led a Nichols College European Summer Study Tour that examined business, political, and economic conditions in locations such as London, Brussels, Germany, Austria, Venice, Milan, Zurich and Paris.[31] This satisfied the summer work program requirement as well.

At the same time, the Nichols College Evening Division was accelerated because it was felt that the "College owed a debt to the community and its citizens."[32] Its courses, by 1964, were the same as those offered in the day program.[33] This was the College's second effort to introduce what was then termed "adult education."

One who held that there had been little basic change in the College was President Conrad. The purpose of the College as stated in 1931 was to establish "an institution where a student can secure a college education in business administration and at the same time enjoy the advantages of dormitory and campus life in an rural environment."[34] In his opinion this remained the case. Furthermore, he would argue that, despite the increased size of the College's enrollment – from 362 in 1958, the last year of the two-year college, to 642 in September 1964 with four classes – the size of the entering or first year class was virtually unchanged. In 1958, the freshman class was 213; in 1959 it increased slightly to 220. By 1964 the freshman class size actually dropped to 203.[35] The College had no boarding vacancies over this period.

In his welcoming address to freshmen in 1964, Dean of Men and Registrar Robert H. Eaton explained the College's purpose this way: "A basic philosophy at Nichols is that we are interested in developing the entire student; in other words, Nichols is interested in seeing its students do well academically, socially, and athletically. Nichols has many extracurricular opportunities, so be sure and avail yourselves of as many of these as possible."[36] The number of students involved in student activities confirmed their continuing part in life at Nichols. An analysis done in 1963 by the Office of Student Activities determined that 83 percent of the student body that year was participating in campus activities (athletics and student organizations).[37]

Nichols students tour foreign facility with Professor Lawrence H. Nath, 1961.
Source: *Nichols College of Business Administration, Bulletin, Catalog Issue* 1963–1964, 62.

As for additional growth, President Conrad stated that no further enrollment increases were planned. "Our aim," he said, "is to further improve the academic standard . . . to a level where a Nichols man will not only be regarded a well-trained expert in his business but a gentleman of the highest qualities as well."[38]

Nevertheless, some unappreciated forms of student activities still appeared. In February 1959, 50 or so students from Nichols participated in unapproved trips, sometimes referred to as "panty raids," to several nearby junior colleges. After a meeting of the Nichols Disciplinary Board, 41 students involved were expelled when no one was willing to turn in the names of students fully involved. According to the *Bison*, "Eventually, each boy gave himself up, most were reinstated, but 33 were campused and eight suspended with two from the group expelled "justifiably and fairly."[39] It also was suggested by the *Bison* that they "Grow Up."[40]

In yet another incident of near similar magnitude, several varsity basketball players were declared ineligible for the remainder of one season thereby putting an otherwise excellent season in jeopardy. A remainder of the Chalmers-coached varsity team, with added junior varsity members and a former varsity player, then won games against formidable opponents, in one case, beating one of the strongest small college teams in New England. One faculty member who also was a coach referred to this as a tremendous team effort.[41]

But, while some students complained about the food and the need for a more liberal cut system, others at Nichols during the 1960s later recalled the "wonderful small school atmosphere" and some believed that being at an all-male school was "great." One concluded that this was "never a better time to be at Nichols." Another remembered the experiences of going from a two-year college to a four-year school "with all the excitement that it brought."[42] The element of obvious growth, institutional achievement, and shared success clearly was an empowering experience for all involved.

The success of Nichols athletic teams continued. Despite some fears that established four-year colleges might not be interested in entering into athletic competition with Nichols, this was not a problem. Moreover, Bison teams had excellent records against four-year colleges from the start. President Conrad reported that the 1960 soccer team (11–1–1) was one of the best that the College ever had featuring players from seven different foreign countries in its starting lineup. Actually the 1963 soccer team (12–0–1) may have been better and the 1965 squad better still with a 12–0 record.[43] Baseball in 1964 was 16–0; from 1958 to 1966, the Chalmers-coached baseball team's record was 86 wins and 12 losses.[44] New teams also appeared in cross-country and swimming. In 1965, the fall athletic teams came up with a remarkable 26–1 record.

Not surprisingly some changes occurred on the wider athletic front. According to athletic director, Hal Chalmers, who had the task of redoing all schedules of Nichols teams, 90 percent of new Nichols opponents were competing on the four year college level.[45] Each year, new teams might appear briefly on the Nichols schedule as was the case in 1966 when Notre Dame and the University of Pennsylvania faced the Bison hockey team. The Bisons beat a new and inexperienced touring "fighting Irish" hockey team 9–0.[46] It lost to the University of Pennsylvania in the final round of a brief weekend tournament.

Then too, in 1962 Michael Vendetti became head coach of football and track and was to direct the College's physical education and intramural programs. Vendetti, a former tackle from Leominster, Mass., played his college football at Boston University. He later coached at B.U., Leominster High School, and was serving as Assistant Football Coach at the University of Vermont before he came to Nichols.[47] He followed Harry D. Gafney.

Did greater emphasis and awareness of numerous growth factors, as in athletics, constitute substantive change? The student newspaper, the *Bison*,

Records for Nichols Fall Athletic Teams, 26–1, 1965.
Captains: Kurt Burhoe, football; Fred Erwin, cross country; Donn Norton, soccer; holding total record, Adam Kreuter.
Source: *Bison*, November 22, 1965.

believed it did. A headline for its October 25, 1963, edition published on Homecoming weekend and for alumni eyes, proclaimed "It's Changed!!! . . . It's changed, hasn't it?"[48] This article cited as examples the new dormitories, gym, a "beautiful senior dining room," and a four-year forestry program. It also mentioned the "growth in student desire to gain recognition for academic achievement" that was formally acknowledged in 1962 by the introduction of the Nichols College Honor Society, Zeta Alpha Phi, with 18 charter members. It also could have included a reference to a student work day on the campus which also involved Webster-Dudley organizations such as the Webster-Dudley Boys Club.[49]

A number of developments, however, did point to changes in the nature of the student body itself. In 1958, 28 percent of the Nichols student body had come from New York state, the largest state representation at Nichols. By 1965, six years after the four-year college began recruiting students, the largest population at Nichols came from Massachusetts now having easily overtaken New York. That year, Massachusetts boys made up 43 percent of the Nichols student body; New York was at 17 percent. (For broader comparisons, see Chart 4.1.) This was a significant change, as was the fact that the number of foreign students declined significantly when the college moved from a two-year to a four-year school.[50]

Another indication of an approaching change in the nature of the student body can be found in the responses of Nichols College students in national elections. In a 1960 poll, Nichols students, long supporters of Republican presidential candidates, voted as in the past for the Republican candidate, Richard Nixon. Sixty-nine percent of Nichols students polled were for Nixon, with eventual winner, Democrat John Fitzgerald Kennedy, receiving the support of only 31 percent. However, four years later Nichols students selected Democrat Lyndon Baines Johnson, over Barry Goldwater, 67 percent to 33 percent.[51] Political allegiances appear to be changing, but it would take some time for this potential shift to occur.

Conservation and Forestry – A Four-Year Program

Perhaps the growth of the conservation and forestry program was one of the College's most impressive examples of institutional development during the 1960s. The new two-year specialization had easily been added to the Nichols Junior College curriculum in 1954. This group then involved fewer than 60 students. Its program originally had been designed to meet an industrial demand for foresters with business training.[52] Due to its early success, in 1962 the conservation and forestry program was approved by the College trustees to be part of the four-year business specialization with its concentrations in forest, park, and wildlife management.

Conservation and forestry now functioned in Forestry Hall with appropriate laboratories and classrooms. At the same time, its impact was moving far beyond these confines. It had grown from classes and labs on Dudley Hill and summer work periods at the Rutland Forest of the Daniels School to include summer sessions that functioned on state land in the nearby 1,600 acre Douglas State Forest and later at the Cape Cod National Seashore Park.[53] Its success had been so remarkable that a step to a bachelor degree program seemed almost automatic.

Importantly, this program easily functioned in the structure and spirit of the "New Plan" originally announced by President Conrad in 1931. Actually, it flourished. The College offered the opportunity for the development of leadership skills made all the more effective by extensive extracurricular activities played out in an ideal rural location.

Specifically, the forestry program's success at Nichols resulted from a number of factors. The enthusiasm and abilities of students involved, the integration of the technical forestry and conservation courses and science orientations with the business courses, the presence and support at Nichols of aggressive extracurricular activities as well as intercollegiate athletics, the College's existence in a rural area, impressive leadership from student ranks and from Dr. Paul White, all combined with a strong administrative approval and commitment to contribute to a unique bonding experience. This helped to unite foresters with each other and with their Nichols classmates. When coupled with the new four-year business focus, the four-year forestry course can easily be seen as the College's most advanced effort to achieve the full benefits of the "New Plan." It seemed it could not have worked out any better.

Paul White,
A.B., M.A., Ph.D.
Director, Forestry Program,
1956–1968.

Foresters in action.
Source: *1960 Ledger*, 73.

In 1960, the *Bison* commented about a new level of school spirit at Nichols when discussing the foresters' contributions. Its editor believed an achievement award for building school spirit that year should go to the director of the forestry program, Dr. Paul White, and his group of forestry students and other Nichols students, all part of the "Nicon Forestry Club." This group "hosted" some eight other northeast colleges for the annual Woodsmen's Weekend competition held that year at the foresters' summer camp in Rutland.[54] Participants in the 17 scheduled foresters's events, featuring skills such as log rolling, speed chopping, and pulp throwing used by good woodsmen, came from teams representing the University of Maine, Dartmouth, Colby, Middlebury College, Paul Smith's College, University of New Hampshire, the U.S. Military Academy, University of Massachusetts, as well as Nichols. During the 1965–66 year, Nichols' Woodsmen's teams competed at Middlebury, MacDonald College in Montreal, Canada, and at Dartmouth College taking first place in all three weekend competitions.

Their success was immense; their spirit was infectious. Annual game dinners put on by the foresters were a treat as were their demonstrations of woodsmen's skills at football and soccer games. And, on occasion, their small, penned deer caused much local excitement when they escaped. One former student remarked that the foresters helped to create "a unique campus atmosphere equaled in few schools in the country."[55] No one at Nichols disagreed.

However, as successful as its conservation and forestry admissions and placement efforts appeared to be, by 1965 the support of a complex four-year academic program had become a challenge for the small college. New courses ranging from business and liberal arts through science and forestry, including laboratory and fieldwork, were beginning to tax the ability of the College to support their needs.

As for the institution's future, President Conrad, then in his last year as president, determined that the College would likely have the opportunity to enroll about 150 transfers and graduates of community colleges each year. This, he felt, could increase the day enrollment to nearly 1,000.[56] He also added that the College was planning for a small graduate school of business administration.[57] President Conrad said, according to a local newspaper reporter, that someday Nichols would be more important to the area than the American Woolen and Packard Mills combined.[58] These once thriving mills no longer exist. Surveying the situation at Nichols in 1960, a *Bison* editorial put it this way: "If we keep up the momentum of growing, we should be quite a school."[59]

In the course of the institution's complex emergence, one of the main features of the Nichols Commencement in 1963 was an important address given by Karl A. Hill, then dean of the Amos Tuck School of Business Administration at Dartmouth College. Dean Hill was back on friendly ground since he was a member of the faculty at Nichols Junior College twenty-five years before. One point that Dean Hill raised was that management techniques were on the verge of being revolutionized by the computer and related technological systems. This, he claimed, would eliminate thousands of white collar and mid-executive jobs. In such an environment, change was to be commonplace and a "never-ending process of learning" was necessary to cope with an accelerating world.[60] This was enlightening, although it seemed somewhat distant at the time.

Milestone Events at Mid-Decade

During the months between February 1965 and July 1966, Nichols College experienced four events calling for immense celebration. First came the Sesquicentennial Celebration of Nichols with festivities extending over half the year. Then, several months later, Nichols received word that it had been accredited by the New England Association of Colleges and Secondary Schools (now New England Association of Schools and Colleges). That year Nichols also became a member of the National Collegiate Athletic Association (NCAA). This was followed in July 1966, by the retirement of the only president of Nichols Junior College of Business Administration and the first president of Nichols College of Business Administration. Quite suddenly, but appropriately, these significant events concluded a spectacular period in the institution's history.

Sesquicentennial Celebration

In late 1964, the Nichols community began to make plans for celebrating the 150th year of its existence. After much discussion, this Sesquicentennial Anniversary Celebration was planned for 1965 and designed around three primary events or phases. Each in its own right could be classified as one of the finest events ever presented on the Nichols campus. The first featured the "Brothers Four, In Concert," pioneers in the 1960s folk revival in the United States. This occurred as part of the College's annual Winter Weekend and was open to all Nichols students and their guests at no charge. The Brothers Four concert was expected to attract an estimated 1000 guests invited from 15 area colleges.[61]

Crowd enjoying the Brothers Four concert in Field House, 1965.
Source: *1965 Ledger*, 6–7.

Next, was a two-day Sesquicentennial Celebration in April. A convocation for parents and alumni was held one day and an academic convocation the next, all in the new field house now colorfully adorned with 91 different flags from every state and nation represented by Nichols College students since 1931. In his introduction to the academic convocation, President Conrad set the tone for this occasion:

> As a result of the planning for, and the celebration of, our Sesquicentennial anniversary, there occurs in the process an awareness of our real appreciations. . . .
>
> The names of the greats of our heritage, the Nichols, Conants, Slaters, Healys, Larnards, Goodells, Corbins, Merrills and numerous others will always be revered and kept prominent in our lore, but it becomes increasingly apparent that throughout our one hundred and fifty years, we have a deep obligation to many unknown and unheralded men and women who have been loyal, contributive, and dedicated to Nichols.
>
> In the continued growth and longevity of Nichols, may we continue to be fortunate in adding to those who by force of character, vision, and

contribution, will have their names etched indelibly with the older greats on the scroll of Nichols' honorable history, but we, the majority, of more ordinary capabilities, be joined with our predecessors with no fanfare, content to give of ourselves unselfishly to the end that on our bicentennial or tercentennial, the force of our influence for good, our loyalty, and our faith, will be recognized and an inspiration to those responsible at that time, just as the splendid record of our predecessors has been to us of the present that they, as we, will dedicate themselves to the end that Nichols will continue to represent the virtues of our College seal: Loyalty, Service, and Culture.[62]

The featured speaker for this occasion was Dr. Carter Davidson, president of the Association of American Colleges, whose address was titled "A Liberal Education For Business Administration." Representatives of 68 educational institutions were listed as attending this celebration. One observer remarked that it was "something to remember."[63]

Academic Convocation for Sesquicentennial Celebration held in Field House, 1965.
Source: *Nichols College Bulletin, Alumni Issue, September 1965; 1965 Ledger*, 80.

This convocation weekend was followed on May 1st and 2nd by the 18th Annual Northeastern Intercollegiate Woodsmen's competition featuring Nichols Woodsmen's teams and 14 other competitors. In a remarkable show of skill and determination, Nicon (Nichols foresters) teams finished first, fifth, and eighth in a competition called the biggest athletic event the College had ever held. It may have been watched by as many as 800 spectators.[64]

Accreditation

Once Nichols became a four-year college, a primary objective was to gain regional accreditation. This was an issue not unfamiliar to the former junior college where transfer ability depended on the willingness of institutions of higher learning to accept credits from another school. However, where once accreditation was desirable, it now was indispensable.[65] Nichols had been a member of the New England Association of Colleges and Secondary Schools as a specialized two-year college since 1952. Initially the New England Association had been somewhat reluctant to evaluate its area members; eventually it became one of the last regional associations to do so.[66]

After Nichols College of Business Administration graduated two classes, College trustees welcomed a visit from the New England Association regarding the institution's accreditation.[67] This was not to be a simple matter since the Association was experiencing difficulties evaluating specialized institutions.[68] After visits by a New England Association Committee in 1963, discussions began regarding concerns about Nichols faculty needs and qualifications, salary levels, a need for a liberal arts balance in the freshman and sophomore years and the absence of science courses with laboratories.[69] As a result, the Nichols curriculum was adjusted for students in their first two years.[70] By the following spring, new biology and English literature courses were added in preparation for a second Association visit. This second visitation was scheduled at Nichols from September 29 through October 1, 1965.

On December 3, 1965, at approximately ten minutes after three in the afternoon, College bells rang for about five minutes notifying the campus that Nichols College had been accredited. President Conrad announced that "This recognition is the finest Nichols has ever received, to me the most outstanding feature is the complete unity of the College in wanting to accomplish this end."[71] Nichols students now had better opportunities for entrance to graduate schools and Officer Candidate Programs, more chances to take part in post season tournaments and to receive other awards, while its faculty had the opportunity for greater recognition and the College stood to benefit from more outstanding students along with its institutional achievements.[72] And, within several months, the College became a member of the National Collegiate Athletic Association (NCAA). This occurred in part due to its long-time commitment to intercollegiate athletics.

A President Retires

At this point, Colonel Conrad entered his final year as President. In reflection, it is not surprising to find his "stewardship approach" had extended far beyond the Nichols College community. At a Nichols alumni program, Dr. Edward Carlson, Class of 1940, remarked that President Conrad had made every effort to assist small colleges with their growth and development. This certainly was the case. The Nichols president was committed to helping emerging junior colleges as vice president and then president of the New England Junior College Council from 1951 to 1955. He believed that this was the only way to improve the images of junior colleges in Massachusetts. He followed this by serving as national chairman of the Legislative Committee of the American Association of Junior Colleges from 1954 to 1959. When Nichols became a four-year college, he became a director of the Council for Advancement of Small Colleges from 1963 until his retirement in 1966.

During his presidency at Nichols, Colonel Conrad served one year as executive director of Worcester Academy, Worcester, Mass. He also was the first president of the Webster-Dudley Boys Club, and a director and incorporator of several local banks. In 1958 he retired after thirty-five years of continuous military service (active and reserve). He served, too, as president of the New England Quartermaster Association for one year. His last few years at Nichols, however, found him limited somewhat by reoccurring health problems.

He was honored, as well, by the larger educational community. Honorary degrees and certificates were presented to the Nichols president from Western New England College, Villanova University, Nichols College, and Leicester Junior College. Beyond this, he also was acknowledged by the local community. As he retired he was honored by the Webster-Dudley Chamber of Commerce with an Outstanding Citizen Award, the Exchange Club presented him with its "Golden Deeds Award," and the Boys Club of America gave him its "Silver Keystone Award" for his leadership in creating the Webster-Dudley Boys Club. In accepting his award from the Chamber of Commerce, he remarked: "The growth and success of Nichols College is a two-way road, due to no one man but to the cooperative efforts of the community with the College and the College with the people of Webster and Dudley."[73]

There were many other accolades, awards, and ceremonial presentations received by the Nichols president upon retirement that need not be repeated here. There is one, however, that must be noted since it seems to best summarize his goals. Quite appropriately, this came from the Nichols student body as presented by the 1966 Justinian Council President, Donn Norton:

> This physical growth [of the College] is a great accomplishment indeed, but we feel that in the Colonel's mind, and in those who worked around him, his greatest accomplishment can be seen in the complete education of the Nichols man. He has emphasized to us that we should act as men of virtue – with strong character and personality. He has taught us to accept responsibility and to react to all situations to the best of our ability. We are all honored to have been directed by a man who possesses all these characteristics; a man who has sacrificed his time and effort to build good men and a great institution. . . . [74]

Graduation 1966 – A Final Degree. President Conrad and a Nichols graduate.
Source: *1966 Ledger*, 119.

President Conrad delivered his final message, a "Retired President's Report," to the Nichols Board of Trustees on June 30, 1966. He referred to this report as "an accounting of a 35-year stewardship." His concluding remarks discuss the full dimensions of this "stewardship:"

> It is practically impossible to encompass a way of life over a period of thirty-five years, where no other issue exists other than the welfare and good of the College be paramount. No sacrifice, no personal effort being too great, time no issue, a complete giving of oneself, with no sense of martyrdom, but the satisfaction of dedication to a belief or an ideal. Now, it is good to know that within reason, every objective has been achieved, accreditation, the splendid recognition accorded us by the many, and all of the outstanding colleges and universities of New England at our Sesquicentennial Convocation, our international acceptance by students, the growth and contribution of our 23 Alumni Clubs, the continued contribution and loyalty of the Advisory Council, the tributes of the Military Authorities for our contribution, the growing and substantial respect of our townspeople, the fine image created by our students in the surrounding communities, and the many other reflections of the goods of the fine people of a college community accepting their responsibilities. . . .[75]

In the celebration surrounding the Sesquicentennial, the elation caused by accreditation, and the finality of a retirement, there was little opportunity to consider that an era was ending for the College on the Hill. Nonetheless, change was in the air.

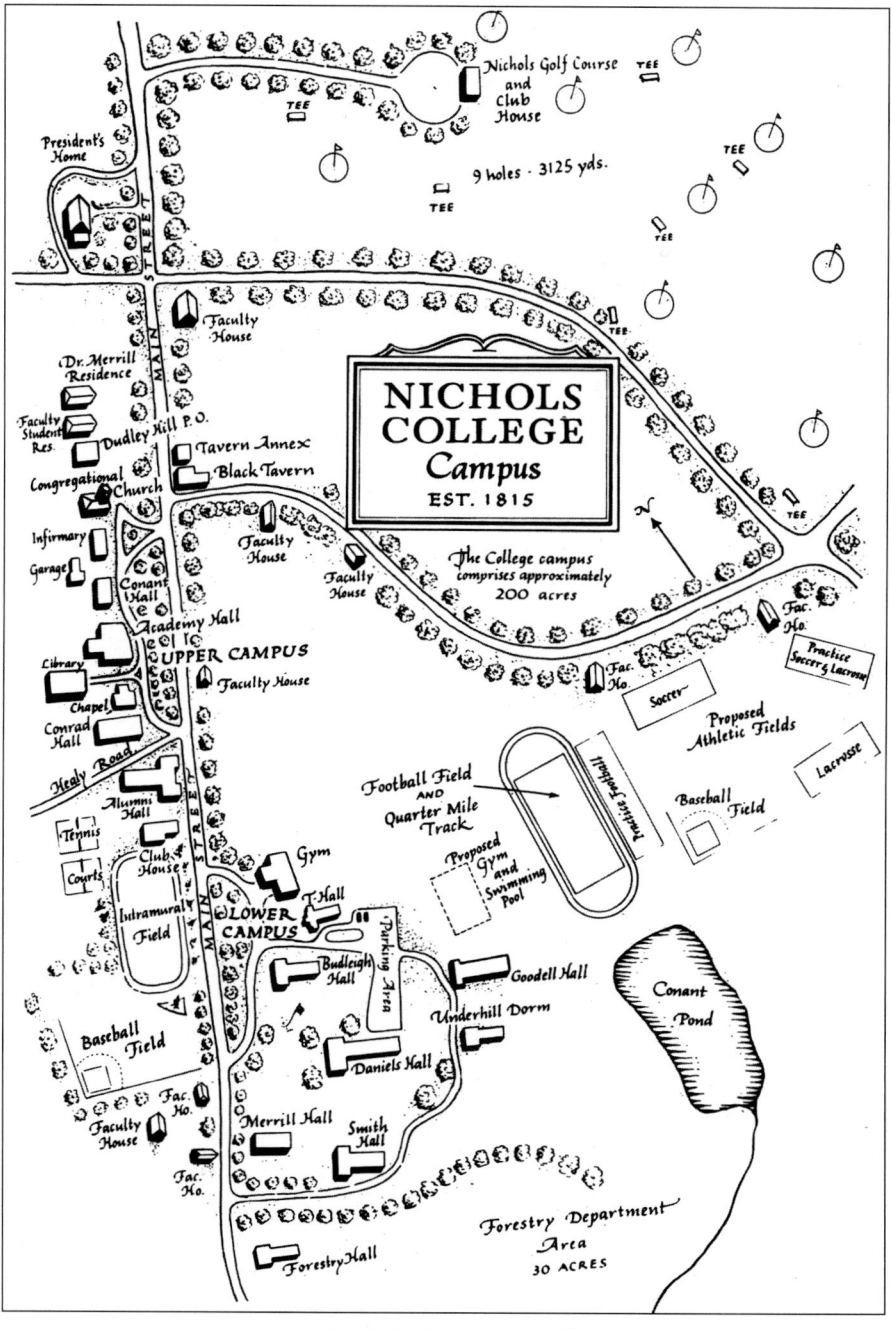

Map 2. Nichols Campus, 1965.
Source: Catalog, *Nichols College of Business Administration Bulletin*, 1966–1967, 30.

Other Notable Events, People, Items, and Pictures 1946~1966

1946   Course in News Analysis required (*NY Times* to be read daily).
Students then living in President's house moved to Tavern Annex.
Glee Club singing on WTAG, Worcester.

1947   Dr. P. S. Merriman creates weekend loan fund for students.
49 Nichols graduates from pre-1938 years to receive ABA degrees, with some stipulations.

1948   Nicholodians created, Glee Club singing throughout Worcester County.
Ski team being formed.
January graduation for 40 Seniors.

1949   "Who Said That," written by Fred Friendly '36.
Enrollment: 296.
Metonomes (octet) first appearances.

1950   Lacrosse recognized as a major sport at Nichols.
Board, Room, and Tuition for year (1950–1951): $1,200.

1951   Sunbathing on Budleigh roof.

1952   Nichols Junior College accredited as specialist junior college by NEASC.
Chalmers-coached basketball team in Junior College championships at Lake Placid.

1953   Nichols College Woman's club organized.

1954   Mark Kato from Japan graduates at the top of his Nichols class, said to be first junior college graduate to transfer to Harvard University; he graduated from Harvard with a B.A. in Economics and returned to Japan.
Physical fitness program required of all students.

1955   Nichols grad, Wilbur Whedon '50, got two aces in one round in a PGA tournament, the Insurance City Open, won by Sam Snead.

1956   Margaret Conrad Chalmers dies.
Nicholodians sing on Jack Parr show in New York.
Largest Nichols enrollment: 345.

1957   Nichols basketball team New England Junior College champions.

1958   Freshmen beat Seniors at annual field day.
Nichols baseball team makes "southern trip."
Faculty winners in intramural volleyball tournament.

Listing continues on page 145

1946–1966 College Buildings or Renovated Structures not Pictured in these Chapters (and as they appeared during this period).

Administrative Building
(formerly Way House)
1965–

Black Tavern
1946–1983

Dining Hall in Alumni Hall
1948–1974

Black Tavern Annex
1946–2003

Bazzie's (Club House)
1946–1972

Daniels Hall
1954–2004

Other Notable Events, People, Items, and Pictures 1946~1966

Forest (or Forestry) Hall
1959–2001

Olsen Hall
1969–

Goodell Hall
1961–1993

O'Neil Hall
1963–1993

Houlberg House
1964–1980

**Ridings Memorial
(attached to Club House)**
1954–1972

Smith Hall
1960–1996

Underhill Hall
1961–1993

T-Hall
1959–1962
Olsen Hall
1963–1969

1841 House
1953–1998

Other Notable Events, People, Items, and Pictures 1946~1966

Listing continued from page 141

1959   October, new football field ("Bison Bowl") completed off Tanyard Road.

1960   Master Card introduced.

1961   Chalmers Circle (next to old gymnasium) created and named for Hal Chalmers, a Gift of Class of 1961.

1962   Red School Building (Center School) acquired by College later to become Merrill Infirmary, then Currier Center.
New Library Building opens.
College Honor Society (Zeta Alpha Phi) installed.
Board, Room, and Tuition for year (1961–1962): $1,800.

1963   Dave Geer, North American Speed Chopping Champion gives demonstration for Nichols Forestry Club.
Pio's Barber Shop operating in Bazzies.
Nichols Summer Work Program begins; said to be "Key to Career Planning."
Four-year Forestry program approved by College trustees.
Nichols Fire Department buys new "used" fire truck.
Bob Sharpe '63 begins racing career as sports car driver.
Seth Kisenge '63 from Tanganyika to return home after graduation, to work in government position.

1964   Budleigh flag pole came down. [From *1967 Ledger*]

1965   Dick Paterson on Nichols cross country team sets a number of different course records.
Over 2,000 attended Sesquicentennial convocations.

1966   Nichols Chapter of A.M.A. recognized.
Most Reverend Bernard J. Flanagan, Bishop of Worcester Diocese, offers Catholic Mass in Nichols Chapel.
Nichols Hockey team beats Notre Dame, 9–0, but loses to Univ. of Pennsylvania, 2–7.
"Who discovered the Mohegan club?" the "TSKK?"
Board, Room and Tuition for year (1966–1967): $2,100.
Nichols *1963 Ledger* awarded a "Second Honor Rating" by Associate Collegiate Press.

NICHOLS: A COLLEGE FOR THE HILL

On and Around Campus, 1946–1966.

~ Other Notable Events, People, Items, and Pictures 1946~1966

1. View of first athletic fields to the west of Center Road; **2.** Amasa Nichols, Symbol of Sesquicentennial Celebration, 1965; **3.** Post Office, Dudley Hill; **4.** Coaches and Football team on first football field; **5.** Golf team on Nichols Course; **6.** "Bazzie" holds court – "You asked for it."; **7.** Sailing Club on Webster Lake; **8.** Nichols vs. Notre Dame; **9.** Nicholodians; **10.** Swimming team in Hermann Pool; **11.** Required Typing Class; **12.** Glee Club; **13.** Track, Bison Bowl; **14.** Dean Chisholm crowns Winter Carnival Queen; **15.** Grand March, 1957

147

NICHOLS: A COLLEGE FOR THE HILL

On and Around Campus, 1946–1966.
Continued

NICHOLS ATHLETIC PLEDGE

I'm playing the game 'cause I like it.
I've started and I never will quit.
I've given my word and I'll keep it.
To play hard — to play fair — and keep fit.

Through the grind of practice
And in the heat of the game
I promise I'll do nothing
That will ever mar our name.

Whatever the game may call for
I'll give unstintingly
I give my word unreservedly
For our college, for you, and for me.

148

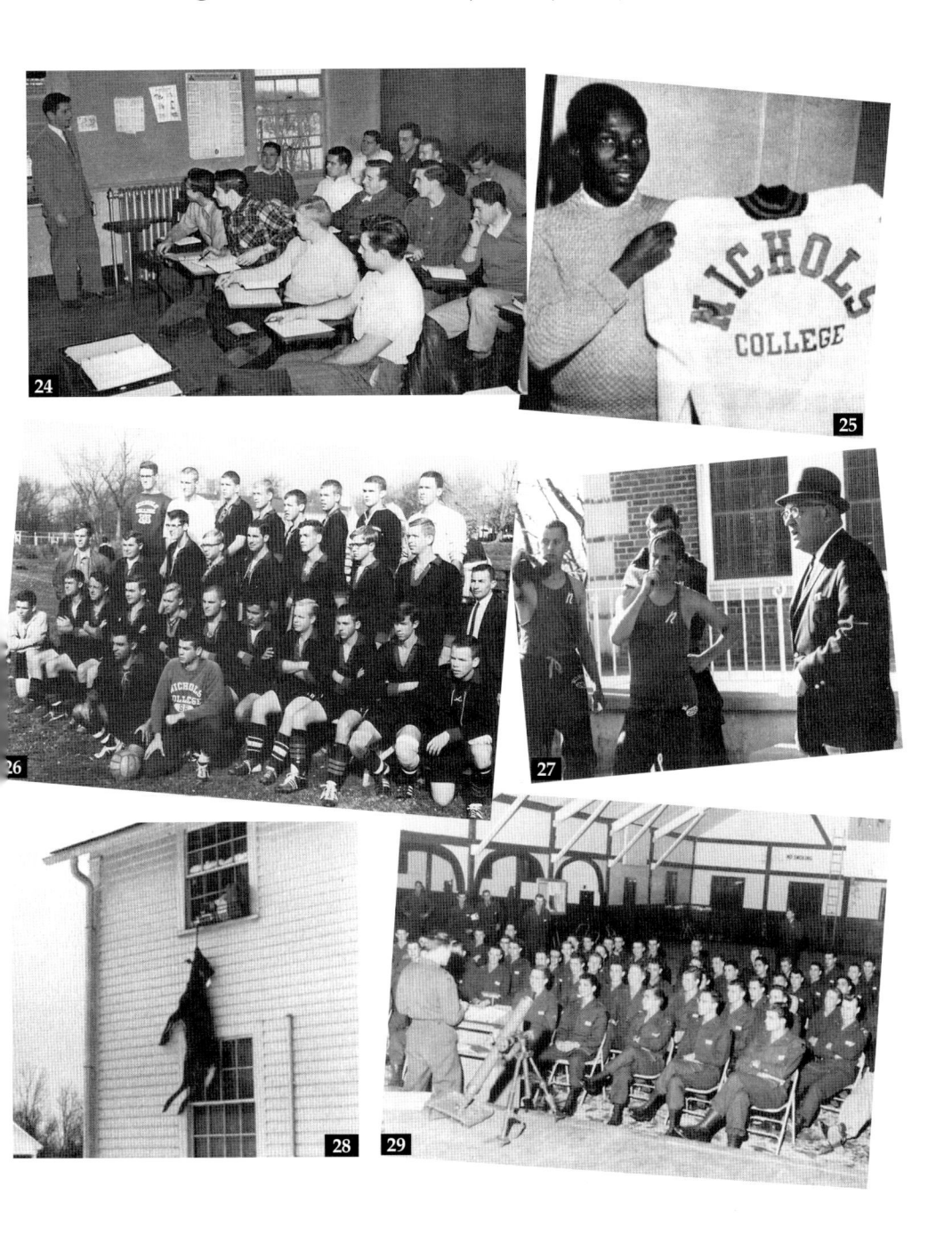

~ OTHER NOTABLE EVENTS, PEOPLE, ITEMS, AND PICTURES 1946~1966

16. Intramural – faculty vs. students; **17.** Nichols Athletic Pledge, 1954; **18.** New Grid Coach, Michael Vendetti, welcomed by Athletic Director, Hal Chalmers; **19.** Soccer on first field; **20.** Action on new football field (Bison Bowl), 1960s; **21.** "Roundhouse" Rob Phelps; **22.** College Mug; **23.** Lacrosse, 1964; **24.** A Nichols Class 1960; **25.** Seth Kisenge from Tanganyika with new Nichols Warm-up; **26.** Undefeated soccer team (12–0–1); **27.** Coach Chalmers talks with his cross-country team; **28.** A forester trophy; **29.** ERC Meeting in gymnasium

149

CHAPTER 6

The College "Transforming," 1966~1978

Nichols College Seal, 1972.
When the first fall edition of the Nichols College newspaper, the *Bison*,
appeared on September 7, 1972, a new College seal was on its masthead.
A previous edition in May carried the seal of Nichols College of
Business Administration. This new seal followed the school's name
change to "Nichols College" in 1971. Adjustments were made in the new
seal's border which now simply states "NICHOLS COLLEGE" and "1815."
Several decorative leafs also are placed in this border. The interior shield,
fasces, and symbols of virtues remain unchanged.
Source for seal (1972): The *Bison*, September 7, 1972, 1.

Success in the 1960s seemed capable of carrying Nichols College of Business Administration far into the next decade. A seemingly long-tested organizational and operational structure had evolved around a central theme that stressed a student-centered approach overseen by experienced administrators, including the president. Change, however, came to Nichols more rapidly than was anticipated.

Despite the earlier successes of Nichols College of Business Administration and the generally favorable outlook in the 1960s for most institutions of higher education, Dr. Gordon B. Cross, the second Nichols president, faced significant obstacles when he began in 1966. At this point, American higher education was experiencing an unparalleled opportunity for growth causing Nichols, still small and vulnerable, to make unplanned changes. President Cross was at Nichols for eight years from 1966 to 1974 spending his last year as dean of the College. He was succeeded as president by Dr. Darcy C. Coyle in 1973.

The Nichols experience immediately after 1966 supports a general view of this period in higher education as one of extreme and permanent change. In fact, virtually all American institutions were experiencing both the benefits and drawbacks of what Clark Kerr, a former University of California chancellor, called the "Great Transformation."[1] For Kerr, it was the third such transformation in American educational history: the first was prior to Civil War; the next extended past World War I; and the third occurred in the 1960s.[2]

Nichols became Nichols College of Business Administration in 1958. Thirteen years later, in 1971, the institution's name was changed to Nichols College when it became a four-year, multi-degree granting college offering degrees in the liberal arts as well as professional fields. Nichols also became co-educational in 1971; three years later it offered the Master of Business Administration (MBA). These developments greatly altered the College's essential nature and culture.

Between 1966 and 1978, Nichols administrators also were confronted by newly competing institutions from within the business education field. By 1974, an expanding group of business colleges had come forward in large part due to the rapidly increasing popularity of business administration programs. Once Nichols, as a specialized college, was granted the authority to offer four-year bachelor degrees, others could follow. This group included colleges with campuses in Waltham, Massachusetts (now Bentley University) and in Smithfield, Rhode Island (now Bryant University), while Babson Institute became Babson College in 1969. All were to offer more extensive athletic programs similar to the Nichols model. Beyond them, many former liberal arts colleges added majors or concentrations in business administration as well. In addition, long-established universities, including many land-grant institutions, expanded the landscape of business education with new business programs and increased enrollments. Some eventually became members of the Association to Advance Collegiate Schools of Business (AACSB). In short, what had been a "new" idea for Nichols in 1931, and even in 1958, was beginning to be standard and accepted in American higher education.

The Great Transformation, 1960~1980

According to Clark Kerr, the period from 1960 to 1980 was a special time in the history of American higher education. Nichols and others experienced conditions that forced a long-standing system of higher education to change dramatically and permanently – a "great transformation."[3] Kerr listed a host of factors he saw responsible for these changes: military challenges, demands for greater equality of opportunity, recognition of the full importance of human capital, changing demographics, and the emergence of a youth culture opposed to traditional virtues or to any authority, all complicated by the increasing involvement of the federal government.[4] As a result of student employment difficulties during this period of change, many sought the security of jobs and careers thought to be provided by specializations in business administration. Concurrently, government involvement in higher education became nearly overwhelming thereby contributing to the belief that there was little likelihood of any return to pre-1960 days.[5]

This transformation described by Kerr is best understood by comparing American higher education in America in 1980 with what existed in 1960. For instance, enrollment in higher education grew from 3.5 million students in 1960 to 12 million two decades later, or a total increase of 8.5 million – nearly 2.5 times in 20 years. Of this group of students, the percentage enrolled in professional programs such as business increased from 37 to 58 percent. Further, the percentage of women enrolled in higher education expanded from 37 percent of the total student enrollment in 1960 to 51 percent by 1980.[6] During the same period, federal aid grants to professional school students far exceeded those grants received by students enrolled in liberal arts departments.[7]

As for the institutional landscape of American higher education, it too changed dramatically. Logically, the total number of colleges and universities should have grown with additional students. The resultant enrollment explosion, however, was not reflected by a balanced across-the-board institutional growth. While the number of public institutions doubled (700 to 1,500) over this twenty-year period, the number of private colleges and universities in America increased by only 400 from 1,300 to 1,700. Enrollment in community colleges during this twenty-year period increased nine times (400,000 to 3,600,000) and enrollment in public comprehensive colleges (including former state normal schools) went from 600,000 to 1,800,000.[8] These change-producing features greatly challenged private education.

In such an educational environment, increases in institutional numbers and a demand for a greater selection of professional and career choices resulted in necessary adjustments by the Dudley Hill institution. The second president of Nichols, Gordon Cross, had to guide his institution into uncharted waters of institutional growth. And this had to be done in the shadow of the achievements in place for 35 years. There was one subsequent reality: the Nichols College of 1977 was to be significantly different from the Nichols of 1966.

Gordon B. Cross, B.A., M.B.A., Ph.D.
President, Nichols College of Business
Administration and Nichols College, 1966–1973.

Gordon B. Cross and a "Rush of Decisions," 1966~1971

Gordon Cross was 55 years old when he became president of Nichols on July 1, 1966. At the time of his appointment, he had been Dean of the Barney School of Business Administration at the University of Hartford since 1959. He was born in Canada, received his undergraduate degree from Bates College, his MBA from the University of Miami, and a doctorate in business from New York University. He also served in the military during World War II and was a retired commander in the United States Naval Reserve. His background included extensive time in business. He once said that this experience made it easier for him to understand what students needed for their careers.

With a background as a teacher, consultant, and author of several publications, he was well qualified as a business educator. And, arguably, he was the best pool player on the Nichols campus. His daughter, Melissa Cross, graduated from Nichols in 1977.

His years as Nichols President can be divided into three distinct periods. The first ended in 1968 when the College received a full ten-year accreditation while the second was capped in 1971 by a "rush of decisions," as the *Alumni Bulletin* put it. The third then featured institutional changes resulting from the demands of Nichols students in an era of aggressive student activism.

When he arrived at Nichols in 1966, his primary task was clear. As a leading New England business educator, he observed discussions between President Conrad and members of the visiting teams from the New England Association of Colleges and Secondary Schools (now New England Association of Schools and Colleges or NEASC) as they worked on the accreditation of Nichols between 1963 and 1965. Nichols then received provisional accreditation with

THE COLLEGE "TRANSFORMING," 1966~1978

the condition that several weaknesses be corrected.[9] It was intended that discussions continue regarding the qualifications of the Nichols faculty and administrators as well as beginning a review of the liberal arts and professional courses in the Nichols curriculum. President Cross's initial responsibility was to prepare Nichols for the next accreditation visit in 1968.

Originally, the Cross administration demonstrated firm support for the long-existing Nichols approach to business education.[10] It continued to see Nichols as a single purpose college offering a course of study leading to degrees in business administration.[11] In 1967, according to a new Nichols catalog:

> the ultimate objective of a Nichols College education was to provide an opportunity for a cultural, social, and technical academic experience that will enable the student to be a contributing member of society, to be morally and ethically appreciative of values, and soundly trained in the profession of business. . . . The outlook for Nichols College for the future is to be a leader in the field of small colleges of business.[12]

CHANGES BEGIN

President Cross's first task in 1966 was to consider the concerns originally expressed by NEASC at the time of the College's conditional accreditation. He later explained that the New England Association granted membership to the College "with the provision that several weaknesses be corrected."[13] He accepted its position that it was necessary for at least two experienced administrators from a college of business administration to lead Nichols. To accomplish this, Dr. Cross (while remaining President) also became Dean of the College. Nichols Dean of Faculty, Charles Quinn, with no experience in business education before his time at Nichols, eventually became Executive Vice President. But this allowed two administrative positions (the president and dean of the college) to be held by an experienced business educator.

Second, President Cross reviewed faculty records and backgrounds. Again, using New England Association standards as guidelines, he concluded that the qualifications or credentials of many members of the Nichols faculty, some at the College since junior college days, had to be carefully reviewed. One of his first steps was to search for qualified and experienced faculty to provide leadership in critical academic areas. Philip H. Ragan, former Dean of the College of Business Administration at Boston University, was appointed to lead the Nichols business program as professor of management and chair of the management department. George Winston from Lafayette College and Syracuse University was selected to head the Nichols English and humanities department. Throughout, President Cross remained committed to his goal of a stronger and better credentialed Nichols faculty. A review of a list of Nichols faculty members in 1969 showed a 70 percent turnover since 1966.

Next he focused on the Nichols conservation and forestry department. Its program, insightfully and correctly referred to by a former student as an "unorthodox, conservation-based business major," was arguably the most popular program ever to appear on the Hill. Forestry students comprised an elite group in all respects. Nonetheless, six months after his arrival, President Cross and the College trustees recommended that it be discontinued because its objectives were not seen as compatible with those of a business college.[14] At the same time, in a less controversial decision, President Cross recommended to his board of trustees that the Nichols evening program be dropped. He concluded that the Dudley area was not large enough to support this program.

According to the Nichols student newspaper, President Cross said that Nichols was returning to its original objective – "that of being a specialized

No More Foresters.
The Nichols Bison, October 12, 1970, 2.

college of business administration, chiefly residential in character." During his review of the forestry program, the new Nichols president appeared to use standards and a review process more appropriate for a four-year liberal arts college or university. He apparently did not consider the strong relationship between the Nichols forestry program and the business curriculum. He also determined that the cost of supporting forestry courses was "too much to continue."[15] When the last foresters graduated in 1970, a special tablet was placed near Budleigh Hall in their memory stating "1954 – 1970. The Best Damn Group that ever lived."[16] Ironically, at precisely this point in time, Nichols trustees and President Cross were considering the addition of more degree-granting programs.

These actions by the Cross administration resulted in Nichols receiving a ten-year accreditation in 1968, three years after its initial conditional accreditation. The New England Association's visiting committee in 1968

Administrative Committee, 1969. *Left to right:* Hal Chalmers, athletic and alumni director; Charles Quinn, vice president; Gordon Cross, president; Robert Eaton, registrar and dean; George Gromelski, treasurer.
Source: *Nichols College of Business Administration, Catalog Issue, 1969–70*, 87.

concluded that ". . . Nichols College has the facilities, the solid base of human resources, and the clear sense of purpose to progress toward its goal of being an excellent small college of business administration. . . ."[17]

And, once President Cross's faculty began to evolve, he could focus on other College issues. Although he had excellent qualifications as a business educator, Dr. Cross had not dealt with the mounting problems of small colleges. Few had. To support a review process that he believed necessary, he preferred to receive recommendations from special long-range committees composed of faculty, administrators, and some students.[18] These committees were chaired by senior members of the administration including the President, Vice President Quinn, Treasurer George Gromelski, Athletic and Alumni Director Hal Chalmers, and Registrar and Dean Robert Eaton. On occasion, Nichols trustees and additional students were added.

Long-range committees introduced and discussed all recommendations. For instance, one group immediately supported a plan for a gravity-flow campus sewer system to tie into the municipal network, the renovation of Academy Hall, the use of Conant Hall for faculty offices, enlargement of the athletic fields, and a four-story addition to the relatively new Library building.[19] And, when President Cross decided to drop Saturday classes; few on campus objected. He also introduced an IBM 1130 computing system that was installed in July 1968 in Conrad Hall for students, classes, and the general processing of all Nichols records.[20] As for the athletic program, the new Nichols president assured the alumni that "we consider them [athletics] to be a part of the academic program and have no thought of reducing them."[21] A new baseball field was in place by 1970.

A Bison statue, called at various times "Nick," "Dimes," and "True Blue," a gift of the Class of 1968, eventually was placed next to the auditorium on Chalmers Circle. Source: *Nichols Alumnus*, Winter 1973, 19.

His long-range planning committees went further. They discussed additional topics such as the institution's size, student government, off-campus living, dormitory parties, the nature of the College, strengthening the liberal arts, scholarship assistance, women at Nichols, a new dining hall, a hockey rink, and the MBA degree. During this period, the Class of 1968 presented a statue of an American bison to the College thereby reaffirming its commitment to the school.

Committee recommendations were in by 1969. For instance, one committee recommended that the College enrollment be 1,000–1,500, become coeducational, and that the title of "Business Administration" be dropped from the college name.[22] Another recommendation included the construction of a student union with dining facilities.[23] A new dining hall designed to seat more than 400 students was eventually constructed in 1972 on the site of the former "club house," or "Bazzies." This required its razing, an action that, in itself, ended an era.

Not surprisingly, various College constituencies had interesting opinions on these important topics which were passed on through contacts and meetings with President Cross. For instance, according to the Nichols president, the College's alumni generally opposed the school becoming coeducational. The Nichols faculty, however, was far more supportive of this move seeing coeducation necessary for survival. (In the 1960s, single sex colleges and universities made up 25 percent of the number of American colleges and universities; by the 1980s, this percentage would fall to six percent.[24]) On institutional expansion, most from Nichols agreed on a total enrollment of

1,000, although some wanted additional students in order to build better athletic teams.[25] Most approved of liberal arts programs being added, although the alumni only "slightly favored" this step.[26] A final conclusion of an All-College Senate was emphatic and straightforward: "Nichols should be a small, private institution which has various activities and produces a well-rounded student."[27] In April 1972, the Nichols Board of Trustees supported the further development of Nichols College as a resident college thereby rejecting student requests to live off-campus.[28]

"WIDEN THE HORIZON," A NEW CURRICULUM, 1971~1973

In what seemed like a period of only a month or two in 1970 and 1971, new programs leading to significant changes were prepared for the approval of the Nichols trustees and the Massachusetts Board of Higher Education. Quite understandably, the *Nichols Alumnus* in the summer of 1971 asked the logical question: Why the "rush of decisions?"[29]

Answering this question, the Nichols Development Office reported that the College was about to face significant financial problems. This finding, based on projected financial trends, required immediate attention. Consequently, the "rush of decisions" was intended to quickly add more students and additional degree programs "in other applications of management and administration," including the social sciences. President Cross and the Nichols trustees determined that the College had to have a student body numbering 1,000 by 1975–1976. Nichols enrollment in September 1971 was 697 (this included 690 males), up from 673 (including 96 foresters) in 1966.[30] In fact, however, the projection of 1,000 day students was not achieved until 2007. President Cross eventually concluded the College was able to sustain and renew itself through its own operations – although he foresaw a financial future that posed a "great danger for private colleges."[31]

Nichols' curriculum originally was designed for a two-year college of business administration. Some important changes did occur in 1959 when the college evolved from a specialized two-year college to a specialized four-year college. Nonetheless, by 1968, its curriculum, as stated in the 1969 College catalog, had been long-established. (See Chart 6.1.)

When it became evident in 1970 that the enrollment had to be increased, the trustees and President Cross decided to "widen the horizon" by adding new programs.[32] Once this decision was made, the action to expand the curriculum followed. Previous discussions by long-range committees directed the College president and the trustees to areas for change. (See Chart 6.2.)

Without question, extreme changes in the College's nature occurred between 1971 and 1975. In virtually one move, Nichols dropped its traditional all-male enrollment, ended its exclusive focus on business education by adding

Chart 6.1. Nichols Curriculum, 1969

> The programs of study are designed to provide the students with a professional major in one of five areas – Accounting, Economics, Finance, Management, and Marketing. To qualify for graduation, the student must have completed successfully one of the prescribed Curricula, and in addition, satisfactory work experience of eight weeks' duration between the Sophomore-Junior and Junior-Senior years.
>
> The Freshman and Sophomore year programs contain required courses only. In these two years, the student is exposed to introductory courses in each of the majors. By the end of the Sophomore year, the student must determine in what areas he wishes to specialize. During the Junior and Senior years, Nichols men concentrate on professional courses but are permitted to choose other technical and cultural courses as electives. The College requires a minimum of sixty-three semester hours of courses in the general studies area during the four years to insure a broadened background. Thus the student takes more than fifty percent of his work in general studies or liberal arts courses. The Nichols graduate is prepared to enter the business community professionally qualified as well as being socially and ethically oriented toward his fellow men.
>
> | General Pattern of Business Curriculum | Credits |
> |---|---|
> | Business Core Courses | 27 |
> | Accounting, Finance, Marketing, Management, Business Law, Statistics, Quantitative Analysis, and Senior Seminar | |
> | Liberal Arts Core Courses | 54 |
> | Composition, Literature, Mathematics, Sociology, Psychology, History, Speech, Economics, Political Science, Logic, Science, Ethics, and Fine Art | |
> | Concentration (Professional Major) | 21 |
> | Liberal Arts Electives | 9 |
> | Unrestricted Electives | 9 |
> | Total Required | 120 |
>
> Source: *Nichols College of Business Administration Bulletin, Catalog Issue, 1969–1970*, 44.

Bachelor of Arts degrees, changed the College name from "Nichols College of Business Administration" to "Nichols College," no longer remained exclusively an undergraduate institution, and abandoned a total reliance on income from tuition, short-term borrowing, and special gifts.

Moreover, a supplementary program in education became part of the curriculum by 1971. The work of designing this education program and obtaining its approval from the Division of Teacher Certification of the Massachusetts Department of Education was overseen by Professor of Psychology, Daniel Van Leuvan. This program prepared students for teaching

Chart 6.2. A Chronology of Change, 1971–1974

1.	January 1971	Nichols Trustees approved Nichols to be a coeducational college.
2.	June 1971	Education courses for teacher certification approved by Division of Teacher Certification, Massachusetts Department of Education.
3.	July 1971	New degrees (to replace BBA) – Bachelor of Arts; Bachelor of Science in Business Administration; Bachelor of Science in Public Administration – approved by Board of Higher Education of the Commonwealth of Massachusetts. Name to be changed to "Nichols College."
4.	August 1972	Nichols Trustees applied for a bond issue of $1,400,000 later approved by the Massachusetts Higher Education Finance Authority (HEFA). This was the College's first long-term debt.
5.	October 1974	Authority to award MBA granted by the Board of Collegiate Authority, Massachusetts Board of Higher Education.

Sources: *Nichols College Catalog*, 1971–1972, Addendum; *Nichols Alumnus*, November 1974, 3.

in secondary school business education programs, although it could be applied to other concentrations or majors as well.[33]

Taken altogether, these changes were seen by the Nichols administration as creating a "school of administration." This replaced the "school of business administration."[34] In the process, the business administration program remained in place, although it now was sharing institutional commitment with programs in public administration and the liberal arts. One institutional announcement said simply that "after many years of specialization as a college of business administration," Nichols "now offers programs leading to administration careers in business, non-profit institutions, associations, education, as well as business." "Administration" was seen as a multi-dimensional social phenomenon with supporting programs needed in the related fields of economics, history, psychology, and sociology.[35]

This move seemed to broaden the College's appeal and add numerous courses to the curriculum. However, it may have lessened its attraction for those interested in a strictly business education. Some have concluded that becoming "Nichols College" and coeducational signaled a change from a strictly business education "to one influenced by the liberal arts." Perhaps, but most women who attended Nichols evidenced a greater interest in business.[36]

161

How did Nichols students react to this change? Positively! According to a lead article in the college newspaper, the *Bison*, in 1971, Nichols students saw the College setting out "to attain its most significant level of advancement and progress since becoming a four-year college in 1958."[37] Nichols was understood as "meeting the challenge of a super-changing, what sometimes appeared to be explosive, world with its new expansion, diversification, and adjustment programs." The *Bison* concluded that "Nichols will not merely survive, but it will prosper, grow and progress to levels commensurate with the fine things that Nichols is and stands for."[38]

A brief breakdown of the new programs as presented in the 1974–1975 catalog follows. (See Chart 6.3.)

Chart 6.3. The Curricula, 1974–1975

After many years of specialization as a College of Business Administration Nichols has widened its horizons and now offers programs leading to Administrative careers in government, non-profit institutions, associations, and education, as well as business. Since administration is fundamentally a social phenomenon, programs are also offered in the related fields of Economics, History, Psychology and Behavioral Sciences.

Programs are offered leading to the following degrees:

Bachelor of Science in Business Administration with specialization in:
    Accounting
    Economics
    Finance
    International Business
    Marketing
    Management: (two options)
        Business Systems Analysis
        Personnel and Industrial Relations
Bachelor of Science in Public Administration
Bachelor of Arts with majors in:
    Behavioral Sciences
    Economics
    History
    Psychology
    Sociology

Nichols also offers a supplementary program in education for students who wish to prepare for secondary school teaching.

Source: *Nichols College Catalog, 1974–1975*, 34–35.

IBM 1130, the first Nichols Computer System.
Source: *1969 Ledger*, 7.

LIFE IN AN ATMOSPHERE OF CHANGE AND INNOVATION

For most young Americans, the decade of the 1960s was an explosive time in their lives. Many students and young people reacted against the war in Vietnam, social injustice, and myriad social ills, including the perceived elitism of the previous generation. As a result, the sixties experienced more student revolts, greater campus politicization, and generally seemed to suffer from inadequate institutional governance. And, while achieving significant campus academic reforms, students experienced equal dashes of reality and disappointment.[39]

There can be no questioning the existence of turmoil in the 1960s or the intensity of the motives which drove student activism. But it did not continue. At least one study has determined that the student activist movement collapsed by 1972.[40] This was followed by the emergence of the "me-generation," sometimes referred to as Generation X, that saw students focusing more on personal values and needs than did students a decade before.[41] In a general sense, by the early 1970s, some college students actually may have appeared more conservative, although they still were active in student causes.

While the rising tide of student activism in the sixties was extreme, the continuance of institutional features during this period cannot be ignored.[42] Some long-standing self-images, basic forms, and historical traditions continued to influence individual activities and student thinking during the 1970s. For instance, a reliance on Nichols dormitories as social centers did not change nor did the social role of Bazzie's snack bar literally existing as it did at the center of campus. Furthermore, the essential conservatism of Nichols students was again reflected in the political positions taken in 1976 when 54 percent of Nichols students supported Republican Gerald Ford for president while only 24 percent backed the eventual president, Democrat Jimmy Carter.[43] Furthermore, in 1972 Nichols students received much acknowledgment in the press for supporting President Nixon's policies in Vietnam when most American college students were opposing his positions.[44] This should not suggest that Nichols students did not seek changes. These changes, however, generally dealt with life at Nichols.

Initially President Cross's approach to student problems was appreciated by the student body. The *Bison* quickly viewed him as "one of the most spirited and dynamic individuals the college has had." This praise went further: "The man has done more for the college and the student body in the way of improvement than any other before him . . . [he] has instilled in every organization and function, an attitude of progress and innovation."[45] They applauded his administration's action in improving the curriculum, ending Saturday classes, revising the cut system, developing a new grading system, creating professional clubs in each major, modernizing the Academy building and hall, and appearing to show a greater interest in the image of the school.[46] He also supported the creation of a new student government replacing the old Justinian Council system.

By 1970, however, student opinions began to gradually evolve. While the *Bison* recognized some "victories for change" under the Cross administration, it also concluded that the new administration was taking a passive attitude towards the Nichols sports program and was doing nothing to help build school spirit or tradition. According to the *Bison*, although the new system at Nichols had been praised at first, arguably "it was still the same."[47] A student demonstration for parietal hours in 1970 suggested a significant change in attitudes regarding the College's second administration.

Looking beyond the large issues to specifics, it is difficult to picture the every-day life of the average Nichols student of the post-1966 period. Fortunately, an "Around the Campus" column in the *Bison* in 1969 written by Alex Gottfried '69, did this most skillfully. His account of student life on Dudley Hill captures the essence of a small, all-male college in a rural community developing its own brand of activity and humor involving students, faculty, administrators and their community. Gottfried's column "Nichols is [in 1969]," follows.

Student Activism and New Social Rules

Not long after Gordon Cross became president, student requests for new rules of social conduct began to appear on his desk. While the pattern of college life in Dudley during the Cross administration did not mirror the social activism on many college campuses in the 1960s, significant changes were in the offing.

Around The Campus
by Alex Gottfried

NICHOLS IS:

An afternoon nap.
Taking Social Psychology.
Accounting with an overhead projector.
Bringing coffee and donuts to 8 A.M. class.
Changing your major to Biology in your senior year.
Having your 21st birthday party at the Mohegan Club after going there for three years.
Sandwiches and Milk.
Cutting a class and running into your professor at Bazzie's the next period.
A warm beer and a cold shower.
A conference with Dean Eaton.
Getting a date.
Watching color TV at Bazzie's.
Breakfast at Sneaky Pete's.
A party at the Nichols Motor Lodge.
A smile from the lady at the Post Office.
An evening snack with "The Big E".
Talking Herbie out of a ticket.
Going to the Library to read the magazines.
Bolting on your check at the Main Lunch.
Buying clothes at Kerry's.
A monogrammed shirt.
Going home for the weekend.
Bouncing a check at Bazzie's.
A night at the Summit Lounge with Bernie Durning.
Having an old buddy come back for a visit.
Watching Laugh-In.
Disecting the Pig.
A shut-out at the Post Office.
Playing intramural softball.
A 9-Hole golf course.
Cutting class and later finding ont your Prof. didn't make it either.
Hitch-hiking back from Boston in February with no socks.
Carrying your books to class in a waste basket.
Having Jay Sherwood come over to visit you at 2 A.M.
Taking your shirts to Twin Cities.
Picking up your College Mug in B-314.
Making a collection of motel keys.
A mixer at Endicott.
Going to Bermuda.
Being a day student.
Having a part-time job.
Studying for that important test.
Trying to grow a mustache.
A phone call from Mrs. Hannon.
A crash course in Computer Programming.
Making the Dean's List.
Talking to the Army Recruiter.
Going fishing.
Falling in love.
Getting married.
Watching your dorm burn down.

Wearing your freshman beanie.
Trying on your cap and gown.
Many groups of very close friends.
Skiing at Mt. Snow.
Getting a Dear John Letter.
Putting on your snow tires.
Sunday Night at the Top Hat.
Putting your convertible top down.
Accidently leaving your cigarettes in the cigarette machine.
Getting a speeding ticket on the Mass. Pike.
Wearing white socks.
A drive through Webster.
A Spring Cookout.
Getting a blind date and later wishing you were also blind.
A hockey Game with Holy Cross.
Being snowed in on the weekend.
Dropping the side burns.
Begging someone to type your term paper.
Begging someone to write your term paper.
Asking your roommate to hand in your term paper.
Having Chicken—La-La for Lunch.
Calling "Here" for a friend who cut class.
The morning after the night before.
Wolfing down a Bazzieburger.
A trip to the Park and Steal.
An evening at the Watering Hole.
Wearing a tie and jacket to dinner with a zipper front sweatshirt.
A dirty sneaker.
Buying furniture at Catholic Charities.
Playing Lacrosse in the mud.
Running into Psycho in the Library.
Anxiously waiting for Pierre Salinger.
Seeing Don MacQuarrie with a date.
Watching **Barefoot in the Park.**
A warm letter from Mom and Dad.
Going on a Green Mountain road trip.
A birthday card from Col. Conrad.
A soul band at one of the big weekend.
An extra semester for good performance.
Murdering the last test.
Listening to WNRC.
Calling Dean Eaton's Office from the Budleigh Lounge informing them that you are snowed in, in Boston.
Putting on your bumper sticker.
Losing all your change in the telephone.
A place of long and lasting friendships.
A woodman's weekend.
A place you can really fall in love with.
NICHOLS IS YOUR COLLEGE.

Alex Gottfried, "Nichols is [in 1969]."
Source: *The Nichols Bison*, May 10, 1969, 4–5.

These reflected the nature of the times and then worked to fuel the transformation of Nichols College. Actions taken in 1971 by the Nichols Board of Trustees resulted in the emergence of a coeducational institution and a new curriculum. While these changes were being introduced, Nichols students asked the College to look at existing campus rules as well.

President Cross, his long-range planning committees, and the Nichols trustees were extremely active during this period. They considered such social issues as permitting a bar on the Nichols campus (for students 21 or older), parietal hours (the ability of women to remain in student rooms for extended periods of time), kitchen facilities in dormitory rooms, the use of marijuana, standards of conduct, liquor licenses for the field house, grooming and dress codes, and the ability of the Nichols student to live off-campus, among others.

Perhaps the two larger issues to come forward during the early Cross administration were the creation of a bar on campus for students 21 or older and the establishment of parietal hours. The request for a campus bar was eventually allowed after discussions between student leaders and members of the board of trustees. The Nichols Bar had been originally promoted by students Jack Hills '69, said to have "founded and organized the constitution of the school bar," and Richard Paterson '68. Later called the "Bison's Den," it was located under the renovated auditorium and opened in October 1968 as a bar for students 21 or older. The lounge was to be open for weekdays from 4 P.M. to 1 A.M. serving students four brands of beer and wine.[48] From the student point of view, it was "just one more new development that Nichols students, administration, and alumni can point to with pride."[49] It should be noted that not all on the campus agreed with this conclusion. Students 21 or older also were allowed to drink in their dormitory rooms, although kegs were not permitted.[50] Keg parties became an issue for the future.

Once the bar was approved, students focused on parietal hours. The ability of the Nichols students to open their doors to women was seen by the student body as necessary to build spirit and "pride" in the College. According to the *Bison*, social occasions would improve, attendance at sporting events would be greater, and the dorm room could become a "primary social place."[51] Initially the Nichols trustees were told that 96 percent of the students favored parietal hours. Quite legitimately, however, the trustees questioned the legal implications, the need to keep dormitory rooms open, the nature of control for dormitories, and faculty reaction.[52]

At that point, however, the first major demonstration in the history of the modern college occurred. This happened in 1970 when students boycotted classes after what they believed was the refusal of the Nichols trustees to hear their side of the parietal matter. Students saw this as a blatant disregard of their interests.[53] They also presented the trustees with a list of grievances including issues such as grading policies, use of alcoholic beverages, and the need for new and better qualified students.

President Cross concluded that the three-day boycott of classes which followed was only 90 percent effective. However, he was greatly disturbed that it received significant newspaper and TV coverage.[54] This three-day strike caused President Cross to vow not to let the students control the policies of the school.[55] Nonetheless, in his description of the 1970 confrontation, he reported to Nichols alumni that radical student elements did not exist at Nichols.[56] Certainly Nichols students were more conservative – but they still could be aggressive. An editorial in the *Worcester Evening Gazette* after the boycott recommended that the Nichols students return to their academic duties and then push for their request – with perseverance but "without a self-defeating boycott."[57]

This demonstration brought results. First, the trustees angrily moved to strengthen social rules outlawing the disruption of the educational process, forbidding the destruction of property, and protecting the rights of all members of the community.[58] The board would tolerate no further similar boycotts. Second, parietal hours for students were approved by October 1970 to begin at noon on Fridays, Saturdays, and Sundays, lasting until midnight except on Sunday, when they ended at 8 P.M.[59] The faculty then recommended that absences due to the boycott should be excused.

Not surprisingly, the issue of parietal hours was not closed. The following year a request for adding to parietal hours was received by the President and Nichols Board of Trustees. They then agreed to extend the times of parietal hours from midnight to noon of the following day (after beginning at noon the previous day). In accepting this triumph, the *Bison* cautioned the Nichols students to "just use the sign-in log and be cool and we will maintain what so many have worked so hard to get."[60]

Student activism on the national level, however, actually had drawn negative comments from the *Bison*. In 1968, the Nichols student newspaper wrote in opposition to a student-led riot at Columbia University regarding the University's affiliation with the Department of Defense and the construction of a new gymnasium seen by many at Columbia as discriminatory. "According to the *Bison*; It [the Columbia student riot] is a question of irresponsibility over reason."[61] Apparently Columbia students were seen "frustrated by an administrative apparatus which had passed largely beyond their control." Nonetheless, according to the *Bison*, "this is no excuse for lawlessness."[62]

Nichols students took positions on other broad issues as well. According to the results of *Bison* questionnaires completed by Nichols students and faculty (fifteen percent of the respondents were veterans) on Vietnam in 1970, most Nichols responses (75%) predictably did not agree with the then present American policy. The majority (55%) would not have supported a presidential decision to escalate the war.[63] However, on the political front, with President Nixon on the verge of impeachment after Watergate, the percentage of Nichols students urging him to resign was far less than what generally existed across the nation.[64] On an issue closer to home, the results of the *Bison* questionnaire on the school's traditional Advisory Council Day revealed that while most (90%) thought it was a good idea; a surprising number (55%), favored getting better participants the next year. Another questionnaire on the dining hall determined that its food was "not the quality it should have been."[65]

Coeducation

Results of talks regarding the financial future of the College led to the decision by the Nichols trustees to "broaden the concept of administration," to add liberal arts and public administration degrees, and to allow women to enroll. Some at Nichols must have been surprised at the latter decision made by President Cross. As late as 1968, he said "no serious consideration has been given to thoughts of admitting female students . . . [since] there was no substantial demand [from women] for a four-year business program."[66] He also stated "Nichols College is a school for men . . . and it's going to stay that way."[67]

Soon, however, he decided that changes at Nichols would make the College "more attractive to women students." But he also added that he "didn't expect many [women] – if any – the next year."[68] He was wrong there as well. In support of his decision, he explained that Nichols recognized the fact that coeducational institutions of higher education were more compatible with the present-day pattern of living. He also accepted that a coeducational environment would improve student life on the Hill, both socially and academically.[69] Then too, some believed that an expanded curriculum, including liberal arts courses, might make the Nichols program more attractive to women.[70] The Nichols student newspaper was more emphatic and straightforward: "Coeducation is not only much desired by today's young people for the social aspects, but has proven to be a stimulant to more creative responses to the environmental challenges which are crowding our nation's lifestyles."[71]

Women enrolled at Nichols for the first time in September 1971. Although their numbers were small, they immediately introduced a new dimension to student life on the Hill. One, Janice Ducharme, wrote an article for the *Bison* a few weeks after registration titled "709 to 6." She recalled that the few young women who were scattered throughout the auditorium at their first class meeting heard most speakers being reminded to say "ladies and gentlemen" when addressing the class.[72]

One year after their arrival, women students at Nichols indicated to the *Nichols Alumnus* that they "liked best" the Nichols academic program, the

Part of first group of seven women to graduate from Nichols College in 1974.
Source: *Webster Times*, June 12, 1974; *1974 Ledger*;
"Women at Nichols," *Nichols News, Newsletter, Special Edition,* January 1993.

small friendly campus, the willingness of faculty members to go out of their way to help, and the readiness of the administration to pay attention to their interests. But they also believed that Nichols should focus on more co-ed sports, more campus activities, and private rooms for co-eds. The *Nichols Alumnus* writer perceptively concluded: "Although they are few in number, at the same time co-eds are part of Nichols and in the future they are sure to make their mark on the history of the college."[73] And, with little fanfare, The Nichols Alma Mater was rewritten to reflect the institution's coeducational status.

In another article written at the same time by Professor of English, George Winston, and based on student essays that year, he found both sexes were "happy" with the beginning of the co-educational era. Furthermore, he also reported that all students, according to their essays, "generally wanted more girls, more bands, and more parties."[74] Faculty applauded their presence without any reservations.[75]

Overall, Nichols students were quite successful in achieving change. Aside from some skillfully managed efforts such as the student bar and parietal hours, other improvements and increased student interest was reflected in a rejuvenated student-manned fire department, a much improved student newspaper, a strong intramural program, and a new dress and grooming code (students no longer had to wear ties and sport jackets and were allowed to grow beards), among other rule changes.[76] Student interest in big bands and entertainers saw the appearance at Nichols of some notable performers including: "Ed Jacobs and the Soulrockers," Paul Butterfield, Kenny Rogers and the First Edition, Al Cooper, Sha Na Na, Davis Frye, and John Sebastian and Maskmakham, to name a few.[77] And, in an effort to put their stamp on their social activities, students in the 1970s began to hold concerts away from the College campus for the first time in the school's history.

If students needed further support for efforts in changing social rules, it came from an unexpected source – the federal government. In 1971, the 26th Amendment to the U.S. Constitution granted citizens 18 years of age or older the right to vote. Many state governments then went along with the federal government lowering the legal age of majority to 18. This Constitutional Amendment was followed in 1974 by the Family Education Rights and Privacy Act, also referred to as the Buckley Amendment, introduced by U.S. Senator James L. Buckley.[78] Rights were effectively given to college students (18-year olds) to halt the release of their records to third parties (including parents) and granted them the right to correct these records, if necessary. One comment on the impact of this legislation suggested that colleges might no longer be able to continue to act *in loco parentis*.[79] But, above all, this reaffirmed the broadening of college student rights as well as adding some additional confusion for administrators thereafter. Now the student bar could serve 18-year olds. This had a major impact on the peace and quiet of the campus.

While many things were changing, some remained the same. For instance, a week of informal freshmen hazing continued into this period. This involved rope pulls, freshmen beanies, a requirement that they show respect to sophomores, occasional ridiculous activities including being part of an auction, being required to do distasteful tasks such as shining shoes, carrying sophomore books, and otherwise improving the lives of their sophomore tormentors. Some saw this ritual as a bonding one for the incoming class.[80]

There was, however, an expanding community-oriented side of the Nichols student in 1973. One of its members said about a classmate, "He is a person who can relate to his surroundings and have feelings for the things that make up his community."[81] Nichols students, by 1973, were most active in a "new area" – community service. For instance, according to the *Bison*, the role of the Mayor's Council had expanded from running social functions to promoting civic affairs such as assisting needy families in the area by providing Christmas dinners. The Nichols Community Union, then three years old, helped the community by supporting programs such as the Field Day of the Boys Club and becoming involved in some elementary school programs. Another student group organized a children program which helped them work to achieve acceptable positions in life.

While the *Bison's* claim that "the Nichols man of today is still the same considerate and interested student that was known in the past" seems a bit exaggerated (and wrong, since many students involved were women), there can be no question that these activities were different from those during the 1960s at some colleges. By 1975, 35 members of the Community Union were involved in a Big Brothers Big Sisters type program, assisted in a special swim program, became leaders in a local cub scout troop, and were involved in the Webster-Dudley Hockey League. Still others were offering private tutoring.[82]

THE COLLEGE "TRANSFORMING," 1966~1978

A CONTINUING COMMITMENT TO INTERCOLLEGIATE ATHLETICS

There was one additional part of the Nichols picture that did not change as much as some dimensions of student life during this period. The College's commitment to intercollegiate athletics continued as in the past. A "Governance," statement of Nichols College in 1974 saw the "athletic program at Nichols as a part of the academic program as well as an extra-curricular activity.[83] Indeed, this brief period can be seen as a crowning era of athletics at Nichols with the College recording four significant achievements: the acceptance of Nichols by the National Collegiate Athletic Association (NCAA) in 1966; the dedication of the Chalmers Field House in 1968; the formation of the Nichols College Athletic Hall of Fame in 1972; and the first appearance of women's teams in 1978 officially representing Nichols College in intercollegiate athletics in basketball and softball.

Nichols became a member of the National Collegiate Athletic Association (NCAA) in 1966. It was a fitting acknowledgment of 35 years of active participation in intercollegiate athletics. President Conrad's announcement of NCAA membership just before his retirement in 1966 brought much applause for the Nichols College athletic program and its athletes. Beyond this, NCAA membership made it possible for Nichols teams to be eligible for national championships (in Division III after 1973). Appropriately, just as this acceptance was being received in Dudley, the Nichols College golf team was winning the National Association of Intercollegiate Athletics (NAIA) District 32 golf tournament, a proper conclusion to an earlier chapter in the history of Nichols athletics. Nichols had been a member of the NAIA since 1962, or the year after the first four-year degrees were awarded at the Dudley college.

New Athletic Fields and Field House, 1976.
Source: *Nichols Alumnus, November 1976*, back cover.

For its first 35 years, the College's athletic program was centered in the gym, once an "old barn," sharing the floor with occasional dining operations, convocations, examinations, plays, concerts and dances. After 1964, Nichols athletics moved to a new field house with its attached Hermann swimming pool and physical education building. It looked out over the new football field (first Bison Bowl, now Vendetti Field) off Tanyard Road. Nichols athletics had moved to a different level.

The new Nichols center for athletics was dedicated to Hal Chalmers in 1968. Nothing could have been more appropriate. At the field house dedication to Chalmers, Russell Granger, athletic director at Clark University, referred to him as a "dedicated athlete, a successful coach and a skillful administrator." That he was. President of the Nichols Justinian Council, Donald A. McQuarrie '69, said "because of Chalmers, Nichols is now a member of every major college athletic association including the National Collegiate Athletic Association."[84] This was a significant achievement for a still very small and new college. In the shadow of their new field house, Nichols athletic teams during the 1966–1976 era were competing in baseball, golf, tennis, track, lacrosse, football, soccer, cross country, hockey, swimming, and sailing. A woodsmen's team was included in this list as well.

The dedication of the Chalmers Field House was followed in 1972 by the creation of the Nichols College Athletic Hall of Fame intended to salute Nichols athletes and those who supported them. The new Hall of Fame was the result of a gift from Nathan Phillips '50.[85] Since the College introduced its Hall of Fame at a still early point in its history, the qualifications of all Nichols

West entrance to Chalmers Field House, dedicated 1968.
Source: Newsclip, October 23, 1968.

First Women's Basketball Team, 1978.
Source: *1978 Ledger*, 92.

athletes beginning with 1931 could be carefully reviewed by committee members; some had seen all these athletes in action. The first twelve members of the Nichols Athletic Hall of Fame were inducted on October 11, 1972, at halftime of a homecoming football game. This first group included Hal Chalmers as a Nichols graduate, Class of 1936, Joseph W. Donahue of the College's first graduating Class in 1932, and Colonel James Conrad who was made an honorary member. This was correctly referred to as "a very special day in the history of athletics at Nichols College."[86] Ninety-eight athletes graduating between the years 1932 and 1977 are among Nichols athletes selected as members of the Hall of Fame.[87] (For a list of Nichols College Athletic Hall of Fame members, see Appendix D.)

Featured in the continued growth of the Nichols athletic program and the College's commitment to intercollegiate athletics was the introduction of women's athletic teams at Nichols. By 1978, two women's teams were representing Nichols in intercollegiate activities. The first women's basketball game in the history of the College saw Nichols losing to Annhurst College, 42–33 in February 1978.[88] The previous spring a group of Nichols women had organized a softball team and played several games against Holy Cross and Annhurst College although softball, as noted in the *1978 Yearbook*, was competing only on the club level until 1978 when the team received its first uniforms.[89]

Also of significance during the years from 1964 to 1979 was the performance of Vendetti-coached football teams. Over this period, Nichols football teams had 11 victorious seasons, two seasons when the football team split its games, and experienced just three losing seasons.

A Crossroads

On a wider topic, President Cross said in September 1971 that he was confident Nichols was going to survive coming financial problems. In the process, however, he believed that the College had to call on its alumni, friends, and all other possible sources, for "much" help. He determined that the College had "reached a crossroads." Past surpluses no longer existed. It was necessary to get income from sources outside the College.[90] This was required to repay a 20-year bond issue from the Massachusetts Higher Education Finance Authority (HEFA) for the construction of a new dining hall and the remodeling of Alumni Hall as a student center.[91] At that time, gifts from members of the alumni equaled about one percent of the Nichols budget.[92] After 1974, yearly payments of as much as $128,000 a year had to be made to HEFA.[93] President Cross then decided that he did not have the background necessary to lead the College's effort in dealing with its newly projected long-term debt.

As he left the presidency in 1973, President Cross saw the achievements of his administration best described in terms of quality, rather than quantity. He referred to great improvements in the capabilities and qualifications of faculty, students, and other personnel while living conditions and food service had been sharply upgraded. A new dining facility was being constructed. Two newly built student residences, Olsen and New (later Kuppenheimer) Dormitories, were opened in 1969 and 1970 on the former athletic fields to the west of Center Road.[94] President Cross believed that library, classroom spaces, facilities for athletics and auditoriums all were better.[95] Regarding the changes during his administration, he said that Nichols could "survive on change" believing these adjustments were going to be evolutionary rather than revolutionary.[96] He had not, however, managed to increase the College's enrollment or put the institution on a firm path toward fiscal success. But Nichols College was much different in 1973 than it had been in 1966 when he took over.

Dr. Gordon Cross retired from Nichols in 1974 and passed away in 1993. At that time I wrote that "he was a very fair and reasoned person who understood that the faculty as a group was committed to education so he supported them very strongly. . . . He didn't want to change the small college environment and any of the things that went with it."[97]

Darcy C. Coyle and an Age of Survival, 1973~1978

President Cross declared in 1973 when he stepped down as president that his office now had to function in a development capacity.[98] He agreed to remain as dean of the college where he could continue in his role as chief academic officer.[99] To replace him as president, the Nichols Board of Trustees selected Dr. Darcy C. Coyle, to be third president of Nichols College.[100]

Darcy C. Coyle, B.S., M.B.A., D.B.A.
President, Nichols College, 1973–1978.

Darcy Coyle was born in Kentucky in 1918. He received an undergraduate degree from the U.S. Naval Academy and MBA and DBA degrees from the Harvard University School of Business Adminstration. Dr. Coyle worked as an industrial engineer and business consultant as well as serving as a lieutenant commander on an aircraft carrier in World War II. He had been a college professor at Babson, Harvard Business School, Boston University, and Rensselaer Polytechnic Institution of Connecticut. At Boston University, he was the management department chair; at Rensselaer he was responsible for the organization and the teaching of special programs and graduate degree courses.[101] After serving as president of Nichols for five years, he became president of Upper Iowa University in Fayette, Iowa, in 1978, eventually retiring there as President Emeritus. At Nichols, he considered himself to be the unofficial ping-pong champion. He died in 2002.[102]

After his selection as Nichols president, but prior to his arrival at Nichols on July 1, 1973, Darcy C. Coyle made his first recommendations to the Nichols trustees. His initial concern was that the College remain solvent. Secondly, he intended to "reaffirm" the Cross administration's efforts to work toward academic standards that "would enable the College to become accredited by the American Association of Collegiate Schools of Business (AACSB)."[103] In this respect, he met on several occasions with other New England colleges regarding AACSB requirements.[104]

As a consequence, President Coyle's approach to the presidency traveled along two different paths. To his credit, he fully disclosed financial matters in his yearly "Presidential Reports."[105] He was the first Nichols president to do so. While he achieved a semblance of financial order, the OPEC crisis and a period of significant inflation in the 1970s contributed further to the problem of balancing budgets.[106] As his administration proceeded, he became more optimistic. In 1976, he wrote that "though the College was not wealthy, the College is healthy."[107] He also stated to the Nichols community that "We must learn to practice what we teach."[108] At the same time, the College had to deal with two new laws: Title IX passed in 1972 requiring gender equity; and the Rehabilitation Act in 1973 regarding equal access on campus for people with disabilities.

To achieve his financial goals, President Coyle eliminated a number of faculty positions, including the physical education department. Institutional survival was at stake. He hoped this would assist the institution in developing stronger academic programs. He was proud of the fact that in 1974, for the first time, over 50 percent of the Nichols faculty had terminal degrees.[109] The faculty that year included three full-time faculty members who were women, two more than ever before. President Coyle then sought to have the College work at developing a better articulated sense of mission, goals and policies.[110]

As for the Nichols academic program, President Coyle's administration logically followed the lead of the Cross administration. He also saw Nichols College as a school of administration with secondary but important programs in psychology, history, and social service.[111] With regard to the future, President Coyle said the College was "looking forward to another period of substantial growth and development...."[112]

The MBA Program

At that moment, an MBA program, originally discussed as early as 1963 and essentially designed by President Cross, was accepted by the Nichols trustees and then approved in 1974 by the Collegiate Authority Committee of the Massachusetts Board of Higher Education. The first MBA candidate enrolled in 1975; the first MBA students graduated in 1977. President Coyle believed that the authority to grant the Master of Business Administration degree was "the most significant recent happening" for the College and he hoped this program would raise the quality of the Nichols undergraduate program through a "halo" effect.[113]

President Coyle "expected to set high standards" for part-time MBA students and he did.[114] The College required that MBA candidates be from accredited four-year institutions and have earned a cumulative 3.0 average. Beyond this, the College was taking its first big step into a new environment made up of "non-traditional" students.[115] The MBA enrollment in September 1975 was 44; by August 1977 it was at 71.[116] It quickly became one of the major MBA programs in central Massachusetts. And, to insure a proper level of instruction, President Coyle taught at least one MBA course each semester.

His relationship with the resident student body, however, was not as successful. Quite quickly, it became obvious that many students found it necessary to challenge President Coyle's actions regarding their recently hard-gained "student rights." As reported in the college newspaper, President Coyle and the Student Government Association clashed over changes in dining hall procedures, references he was said to have made regarding the lack of intelligence displayed by some Nichols students, and his efforts to create a quiet dorm.[117] This later move resulted in student opposition on the grounds that parietals then might be lost for the students involved. As they saw it, their newly gained entitlement was threatened by aggressive administrative actions if just one dorm lost its parietal rights. Their rallying cry became "Your dorm might be next."[118] A Student Opinion Poll in May 1974 found 62 percent of those polled believed that the new administration was "moving in regression" while 86 percent did not want to live in a proposed quiet dorm.[119] The introduction of two 75 minute classes a week in 1975 in place of three 50 minute classes did little to improve their opinions of administrative decisions.

During the tenure of President Coyle, the Nichols faculty began to achieve the level of expertise and accomplishment that both he and President Cross hoped would occur. By 1978, the faculty included a significant number of doctorates both in business and in the liberal arts and sciences. Unfortunately, the reality of the College's financial problems resulted in less-competitive salaries causing some to leave for better funded positions. Then too, some were greatly bothered by President Coyle's frankness and aggressiveness. For instance, his published pay scales placed business faculty numbers at a higher level than liberal arts faculty with similar academic credentials. Nonetheless, his manner of handling the College's finances put Lowell C. Smith, his successor, and the College in a much stronger financial position.

And, as frequently happens, the Nichols family, hardly large at best, suffered from some significant loses during this period:

Quincy M. Merrill, MD, Chairman of the Board of Trustees and Treasurer of the College, retired in 1966, died in 1969.

James L. Conrad, President of Nichols for 35 years, 1931 to 1966. Retired as President in 1966, remained a Nichols trustee until 1972, died in 1974.

Hal Chalmers, Athletic Director, Alumni Director, Assistant to the President, Nichols Class of 1936, died in 1975.

George Gromelski, Bursar, Treasurer, Nichols Class of 1940. Joined Nichols administration in 1946, died in 1975.

Charles Quinn, Dean of Faculty, Vice President, served under three Nichols presidents, died in 1976.

When coupled with the retirement of Gordon Cross in 1974, these deaths required the creation of an entirely new administration by 1975. Only Dean Robert Eaton remained. The replacements – President Coyle, this writer as Dean of Faculty, Vice President Albert Sargent, Bursar Thomas McClutchy[120]

James L. Conrad Jr.
A.B., A.M., Ph.D.
Dean of Faculty,
1974–1979.

Albert J. Sargent
B.S.B.A., M.B.A., Ph.D.
Vice President,
1976–1978.

Thomas F. McClutchy
B.S.B.A., M.B.A.
Bursar,
1975–1982.

Michael J. Vendetti
B.S., M.Ed.
Athletic Director,
1977–1986.

and Athletic Director Michael Vendetti[121] – had little direct contact with Nichols administrations prior to 1974. Therefore, such a change did not do much to contribute to a settled campus.

Like other presidents, President Coyle took a strong stand on the nature of the College. When he was about to leave Nichols in 1978, he noted that the "College will be stronger academically and far stronger financially than when he came."[122] He looked to "retain the small college environment, the very personal atmosphere that has always been a major strength of Nichols." He said, "we must guard against this possibility of losing personal contact with the individuals who form our College Community."[123]

Without question, the changes that occurred throughout the 1970s signaled the transformation of a college. Given careful planning for expansion and increased enrollment, Presidents Cross and Coyle, along with the Nichols Board of Trustees, were better able to project their institution's financial future. To do this, they worked to expand the student body by establishing a coeducational institution with numerous programs and courses. At the same time, students requested and achieved changes far beyond anything experienced on the Nichols campus. And there was still more to come.

The "Blizzard of 1978" with students jumping into snow banks off Chalmers Field House roof. Source: "The Blizzard of 1978." Photos by Joe Ortlieb, *Bison*, March 8, 1978.

NICHOLS: A COLLEGE FOR THE HILL

Map 3. Aerial Views of the Nichols Campus, 1975.
Source: Nichols College *1975 Ledger*, inside front and back covers.

From southwest, Library in center.

From southwest, first college athletic field in center.

~ The College "Transforming," 1966~1978

From south, Chalmers Field House is upper center.

From south, New Dorm and Olsen Hall left center.

From east, Chalmers Field House in foreground.

From east, looking at south central campus (Smith, Merrill, Daniels Halls).

From east, a view of northern or upper section of the campus.

From south, looking north up Center Road, with Dining Hall in left foreground.

CHAPTER 7

Beyond the Past, 1978~1996

For those seeking to understand the place of Nichols College in the broader picture, it is important to note that a universally accepted history of higher education in the 1980s and 1990s has yet to be written. In fact, there is much disagreement regarding its course over these two decades.

Some believe the period of the 1980s and 1990s benefited from an appreciated calm after the turmoil of the two previous decades. This understanding of the 1980s and 1990s sees it as a time which experienced relief from an earlier era of student reactions, political conflict, and economic threats – oil shock, inflation, unemployment, and international tension. A number of historians see these decades as a time of general quiet devoid of campus activism, while being buoyed by a partial return of the liberal arts.[1] For instance, Clark Kerr, in his book *The Great Transformation in Higher Education*, points to the 1980s as a "time of normalcy," of "few special problems," and of "comparative tranquility" giving evidence of a "tested system."[2]

With the passage of time, however, others conclude that higher education in the 1980s and 1990s actually lost ground in a changing world then seen contributing to a new society. By the mid-1990s, many were taking part in a new "sport" of "college- and university-bashing."[3] Rakesh Khurana's *From Higher Aims to Hired Hands* believes that "all is not well within the institution of the university-based business school." He understands that business education is being negatively affected by many developments including a number of changes in the corporate world, a "chorus of criticism" aimed at business schools, and the "challenge presented by the rise of for-profit, online, and alternatives. . . ."[4]

America also can be seen as entering a new century that undoubtedly will feature fundamental shifts, new conditions, technological innovations and changing behaviors. George Keller in *Higher Education and the New Society*, writes that colleges must "redesign their structures in fundamental ways to respond to the new challenges . . . ." For Keller, incremental improvements are inadequate because of the significant transformations that occurred in the 1970s.[5] He concludes that higher education simply has failed to take into account the "new society" which is emerging after 2000.

While these alarmists have significant followings, still others see a more balanced educational environment. For instance, Christopher Lucas in *Crisis in the Academy* acknowledges that the public appears to have lost confidence in higher education and believes that the 1980s and 1990s were "troubled times." However, he feels that American higher education is not yet "crisis ridden," although the future is uncertain.[6] As he puts it, "Without some larger vision, some sense for the multiple purposes higher education can and should serve, the alternative is likely to be simply more of the same – a popular but increasingly dysfunctional system of higher education, one ultimately ill-suited to meeting the challenges of the century ahead."[7] Less negative is Arthur M. Cohen's *The Shaping of American Higher Education* that asserts higher education in the United States is secured "by its tradition, value and power" and has demonstrated its "ability to adapt to changing conditions."[8]

This brief introduction suggests the difficulties of making any final evaluations of the higher education experience originating in the 1980s and 1990s. This applies as well to the course of Nichols College. What is available to the historian, however, are the records and reports from 1978 to 1996 related to the significant and numerous activities of the fourth president of Nichols College, Lowell C. Smith, and the College's development during his 18-year presidency. They provide the basis for understanding the College's experience during the Smith years and, perhaps, beyond.

Lowell C. Smith, the Fourth President of Nichols

On April 1, 1978, Lowell C. Smith, 47, then vice president for academic affairs at Bryant College (now University) in Smithfield, Rhode Island, became the fourth president of Nichols College. Dr. Smith earned his BSBA degree from Kent State University, his MBA from The George Washington University, and a Ph.D. in industrial relations, economics and finance from the University of Alabama.

For eight years he was an assistant and associate professor at The George Washington University and for three years a full professor at Loyola University in New Orleans. He also served at Loyola as dean of the College of Business Administration. When there he received credit for successfully obtaining accreditation for both its undergraduate and graduate business programs. From 1967 through 1971, he was assistant to the dean of the School

Lowell C. Smith, B.S.B.A., M.B.A., Ph.D.
President, Nichols College, 1978–1996.

of Government and Business Administration at The George Washington University. In 1974 he became the chief academic officer at Bryant College in charge of long-range planning, the development of academic programs, and budgeting for academic affairs.

Dr. Lowell Smith also was active writing at least one scholarly article a year and frequently testifying before federal committees. A former naval aviator and airline pilot, he was a captain in the Naval Reserves. He lists numerous professional affiliations and in 1973 was selected an Outstanding Educator of America. Upon his appointment, he and his wife, Eleanor Mann Smith, immediately took up residence in the President's House on Dudley Hill.[9]

When Dr. Lowell Smith became President of Nichols he found himself in a seemingly positive position. For one, student activism at Nichols in the 1970s had lessened, although not entirely. Second, Nichols had experienced a transforming period that saw the former all-male business college become coeducational and broaden its curriculum to include some liberal arts majors. This led Nichols to proclaim its emergence as a school of administration. The College also experienced the elimination of student social rules and regulations thus effectively ending a long-existing practice whereby the institution acted *in loco parentis*. And, third, President Smith's predecessor, Dr. Darcy C. Coyle, dealt directly with a number of difficult financial challenges in the 1970s with the College emerging from this presidency with carefully balanced budgets.

In his initial "President's Message" in 1978, President Smith offered his perception of the role and the goals of Nichols College. Sections of his "Message" follow:

> Nichols College is a center for the study of free enterprise capitalism. It is our goal to prepare young women and men to assume productive lives in a society from the minute they enter the front doors of business and government institutions which employ them. We have a long and successful history of having done so. In addition, we have a limited number of liberal arts degree programs.
>
> This mission is accomplished by combining the business and public administration courses with a good mix of traditional liberal arts courses, so that the individual who leaves here is well rounded and not narrowly parochial in his or her accomplishments. . . .
>
> The major goal of Nichols College is to prepare men and women to take an active part in our culture and society and to progress by their own competence and through a program of lifelong learning to leadership positions in the fields of administration for business and public service.[10]

Remarkably, fifteen years later the "President's Message" remained unchanged testifying to President Smith's unwavering commitment to his goals and interests.[11]

Specifically, in his inauguration address in 1978 he projected a Nichols student body of roughly a thousand in the near future, a need for funds from outside sources, and benefits to be gained by having stronger ties with the local community.[12] In this latter respect, he immediately established a yearly Dudley Appreciation Day in 1978 to formally acknowledge the community's effort on behalf of the College. He further noted that the "real strength of Nichols College is not in the buildings here, but in the people who form the core, the philosophy and backbone of the institution."[13]

In her brief history, *Nichols College; The First 175 Years*, written during the Smith administration, Elizabeth Kelly noted that President Lowell Smith's administration was characterized by "enhanced academic programs, supplements to those programs, and plans for developing the physical campus."[14] As well as elaborating on these accomplishments, this present chapter begins by focusing on specific changes made in his first year regarding the role and nature of the faculty. These adjustments caused the College to realign its entire operational structure and thus complete a final phase in its transformation begun ten years earlier. These changes in turn led to institutional advancement for which President Smith should receive much credit. His actions also were dedicated to an evolving and aggressive utilization of College resources including efforts to extend the campus beyond Dudley Hill.

INTERNAL REORGANIZATION AND REDESIGN, 1978

One of the generally overlooked contributions of President Smith is his support of a new *Faculty Policy Manual* being introduced as he was taking office. This *Manual*, published in 1978, was several years in the making and replaced Academic and Faculty Manuals written in the 1950s and 1960s.

When I became dean of the faculty in 1974 during the administration of President Darcy Coyle, I was the first full-time Nichols faculty member appointed to this position in the College's history. The faculty had been growing in size, credentials and abilities under the policies of Presidents Cross and Coyle. Unfortunately new and promising faculty members sometimes left Nichols for other positions after a year or two. Further, it was becoming more and more difficult to hire qualified faculty. Immediately I realized that new operational approaches were necessary. There were a number of easily identified problems: the College required its faculty to teach five days a week rather than four; no clear statement existed regarding a process of faculty evaluation; and no known salary structure was in place.

Previous faculty and academic manuals had been written by administrators with committees usually chaired by the president or the dean of the College. In the 1960s and the early 1970s, the Academic Committee included the president, deans, administrative assistant, several administrators, and four or more faculty department chairs.[15] These committees were responsible for evaluating faculty members, among other tasks.

After discussions with the chairs of the academic departments, I was certain that more faculty involvement was necessary. The faculty experience at Nichols had to be redesigned in order for wider opportunities and greater contributions by faculty members. In 1975, as an initial step in the retention and recruitment of faculty, I recommended to the faculty that we move from 50 minute classes on Monday, Wednesday, and Friday to 75 minute classes two days a week. Seventy-five minute class periods already existed on Tuesday and Thursday. This allowed all faculty to have four-day teaching weeks. After a long meeting, the faculty narrowly accepted this change. The following year, however, a scheduled faculty reconsideration of the 75 minute class schedule found near unanimous acceptance. The nature of the teaching week no longer hampered faculty recruitment efforts.[16]

At the same time, we also began to develop a new *Faculty Policy Manual*. It was important that this new manual clearly set out the process leading to promotion and tenure. This included establishing a standard probationary period of two years and a four-year extended probationary period with formal evaluations of yearly performances using carefully stated standards applicable to each faculty rank. Also added was an expanded statement on due process and other procedural safeguards.[17] Most importantly, the evaluation process was to be conducted completely by the faculty. The resultant manual was reviewed first by President Coyle and then by President Smith, as well as the Nichols Board of Trustees.

In the process, one proposed section of the new *Manual*, Section 7.2, titled "Compensation Reports" did become contentious. It was our goal to have faculty members know and understand the Nichols pay scale. This was not a simple accomplishment since the College had just experienced several extreme inflationary rounds and it was difficult for the trustees to make financial commitments beyond one year. Nonetheless, after several meetings with a trustee committee, the following statement was placed in the *Faculty Policy Manual of 1978*:

> It is the goal of Nichols College to keep faculty salaries at levels which compare favorably to that of other institutions in the Category IIB of the American Associations of University Professors (AAUP) annual compensation report. Annual review of faculty compensation shall be conducted by the administration and the Faculty Senate whose report shall be sent to the appropriate committee of the Board of Trustees.[18]

In order for the intent of the *Manual* to be fully realized, however, much remained to be done. Fortunately Dr. Edward Warren, dean of academic affairs from 1981 to 1996, worked diligently with the faculty to introduce the new committees necessary to support the goals of the *Manual* as well as to develop a standard faculty performance evaluation based on the results of the Educational Testing Service's "Student Instructional Report."[19]

In the process of achieving and refining the goals intended in the 1978 *Manual*, it was necessary to create a faculty committee system that would both accomplish the ends desired and fully utilize the abilities of the faculty. As a result, and consistent with the intent of the 1978 *Manual*, the faculty led by Dean Warren was able to introduce new or restructured faculty committees such as the Committee on Committees while substantially realigning the structure and responsibilities of other committees. This involved the Rank and Appointments Committee, the Curriculum Committee, the Chairperson's Committee, the Professional Development Committee, the Faculty Grievance Committee, the Faculty Senate, and the Faculty Association.[20]

Professor Warren later explained the affect of this process: "The faculty's sense of purpose and responsibility to Nichols and its improvement became a mainstay of the College during the 1980s and early 1990s."[21] Over this period, the Nichols faculty of 35 to 40 full-time members achieved the high levels of professionalism originally intended by Presidents Cross and Coyle. Moreover, a number of faculty members published significant books during this time. They include the following professors listed with their departments: William R. Lasher, Finance; Howard W. Oden, Management; Lilian L. Shiman, History;

Peter R. Savage, B.A., M.A., Ph.D., Dean of Academic Affairs, 1980–1981.

Edward G. Warren, B.A., M.A., Ph.D., Dean of Academic Affairs, 1982–1998.

Thomas G. Smith, History; Donald L. Stancl, Mathematics; Mildred L. Stancl, Mathematics; Karen S. Tipper, English; and George P. Winston, English.

Clearly the *Faculty Policy Manual of 1978*, when added to new Nichols degree programs, coeducation, and a liberalization of student rules consistent with the 26th Amendment to the U.S. Constitution, effectively completed the full transformation of Nichols College.

Advancing the College, 1978~1996

When it came to addressing other institutional problems, President Smith was most aggressive in taking the lead. Furthermore, in all areas he attempted to select qualified people with important experience and applicable talents. This too, was critical, although not always successful. And, like Presidents Cross and Coyle, he believed that "Nichols is moving toward a position of leadership among small colleges of administration."[22]

Institute for American Values
(Robert C. Fischer Policy and Cultural Institute)

One of the problems faced by all professional schools has been the need to develop effective and formal cultural programs. By its concentrated nature and direct focus, a professional school may promote programs seemingly devoid of cultural content. Nichols was not an exception, despite conscious efforts to the contrary. Nichols administrations have always been aware of the need to incorporate a cultural dimension into the College's institutional framework. The word "culture" has been on the Nichols seal since the College's beginning in 1931. Nonetheless, the opportunity to address this dimension was never better institutionalized than during President Smith's years as president.

Initially, Nichols Junior College of Business Administration and Executive Training, with a much smaller enrollment, had introduced an approach to a cultural experience that included as many students as possible. President Conrad, even before the school opened its doors in 1931, stated that a "specialization in business education required training in ethics and should include understanding the value of culture in the human experience."[23] The approach of his early administration was to hold weekly convocations with required attendance intended to bring students up-to-date on institutional issues as well as introducing various programs to provide cultural enrichment. A great part of this approach also included the College's aggressive promotion of Glee Club and Dramatic Club activities calling for extensive student participation. The Junior College's first charter in 1941 cited the school's commitment "to promote the ethical, social and intellectual culture. . . ." (See Appendix C.)

After the Conrad administration ended in 1966, President Cross chose not to follow the previous approach to cultural activity seeking instead to develop a more formalized system. In May 1968, the *Bison* reported that the Nichols administration and Board of Trustees approved "a request by interested faculty members to establish a regular schedule of visiting lecturers."[24] Some later believed that the new Nichols liberal arts courses might be adequate for this purpose. This proved not to be the case. Consequently, President Cross called for a new committee, the Student-Faculty Public Affairs Committee, to discuss the institution's need to "bring a series of lecturers and guest speakers of interest to the entire Nichols community." I was on this committee with Professors Warren, Brooks, and three students.[25]

With the assistance of department chairs, the Public Affairs Committee applied for a consultant grant from the National Endowment for the Humanities (NEH). This proposal, written primarily by English Department Chairman George Winston, stated the institution's goal was "to strengthen our offering so as to bring into focus the underlying humanistic principles of the separate areas and to underline the career values of such studies for our students." We requested help from NEH in developing such a program. Our intention was to make our "offerings cohesive in themselves [but now in scattered places and classes]. . . . to create a humanistic program which will be highly visible as a major factor in the student's pre-professional programs, not merely as an appendix."[26]

Consequently, the College was awarded a consultancy grant and visited by an NEH consultant, Dr. Francis L. Broderick, a professor at the University of Massachusetts in Boston. He concluded that the College was qualified to apply for a substantial NEH grant.

With the Broderick report in hand, I went to President Smith in 1979 to discuss our grant request. I was told that he had decided to go in another direction. He intended to reject any government grants, by itself a controversial decision that also affected the greater issue of government funding for other potential Nichols projects. Rather, he felt it would be better for the College to promote its own needs and responsibilities as a "center for the study of free enterprise capitalism." The end product of his thinking – The College's Institute for American Values – was established in 1980 as a public policy forum.

From its inception, the Institute as designed by President Smith was committed to the "fundamental concepts of personal freedom and the worth of the individual, the primacy of the marketplace with concentration on the individual in our economy, and the assessment of the role of government in American life."[27] Its early introduction was straightforward and clearly stated. According to one of its first announcements, "The College, as a fiercely independent center for the study and teaching of free enterprise, seeks through this Institute [then named the Institute for American Values] to provide a forum for the discussion, study, and dissemination of scholarly information about these issues." The Institute was intended to operate as "a center for outreach" that included regional and national audiences not then being adequately served.[28] Its goals were most ambitious: the presentation of symposiums by the best national speakers; lectures; publishing results of the symposiums; extending the College image nationwide; and promoting the intellectual climate of the College.[29]

Success of the Institute resulted because of a number of reasons beyond its conservative political appeal that was not particularly strong on the Nichols campus. First, in the process of seeking an Institute director, President Smith contacted Dr. Russell Kirk, author of *The Conservative Mind*, and perhaps the leading historian of American Conservatism, regarding a possible candidate. Dr. Kirk referred Robert Fischer to Nichols.[30] He was one of the few candidates interviewed for the position who understood how the Institute and its director should function. Second, the Institute and Director Fischer, a former faculty member and assistant to the president at Olivet College in Michigan, were given a home on Nichols property on Hall Road, adjacent to the campus. This formally established its presence on the campus. Dean of Academic Affairs, Edward Warren, later referred to Robert C. Fischer as "that bon vivant, gracious host, and intellectual traveling salesman for Nichols, free enterprise, and the American way."[31]

Despite its obvious political leaning, this new division was extremely successful. An update in 1983 correctly noted that the Institute "has provided some of the finest minds in the country in intellectually stimulating programs addressing public policy issues across a broad spectrum."[32] Director Fischer's clever programming and appealing personality led to the Institute's acceptance by the College community. The Institute's keynote inaugural address was

Governor George Romney gives the inaugural address of the Institute for American Values (later Fischer Institute), 1981.
Source: *Nichols College Bulletin, 1982–1984*, 9.

given by Governor George Romney on November 18, 1981. His symposium topic was: "Conservatives and the Burden of Political Power." One Institute program actually brought a circus to the campus and gave President Smith a chance to ride an elephant.

There can be no question that President Smith's initiative led to the creation of a cultural experience then being sought by many at the College. If there were any failings, they were in the funding area that he originally said was to come specifically from Institute sources.

Parallel to the development of the Institute, the faculty's interest in a cultural program remained constant. By 1984, the Cultural Enrichment Committee of the faculty led by Dean Warren and the Institute for American

Robert C. Fischer, A.B., M.A.
Director of the Institute for American Values,
1981–1998.

"Circus in America," Institute Program at Nichols on football field.
Source: *1983 Ledger*, 124.

Values directed by Robert Fischer agreed to combine their programs with the College accepting the responsibility of funding the entire project. This resulted in the establishment of a new formal program: "The Cultural Experience: The Arts, Sciences, and Public Policy." As agreed by the president and the dean, this became an administrative requirement for graduation intended "to expose the student to a rich variety of cultural and public policy programs during the academic year."

Each student initially was required to attend 34 programs from the joint offerings of the Cultural Enrichment Committee and the Institute over a four-year period.[33] This combination of programs allowed for a substantial programming potential with great flexibility that touched on current issues, course-related topics, artistic performances and exhibits.[34] It also proved an unique solution to the College's need for a cultural dimension. All programs were open to the public at no cost. (For a partial list of Institute programs, see "The Cultural Experience: The Arts, Sciences, and Public Policy," *Nichols College Bulletin, 1993–1996*, 13–15.) In the late 1990s, the Institute offered several seminars with well-known scholars in residence. This included Jeffrey Hart, professor of English emeritus, from Dartmouth College.

But this had not been accomplished without some conflict. Many faculty were concerned about the Institute's political bent while others felt that this new program would significantly impact the College budget. In 1981 faculty support had been marginal at best. However, Director Fischer's genial attitude and imaginative programming did much to encourage faculty assistance. Moreover, the Institute also attracted a fairly large number of supporters from outside the College. Their interest and appearances added another important dimension to the Institute's vital nature and value. It soon was designated a division of the College. Eventually, those interested created more formal groups – the Alumni Associates and the Advisory Council of the Institute. Furthermore, the President threw his complete support behind the Institute hosting evening discussions in his home after Institute programs and was able, at least initially, to provide support for the Institute through grants.

As for Nichols students, they were quick to express their opinions about what had become a new graduation requirement. Additional graduation requirements are rarely well-received. More than one letter in the *Bison* spelled out their concerns. Some felt that Institute events were not convenient for commuters, programs were not interesting, people were turned off by certain programs, some disliked being forced to attend and sit through programs lacking in quality.[35] Some simply believed the requirement of 34 programs to graduate was too high or "undesirable."[36] For them, the Institute had to prove itself.

Others, however, found the Institute's contributions important. Comments on the College's "Historical Questionnaire" suggested much student appreciation. One noted that the cultural requirement opened the eyes of students to "diversity" – and saw it as a key "to making well-rounded students."[37] And, under the early guidance of Institute Director Fischer, the Elbridge Boyden Society was introduced in 1992 as a candidate chapter for membership in Omicron Delta Kappa, a national leadership society.[38]

THE COMPUTER AT NICHOLS

When the Smith administration took office in 1978, a college computer center was in place in two rooms on the bottom floor of Conrad Hall. No one questioned the need for the College to develop a plan that brought this technology to future business leaders. President Smith went further: he believed that computer literacy was "a must for anyone about to graduate from college and enter the business world."[39] The Smith initiative led directly to the construction of the Mary and James Davis Business Information Center in the lower level of the Library building. He then supported an innovative personal computer plan that was followed by the construction of a major classroom building intended to support the aggressive use of this technology in Nichols classes. While some features of this development were present in other colleges, the all-inclusive, campus-wide nature of the Nichols approach was a singular accomplishment.

By 1985, the Davis Business Information Center became the administrative hub for computer activity involving networking hardware and an academic laboratory. This facility, a new $563,000 computer lab, was placed in an open area on the bottom floor of the Library building and included a 60-seat auditorium and a microcomputer lab with 24 microcomputers. The Center was made possible by a matching challenge grant from the Irene E. and George A. Davis Foundation. Mary and James Davis, for whom the facility

"College Dedicates New Davis Information Center,"
March 22, 1985. James and Mary Davis with President Smith.
Source: *Nichols News, Alumni Newsletter*,
Vol. XXXVI, No. 3, Summer, 1986, 1.

was named, were parents of Nichols alumni, John Davis and Stephen Davis, Classes of 1972 and 1980, respectively. The center was a result of the third significant fund raising effort in the College's history (the first was in 1948 for Alumni Hall, the second for the field house). Ably supervised by its director, Dennis Keohane, the initial intention of the Davis Business Information Center was to introduce the computer as a vehicle for business analysis and to better prepare students for its use as future leaders. It soon became the vital center of Nichols College's new personal computer plan (PC Plan).[40]

In many respects the College's PC Plan was an on-going response to another long existing need. Communication has always been a necessary focus of business education beginning with courses in penmanship in the 19th century followed by the ubiquitous typewriter and various business machines. The two-year college, as well as the later college of business administration, required all students, interested or not, to complete a typing course. The introduction of the computer and electronic communication moved this communicative technology to another dimension. In the process, Nichols students increased their abilities to analyze corporate data required for business decision-making.

Within a year, the program required that all undergraduate students own MS DOS compatible personal computers as part of the Nichols PC Plan. Nichols thus became one of the first colleges to make such an all-campus commitment. Apart from supporting its general informational role and coordinating the use of PCs, the center and the College then demonstrated the intention of using PCs in state-of-the-art classrooms in a new academic building by 1991. The ultimate goal was to create a campus-wide system that fully integrated the microcomputer into the entire curriculum. Eventually nearly universal ownership by students of computers prior to their arrival on campus made it possible for the College to reduce its direct involvement in this part of the PC Plan. Nonetheless, a supportive environment for its utilization was introduced to the campus.

When the student newspaper, the *Bison*, said that Nichols was in a "league of its own" after the PC Plan was in place, it was right.[41] The decision to introduce the PC Plan, according to the *Nichols News*, was seen as "one of the most significant in the history of the College. . . ." Business education at Nichols was seen taking a "quantum leap" forward.[42]

My personal awareness as to where the College stood on the question of student computer usage compared with other colleges and universities crystalized for me when I went to an historian's meeting in New York City and attended a seminar on computer use. Several historians discussed the excellent support from their institutions and were accomplishing wonderful things. When I explained what Nichols was doing and how the College was getting everyone involved – with the College accepting much of the cost for faculty computers – they were amazed. No one there was associated with a college-wide program such as Nichols had put in place. As the *Boston Globe* put it, "Computers a must at Nichols College."[43] These aggressive steps in new communication technologies positioned the College to assist Nichols students to become part of a new age and culture.

New Facilities and the "Campaign for Nichols"

A third development during the Smith administration that had long-term implications for the institution and its students was the expansion of the College's physical plant. When Lowell Smith arrived on the Nichols campus in 1978, he found the institution operating at near resident capacity. To increase the enrollment, he first began to convert some campus homes into small dormitories while buying other houses to serve as alternate living opportunities. By the mid-1980s, he was considering new buildings as well. The last structures erected on the Nichols campus were the dining hall (now Lombard Dining Hall) completed in 1974, while the most recently built dormitory, then "New" dorm (now Kuppenheimer Hall), was added in 1970.

As President Smith reaffirmed the nature of the campus proper, he acquired or renovated a number of College and other nearby Dudley Hill homes as housing for Nichols students. Eleven to twenty students, frequently women, were located in these residences – the Houlberg, Justinian, Chisholm, Fuller, Winston, and Gurnett Houses.[44] This effort, however, lasted only a few years as the popularity of this housing option declined. By 2000, or shortly thereafter, only one, the Winston House, remained suitable for student use. Two eventually were sold (the Chisholm House and the Hall Road property) and four (Houlberg, Justinian, Fuller, and Gurnett houses) would be razed. In the case of the 1805 (Fuller) House, its later demolition caused significant debate in the Dudley Hill community because of the building's history and architecture.

Considerably more successful than his plan for alternate living was the College's most ambitious fund raising drive to date. It resulted from the creation of a long-range plan taken more than a year to write.[45] This capital campaign generally was intended to help the College make changes, but not to change Nichols traditions. Its purposes, according to the *Bison* in 1988, were to "provide a quality business education, protect the College's political stance, demonstrate prudent fiscal management, and assist the College in its commitment to quality teaching."[46] Frequently overlooked in an assessment of Lowell Smith's presidency is his achievement during the late 1980s of obtaining the financial support for the College's Business Information Center, Shamie Hall, and Davis Hall.

This "Campaign for Nichols" resulted in the construction of two new state-of-the-art structures in 1990 and 1991. Shamie and Davis Halls joined the buildings put in place by Hezekiah Conant over a hundred years before. The first, Davis Hall, an up-to-date academic center in the middle of the upper campus, was dedicated to the Davis family of East Longmeadow, Massachusetts. The Davis family also had assisted in the construction of the computer center. Davis Hall then became the College's primary academic facility on campus with ten classrooms and two lecture halls; all were part of the College's beginning electronic network. As such, it represented a successful early stage of the College's initial commitment to provide its students with electronic technology in an educational environment.

Second, Shamie Hall, built in 1991, was named for Ray and Edna Shamie, also friends and generous benefactors of the College. It became the largest residence hall on campus housing 246 students, more than twice the number

Davis Hall, a state-of-the-art academic building dedicated to the Davis family of East Longmeadow, Massachusetts, opened in 1991.
Source: *Nichols College 2001 Ledger*, 113.

of Budleigh Hall, the next largest hall. It represented the latest in residence hall construction with individually controlled heating and air conditioning as well as cable and computer connections. It was, according to President Smith, "not a luxury plan" but "a survival plan."[47]

Taken in their entirety, the Smith administration's additional actions led to significant campus growth. The creation of the Davis Business Information Center in the Library building and the construction of Davis Hall as the

Shamie Hall, the largest residence hall on campus, was named for Ray and Edna Shamie in 1991.
Source: *Nichols College Bulletin, 1997–1998*, 33.

College's primary academic center, both on the campus north of Healy Road, helped to reestablish this area as the College's academic center. At the same time, the construction of Shamie Hall, on what had been the left field line of the College's former baseball field, likewise set the residential section of the college campus to the south of the dining hall for future development.

Not to be overlooked in the rebuilding process was the construction of the Francis W. Robinson, Jr. Tennis Courts and outdoor recreational facility in the shadow of Chalmers Field House. With its adjacent fields, this facility finalized the shift of the College's athletic complex to the eastern side of Dudley Hill. In the process, a rejuvenated college campus was in place by 1993. This was termed by some as the beginning of another era.[48]

A response to the College's "Historical Questionnaire" summed up one experience at Nichols over the 1990–1994 period. A member of the Class of 1994 referred to this time as "exciting" with attendance increasing, diversities rising, opportunities increasing, the College's reputation was improving, life-long friends being made, and memorable professors.[49] Students clearly were excited with the results of the "Campaign for Nichols." Just after Davis Hall's opening, the *Bison* determined that this was "the start of more good things to come to Nichols."[50] With Shamie, "beauty" was seen being added to the

Francis W. Robinson, Jr. '38 Tennis Courts, with
Lowell Smith and Francis W. Robinson, Jr., 1992.
Source: *Nichols Newsletter*, v.21, Spring, 1996, 4;
see also *1993 Ledger*, 42–43.

Nichols College community.[51] Some observers also marveled at the presence of 34 life masks of Nichols people at the entrance of Davis Hall. For graduates writing later about their college experiences, Nichols' building program in this period was seen "providing the college with the opportunity to move forward" or "to go to the next level."[52] These new halls made "a difference," according to another.[53]

The construction of Davis and Shamie Halls was the result of what was seen as "the most ambitious fund raising drive in the College's history." Intended to substantially upgrade the College's physical plant, "The Campaign for Nichols" initially raised 5.5 million dollars. As it was seen in 1989, the Campaign was to go toward the completion of a new academic center, a residence hall, a new student center, the renovation of the academy building, with additions to Chalmers Field House to follow.[54] This was estimated to eventually cost between 15–20 million dollars. In 1996, the *Nichols News* announced that "The Campaign for Nichols" had reached its initial goal.[55] The Davis, Shamie and Robinson families joined the list of notable College benefactors.

REACTIONS TO PROBLEMS OF GROWTH

In his perceptive examination of what he referred to as *Problems in the Transition From Elite to Mass Education*, sociologist Martin Trow noted a number of areas in higher education after World War II most affected when greater and more diverse numbers of students became part of a system originally intended for a specific and limited pre-war group.[56] All aspects of higher education were similarly impacted by a dramatically increasing rate of growth, the size of desired educational systems, and the nature of the age groups involved. Change was inevitable. While institutions might vary in their approaches to these problems, it was no longer possible given the circumstances of necessary growth to distribute new institutional responsibilities among existing administrative personnel or systems as it was done at Nichols and other small colleges in the 1960s and 1970s.

When President Smith arrived in 1978 he found remnants of old solutions still in place. With the deaths of a number of administrators in the 1970s, I was asked with other administrators such as Bursar Thomas McClutchy and Dean Robert Eaton, to add other duties to our primary tasks. We knew this could not or should not continue. In fact, one of the NEASC visitation teams agreed and recommended that changes be made. And, in 1979, Dean Robert Eaton, the last of the pre-1970 administrators, retired.[57] He had been with the College in a full- or part-time basis for 42 years, the last 18 as dean of students/registrar.

His contributions to the growth of the College and to its students were invaluable. It is correct to say that in one way or another he dealt with almost every student to attend Nichols from 1937 to 1979. For the record, he ranked the arrival of the four-year school in 1958 to be "one of the most important developments in the school's history."[58] The new foyer in the auditorium was named for him.

His leaving, however, made it possible and necessary to create a student services office. After an extensive search, Dr. Floyd N. Franke was appointed as the first dean of student affairs. With graduate degrees in higher education, he brought the first formal program of student services to the College. This was an important development. Now student services could be combined in one office under one director. The new office was located in the recently acquired former Fletcher residence on Dudley Hill opposite the Academy building.

Further, Dean Eaton's retirement also resulted in adjustments to the Registrar's responsibilities and procedures. A combination of accelerating demands, as sociologist Martin Trow suggested, plus the retirement of a dean and former cog in an area then dominated at Nichols by procedures of a past day, led to a decade of critical staff growth. Dean Eaton's approach to scheduling students was to meet individually with each one, and then determine class times and actual schedules after taking into account needs and requests of students and faculty. Such an approach could not be continued.

One who later made a significant contribution to the new office was Dean Roger Carney, a former Lt. Colonel in the Worcester-based ROTC program that was open to Nichols students. As dean of students from 1985 to 1998, he did much primary work in setting the stage for new student services programs then about to emerge at Nichols.[59] He later became a successful director of the Fischer Institute after the untimely death of Robert Fischer.

By that time, the College was adding more new people with different talents and backgrounds. It was one of President Smith's contributions that he was

Student Services Center Ribbon Cutting Ceremony in front of former Fletcher House, 1979. Participating in ceremony: Richard Naughton, Mayor of the Hill; John McDermott, Student Government President; Dr. Lowell C. Smith, College President; Dr. Floyd Franke, Dean of Student Affairs; and Dr. Marilyn Eichler, Director of Counseling.
Source: *Nichols News*, Vol. 4, December 1979, 10.

committed to hiring qualified and experienced people for these new openings. It was noted when Robert L. Packard was hired as MBA director, that "adding people of Packard's caliber underscores President Smith's commitment to excel in all levels of business education."[60] Certainly this had been the case with the aforementioned Robert Fischer. He was followed by others including Dennis Keohane, Registrar Peter Engh, Ken Grant, George deRedon, Jim Drawbridge, Edward C. Bradway, and a host of professionally trained dormitory counselors who replaced faculty in residence halls. It also included the new Safety and Security Department that took the place of the College's long-time security officer, Herb Durfee.[61]

A list of new positions and personnel who joined the College between 1980 and 1990 suggests the nature of this expansion. The College's staff and administration, according to College catalogs for the years 1981 and 1990, increased from 21 to 45 people. This featured new positions in career development, safety and security, and student activities. Added were the director of men's athletics, director of women's athletics, director of development, athletic trainer, director of corporate services, assistant to director of college advancement, director of public relations and publications, administrative assistant to director of MBA program, software consultant, assistant director of college advancement, college chaplain, director of advising services, assistant to business manager, operation coordinator, and director of continuing education.[62] Interestingly, during the same period, day enrollment (not night programs) was declining.[63]

Faculty members did more as well. As a group they became student advisors and advisors for majors. Many made special contributions. For instance, Dr. Karen Tipper, professor of English, was the "founder and driving force" behind the College's Learning Resource Center and Writing Lab established in 1980.[64] This project was funded by a grant that President Smith said was a "first" for the College.[65] Professor Tipper also contributed to the beginning of *Windfall*, a new student literary journal. Several years later, math professor William Steglitz introduced a math lab. Professor Frank Pfeiffer contributed much time and skill to the beginning of WNRC-FM. On a more formal level, Dr. Peter Savage replaced me as dean of academic affairs in 1980; the next year he was succeeded by Dr. Edward G. Warren who served as dean until 1998. In another category, Dr. Lilian Shiman, the College's first assistant dean of women and a professor of history, was elected chair of the Faculty Senate, the first woman to hold this position.

And, within the faculty, a restructuring of departments was occurring with the creation of divisional chairs in business and the humanities.

Nichols Students Entering a New World

American higher education had changed dramatically by the 1980s. Christopher J. Lucas in his *American Higher Education; a History*, finds the 1980s and 1990s radically different from what existed just a few decades before. His assessment points to higher education as being composed of an "untidy array" of all sorts of institutions. As for students, they sought different academic degrees and had different expectations requiring both broader and more specialized curricula. This included a closer relationship between academics and occupations and a student environment with less paternalism. Those involved wanted more freedom and more technology all designed to function with broader aspirations. This, in turn, resulted in different standards for judging the performance of colleges and universities.[66]

At the same time, greater student numbers coupled with their evolving needs led to the emergence of substantially larger and more powerful market forces. And, when the federal government chose to fund this growth with loans and grants directly to consumers, the students, rather than to institutions, the power of the student was greatly increased.[67]

This shifting institutional context occurred on the Dudley campus as Nichols students experienced some predictable conflicts. In some areas in the 1980s and 1990s, they followed past performances. *Bison* polls of these students in 1979 found them opposed to raising the drinking age in Massachusetts to 21 (68% to 32%) and favoring the legalization of marijuana (66% to 34%). A significant majority (68%) also felt there were not enough social activities on the Hill.[68]

Floyd N. Franke,
B.A., M.Ed., Ph.D.
Dean of Student Affairs,
1979–1982.

Kenneth E. Grant,
B.S.
Bursar,
1982–1994.

Roger F.X. Carney,
B.S., M.S.I.A., M.A.
Dean of Student Affairs,
1985–1998.

Politically, Nichols students continued to favor Republican candidates. In the 1976 election, according to a campus poll, Nichols students supported Gerald Ford (54% to 24%) for president over Jimmy Carter, the Democratic candidate and eventual winner.[69] In a 1980 poll, they favored Ronald Reagan, Republican candidate and winner over President Jimmy Carter (36% to 24.6% with Independent John Anderson at 28.5%).[70] Eight years later, when considering the Bush-Dukakis vote and election, the *Bison* found the Nichols population was still Republican although "Independents" now exceeded both Republicans and Democrats (40% – 31% – 29%).[71]

Aside from continuing traditional political tendencies, students during the 1980s and 1990s sought and received more from College programs. By 1983 "supplemental" programs included college success skills workshops, a learning resource center, and a career planning and placement service. The formal academic offering also added numerous internships in business, history, and a semester in Washington, as well as a small Army ROTC program attached to a unit at Worcester Polytechnic Institute.[72] Within seven years, the College introduced a new freshman seminar which stressed "fitting in," a formal reading and study strategy program, a New England-Nova Scotia student exchange program, a semester in England at Regent's University described by one student as a "best ever" experience, as well as the opportunity for additional majors at Nichols. And, to assure proficiency in English, a degree requirement was introduced on the "Use of Correct English."[73] Each required additional administrative or faculty oversight.

Not surprisingly, not all students were pleased. As with their colleagues everywhere, Nichols students had their own concerns which were typical or reflected long-existing College conditions. In 1979, the *Journal* (a new name for the *Bison*) found classes too crowded, dorms dirty, and food that had "just gotten worse."[74] A battle also was occurring between the editors of the student newspaper and the Student Government Association (SGA) over the newspaper's proper role, its approach to editorialization, and a number of other issues, including a name change and the right of the editor to make editorial policy.[75] Further, student complaints, some justified, some not, occurred when funding for the *Journal* was threatened by the college administration, an action that involved the SGA as well.[76]

A *Bison* poll in 1980 determined that social life at Nichols needed "improvement."[77] This poll also found that the most popular social function areas on campus were the bar, parties, and sports, then dances and semi-formals.[78] The college newspaper reported that some believed Nichols College was a "dictatorship solely run by the administration. . . ."[79] When Nichols attempted to get its students to agree not to sue the College by having them sign a waiver, a petition signed by 400 students apparently caused the administration to "rethink" this decision.[80]

Although this conflict between and among administrators and students generally tapered off between 1981 and 1989, many old issues sometimes reappeared. Complaints could be heard about excessive dormitory damage, the fact that social life on Dudley Hill was thought to be dying although the College introduced more activities, the need for better-prepared students, and the fact that no meal plan existed.[81] Some complained about the lack of school spirit and wanted more emphasis on weekend activities.[82] In November 1994, one article in the *Bison* summed up student complaints — a lack of activities, poor food service, the Cultural Experience, and a lack of respect from the administration.[83] Ironically, improved local roads and new nearby highways actually reduced the importance of local commercial centers and towns such as Webster and Southbridge forcing off-campus student activities to center on more distant cities such as Worcester and Boston.

One additional issue that students brought forward was the question of possible discrimination on the campus. According to another *Bison* poll, 69% of those responding thought that informal discrimination "probably" existed on campus.[84] It had been suggested that people of color were "not in abundance" at Nichols.[85] An Umoja (Unity) campus group eventually was formed in 1999 to provide a more "welcoming environment for minorities" by having the Nichols community "come together to form a high level of tolerance and respect for their peers." The club worked to destroy ignorance and discrimination and to "unify students."[86]

While these negative criticisms clearly existed, there was much that pleased Nichols students during these years. Certainly the construction of Shamie and Davis Halls in 1991, as already noted, brought many positive comments that focused on the "beauty," comfort, and utilitarian features of these buildings and the campus.

Further, and greatly contributing to a better understanding of the attitudes of Nichols students in the 1980s and 1990s were surveys done by the College administration in 1984 and 1994. Comparisons of 1984 survey results from graduates of the period 1973 to 1983 with similar surveys completed in 1994 for graduates from 1984 to 1993 provide important information. For Dean Warren, these results were "encouraging." Of this 1994 group, 75% of those who completed the surveys rated the selection of course material by Nichols faculty as "above average or excellent." This rating was a significant improvement over the previous survey. The 1994 survey also found 78% of those responding believed the quality of teaching at Nichols to be "above average or excellent;" as to quantitative skills, 87% of the 1994 group believed they were "adequately developed" at Nichols. In 1984 this rating had been 55%. In addition, in 1994, a great majority, 77%, said that they believed the quality of their majors or specializations was above average or excellent.[87]

As for the College's social and cultural offerings, the survey results of 1994 also showed much improvement over 1984, probably the result of the new cultural requirement. Of the group surveyed in 1994, 73% said that social life at Nichols was above average or excellent. The 1994 survey also found that students from 1984 to 1994 "liked best:" small class sizes; good faculty who cared and were available to students; and academic program features – curriculum, course content, and teaching.[88]

One additional element in this examination of Nichols student life from 1978 to 1996 is the part being played by coeducation. In first hand accounts focusing on the twentieth anniversary of women at Nichols, seven women who graduated in 1977 told their stories. Clearly these first years were challenging for them as a small group in a traditionally male environment. Nonetheless, they easily achieved high grade-point averages and quickly became campus leaders. During the years from 1975 to 1985, their numbers increased from fewer than 10 to 311 or 37.56% of the total Nichols day enrollment.[89]

Blue Ribbon Committee on the Future of Nichols Athletics

One event during this period that clearly disrupted the campus was the decision in 1986 of Athletic Director Michael Vendetti to leave Nichols "to seek a change of atmosphere."[90] He coached football and track at Nichols for 24 years and had been athletic director since the death of Hal Chalmers in 1975. At the time of his resignation, he had a career record as a football coach of 103–83–5, the second-most wins of any active coach in New England. At a faculty and staff gathering, I spoke for a group thanking Mike for his 24 years of "desire and spirit for his commitment and dedication to athletics, to Nichols, its athletes, its people and for his examples of loyalty, leadership, sportsmanship, and professionalism. . . ."[91] According to a comment by a former student and shared by many, Michael Vendetti had been "a very big part of creating the Nichols brand of successful student athletes in the 1970s."[92]

Athletic Director Vendetti's resignation led President Smith to review the entire athletic program by appointing what he termed a "Blue Ribbon Committee." Composed of a number of professionals in the field and Nichols faculty members, including this writer, the committee was chaired by the Rev. John E. Brooks, president emeritus of Holy Cross College, Worcester, Mass. After extensive discussions, this committee made the following recommendations to President Smith regarding athletic programs at Nichols:

1. Construct a new field house/gymnasium or build additions to an upgraded field house;
2. Complete renovation and upgrading of existing football facilities, including an all-purpose track;
3. Develop a new, all-purpose athletic field on an appropriate on-campus site;
4. Construct a modern skating arena for ice hockey.

Short-term recommendations also included improving selected areas, appointing an athletic council, and naming athletic directors for men's and women's sports.[93] Importantly, no suggestion was made that the College change its original commitment to intercollegiate athletics made in 1931.

Within a few months and consistent with the Blue Ribbon Committee recommendations, Nichols hired a new men's athletic director and a full-time coach in football and began renovations of Chalmers Field House. Karen Tropp remained the women's athletic director. Thomas R. Cafaro was appointed men's athletic director; football coach, Jack Charney, was appointed to a new full-time position as coach of men's sports and continued to serve as head coach of football and head coach of track and field. A part-time sports information director was to be hired as well. By 1993, the Francis W. Robinson, Jr. Tennis Courts, a new and impressive outdoor recreational complex with six lighted courts, one and one-half basketball courts and a volleyball court, was in place next to the Chalmers Field House.[94] In effect, the Blue Ribbon Committee's report brought about the rededication of Nichols to its athletic program for the forseeable future.

This reassessment of athletics at Nichols did not detract from the day-to-day course of the Nichols athletic program. Perhaps the most notable single development in Nichols sports history during this era was the emergence of women's sports. In the broader picture, in 1980, the College fielded eight men's teams (soccer, football, hockey, basketball, baseball, track, golf, and tennis) in NCAA competition and three women's varsity sports teams (field hockey, basketball, and softball). Thirteen years later, the Nichols varsity athletic program featured seven men's teams and four women's teams (soccer added), and listed three co-ed varsity teams (cheerleading, track & field, and golf). This increase of two varsity teams occurred despite the fact that the Nichols day enrollment declined by nearly 18 percent between 1980 and 1996.

In 1993, Nichols College was a member of the National Collegiate Athletic Association (NCAA, Division III), the Eastern College Athletic Association (ECAC), the Massachusetts Association for Intercollegiate Athletics for Women (MAIAW), the Eastern Collegiate Football Conference (ECFC), and the Northeast Women's Athletic Conference (NEWAC). On various occasions during this period, Nichols teams won championships in football, field hockey, women's basketball, softball, and golf.[95]

As in the past, Nichols athletes continued to be honored by the College. Sixty-one Nichols graduates from the years 1978 through 1996 were elected to the Nichols College Athletic Hall of Fame. Of this group, 17 were women and 44 men. In 1987, Ellen O'Connor Duggan became the first woman elected to the Nichols Athletic Hall of Fame. She was followed by Nancy Rossini in 1988. Of the classes from this period, the greatest number of new Hall of Fame members came from the Classes of 1979, 1983, and 1988 with six each. (See Hall of Fame members, 1972–2011, Appendix D.)

"Nichols Nighttime"

Six months after Lowell Smith became president, the College introduced what was essentially its third attempt to create a continuing or adult education program. In the 1950s the Junior College offered some adult education courses. After the College became a four-year school, it immediately introduced a degree-granting evening division based on what it saw as its responsibility to the community. President Cross ended this program in 1966 when he concluded that the community was not large enough to support its cost.

Much, however, changed by 1978. An evening undergraduate program could be built around the small evening staff already in place for the MBA program. President Smith quickly made the decision to re-establish what was termed a division of continuing education, a move that was later considered a "milestone" by his administration.[96] It was the first adult or evening degree-granting program offered by Nichols Junior College or Nichols College designed to produce additional revenue and intended to expand the College's reputation and its markets. He believed it was a perfect fit consistent with the College's mission of service to industry and community.[97]

Generally a new and greater educational environment for adult and continuing education was emerging quite logically from what was termed then as a "unique" interaction between American life and higher education.[98] Americans everywhere, young and old, were taking advantage of opportunities to enroll in institutions of higher education and to select from broader offerings of courses presented by colleges and universities all with generally acknowledged standards.[99] In 1988, President Smith reminded the Nichols community of the importance to the College of the Continuing Education and

MBA programs. He said: "You may wonder why . . . [evening programs] are so important. These offerings strengthen our day division by bringing in extra revenue, by keeping our name in the news and the public eye, and by keeping the College vital in the face of shrinking numbers of high school graduates."[100] He added that there were no similar evening business programs in the area and concluded there definitely was a need.[101] He was right.

The Nichols Division of Continuing Education offered seminars, workshops, and special programs as well as evening course work. Nichols evening programs awarded the degrees of bachelor of science in business administration (BSBA) and the associate in business administration (ABA), as well as the MBA.[102] In a similar fashion, the MBA program continued to provide its students with courses designed to prepare them for leadership roles in business and society. Its curriculum was designed to respond to social, economic, and technical factors as well as applying evolving knowledge in quantitative and social sciences.[103]

Between 1983 and 1996, Nichols College established temporary satellite campuses for part-time evening programs at Massachusetts locations such as Auburn, Uxbridge, Franklin, Southborough (including a College-owned corporate services and conference center), and Leominster, as well as Dudley. Dean Edward Warren oversaw this approach to marketing the evening programs planned in and around the Worcester area. This program was directed from Dudley or "World Headquarters."[104] As this was occurring, the College was gaining the reputation for a high quality program offered at frequent times at a number of locations. Dean Warren concluded that marketing for the evening made the College better known as a quality school. Surveys of respective Nichols divisions (day, continuing, professional, and MBA) established that students and alumni from all programs most appreciated small classes, numerous locations, and the quality of instruction.[105] Many MBA alumni praised the "real business experience" of Nichols MBA faculty.[106]

Enrollment figures for these night divisions illustrate the significant growth of the Nichols continuing education programs between 1980 and 1995. In the fall of 1980, 820 students were registered in the day division, 142 students in the evening undergraduate program, and 114 in the MBA program for a grand total of 1,076. Fifteen years later, in the 1996 fall semester, the day division enrolled 682, or 138 students (17%) fewer than in 1980; the evening programs enrolled 686 in 1996 as opposed to only 142 in 1980. Then too, the MBA program registered 318 in 1996, as opposed to 114 in 1980.[107] In 1996, the total enrollment of the three Nichols programs was 1,686, or considerably more than the 1980 numbers of 1,076. President Smith had been right when he announced that the evening programs had greatly contributed to the school's success.

In a "State of the College" address in 1993, he declared Nichols was "alive and well," despite the challenges.[108] The Dudley campus, according to President Smith and others, was in the best condition it ever had been in and boasted a number of new, beautiful buildings.

LOWELL C. SMITH, IN RETROSPECT

When President Lowell Smith retired in 1996, then Chairman of the Nichols Board of Trustees, John Dirlam, said that the president's "commitment to his principles was going to be hard to replace. He gave a positive direction to where the school is going."[109] And, on an earlier occasion, the student newspaper, the *Bison* concluded that "Lowell Smith can recognize a problem and tackle it straight on. . . ."[110] To that, President Smith added at his retirement that "the last seventeen years have been a string of unbroken advances with occasional colorful departures. . . ."[111] There is no question that there were successes – but some of the "occasional colorful departures" disturbed many people.

In an assessment regarding the state of the College in 1996, the *Nichols News* posed the question, "Where is Nichols College today?" Its conclusion: "a summary statement might say that Nichols College has never been better, but like all small colleges, we have had some opportunities to take advantage of our striving to be the best institution we know how to build."[112] Aside from the success of the College's evening programs, this article saw numerous achievements including the Institute for American Values, Davis Business Information Center, the PC Plan, Shamie Hall, Davis Hall, the Robinson tennis courts and recreational area, a women's soccer field, a new club house for the golf course, with a number of former single family residences adding alternate living opportunities for students. This included the acquisition in 1989 of the former Oldham residence built in 1792 which once boarded Nichols students and was located across from the Lombard Dining Hall. It was to be utilized as a guest house.

And, beyond these accomplishments, Lowell Smith made his own personal contributions. He and his wife, Nora, frequently served as cordial hosts for get-togethers after Institute programs as well as on a great number of other less formal occasions. When it was possible, he improvised to contribute to the moment. For instance, on two occasions, he challenged members of the Nichols community to exceed the number of laps he could swim in the Nichols pool in a given time period. His purpose was to raise money for proposed tennis courts. The first such competition in 1979 saw "the old man" finishing fourth in a ten person contest and raising more than $5,600 for the tennis courts.[113] In a second challenge swim in April 1988, President Smith, a former

The Old Man (Lowell C. Smith) and His Challengers.
Source: *Nichols News*, Vol. XXXII, No. 4, December 1979, back page.

distance swimmer in his college days, was tied by two other swimmers for first after swimming 250 laps in two hours. This swim made $16,000 for the tennis courts.

But there were moments when his aggressive and direct approach did not always bring appreciated results. A series of events dealing with the college newspaper, an investigation by the American Association of University Professors (AAUP), and a failed attempt to assist Central New England College (CNEC) of Worcester, Mass., did not expand his support on the Hill although they characterized his general approach to his role as president. Further, his inability to increase the Nichols day enrollment suggested potential institutional weaknesses and the possibility of problems in the future.

Before Lowell Smith had been president one year, he saw the need to criticize the student newspaper, then the *Journal* (before, and after, the *Bison*). According to the *Journal*, President Smith was upset by its involvement in local politics, among other issues, and threatened to shut the newspaper down.[114] The newspaper's treatment of certain institutional developments including a faculty tenure decision, criticisms it made of faculty and others outside the administration, and a conflict between the *Journal* and the Student Government Association (SGA) were not appreciated. On one occasion, the SGA asserted that the student newspaper should "clean up its act."[115] Several months later President Smith was reported to have warned the *Journal* editor that "you're in trouble" and the editorial leadership of the newspaper feared the paper was going to be closed.[116] When the newspaper temporarily changed its name from *Bison* to *Journal*, its editor was criticized for the change and remarked, in response, that "Bison" was a good name for a football team but lacked "something" for a newspaper.[117]

Part of the conflict between President Smith and the *Bison* stemmed from the dismissal of a faculty member which resulted in the institution being censured by the American Association of University Professors (AAUP). The issue was ignited when a faculty member was not given tenure and did not receive a year's notice. The policy that President Smith followed was clearly stated in the 1978 *Nichols Academic Policy Manual*. It was not, however, the AAUP's policy. When this faculty member was dismissed by President Smith and the Board of Trustees, the AAUP contended that he was denied his academic freedom.[118] President Smith argued that Nichols policies were followed and that the College was not required to accept AAUP policies. This resulted in censorship by the AAUP.

Several years later, in 1993, he also made controversial remarks about Nichols students that were reported in the college newspaper. His comments were seen as a "personal attack" by the *Bison*. Such incidents did not improve his image as Nichols President.[119]

While the College's approach to continuing education generally met with some success, one significant effort did not. In an attempt to expand Nichols' base in central Massachusetts and to preserve what was then said to be a valuable Worcester college, Nichols College loaned "limited amounts," $700,000 according to some sources, to Central New England College (CNEC) as it was about to collapse.[120] This assistance was inadequate and CNEC failed. In the process, Nichols President Lowell Smith was named CNEC's chief executive officer and Dr. Thomas Lelon was selected to be president and chief operating officer of CNEC.[121] But an undisclosed amount of money was lost as was the time spent on this project by Nichols administrators. Interestingly, had President Smith been successful with CNEC, the future of Nichols College would have been significantly different.

Beyond the failure to revive CNEC, Nichols' inability to build its own day program during President Smith's 18 years must have been a disappointment for the Nichols president. Day enrollment when Lowell Smith became Nichols president in 1978 was nearing 800. Fifteen years later, just prior to his retirement, the Nichols Day Division had 756 students although the number of women had increased from 237 in 1981 to 267 by 1995.[122] In his "State of the College" address in 1983, President Smith reported that "more than a third" of America's colleges and universities experienced a decline in enrollments of greater than ten percent that year. This included Nichols. Smith added that there were "hard times ahead," but Nichols "was in the black, barely."[123] Fortunately things seemed to change for the better as total enrollment in 1986, led by evening programs, reached a "record enrollment year." The College's best fall in 1989 saw more students attending Nichols than ever before.[124] Then came the positive impact of new buildings and the successful "Campaign for Nichols."

Lowell C. Smith's legacy as President should not be underappreciated because of his significant controversies. He established the Institute for American Values, noted as an "amazing net addition to the College's life," he set the PC Plan in place; his new buildings and the successful "Campaign for Nichols" set the tone and standards for the campus without detracting from the traditional structures in place. Philosophically, too, he carefully guarded what he saw as the College's mission – "the center for free enterprise capitalism" – although some disagreed with his anti-government, free enterprise capitalist position. His unwillingness to accept federal monies was criticized by many. At the same time, he reacted strongly against government intrusion, regulation, and its imposed "record keeping burden."[125]

Clearly his direct actions on occasion greatly disturbed many in the Nichols community, including faculty and students. Nonetheless, and despite the unfortunate loss of his wife, Nora, in 1992, it was obvious that he clearly enjoyed his work. Later he married Dorothy Drake. He ended his years as president with this statement: "I can truthfully say that collectively speaking, I love the people of Nichols College and I will miss everyone of you in a very special way."[126] Unquestionably he meant this.

Other Notable Events, People, Items, and Pictures 1967~1996

1967   Enrollment: 663 (including 92 foresters).
Sewer line completed (begun in 1965) encircling the entire campus.
Fred Friendly '36, former president of CBS News, is Commencement speaker.
Discussion of merits of an honor system in *Bison*.
Waterfront Mary's.

1968   New Nichols Alcohol Policy: responsible use by legal age students allowed in rooms.
"Bison" statue a gift of graduating Class of 1968.
EREHWON, Nichols Literary Magazine Club.

1969   Olsen Hall burned to ground.
Faculty teaching requirement reduced to 12 hours per week.
Annhurst College, No. Grovenorsdale, Ct., unofficially considered by some to be Nichols' sister school.
1949 undefeated Nichols football team honored as part of National College Football centennial program titled "An American Tradition for 100 years."

1970   Cost of enrollment (board, room, and tuition): $2,650.
Alpha Phi Chapter of Delta Mu Delta established.
Nichols Ski Slope constructed by foresters next to Chalmers Field House with motorized rope tow and dining hall trays "common form" of conveyance.
Hazel Oldham retires, made Librarian emeritus, Conant Library Reference Room named for her.
Prof. Ernest Phelps appointed Vice President of Development, a newly created position.
New Program for Honor Students directed by Dr. P.H. Ragan.
First six-week summer session for College.

Listing continues on page 221

1967–1996 College Buildings or Renovated Structures not Pictured in previous Chapter (and as they appeared during this period).

Admissions Center
1975–

Dining Hall
(now Lombard Dining Hall)
1974–

Auditorium with Dean Eaton Foyer
1980–

Fuller House (1805 House)
1805–2005

Chisholm House
1959–2000

Gurnett House
1934–2000

~ Other Notable Events, People, Items, and Pictures 1967~1996

Library and addition
1968–

Oldham House (Guest House)
1989–

Merrill Hall
1981–2000

Student Services Center
(Formerly Fletcher home)
1979–2012

New Dorm
(later Kuppenheimer Hall)
1972–

Winston House
1941–

217

Activities and Events, 1967–1996.

~ OTHER NOTABLE EVENTS, PEOPLE, ITEMS, AND PICTURES 1967~1996

1. Swim Meet, Hermann Pool; 2. Nichols Fire Department; 3. Herbie, Nichols security force; 4. New tennis courts; 5. Well house on Conant Commons; 6. Nichols cheerleaders; 7. Community Union; 8. Fred Friendly '35, received an honorary Doctor of Humane Letters degree in 1989, Nichols graduation; 9. Eastern side of Chalmers Field House; 10. Men's basketball in Chalmers Field House; 11. Women's basketball in Chalmers Field House; 12. Cover of Nichols Catalog, circa 1977; 13. George deRedon; 14. Tug-of-war between upper and lower classmen; 15. Bates; 16. Softball; 17. Professor Jim Guimond and friend.

Activities and Events, 1967–1996.
Continued

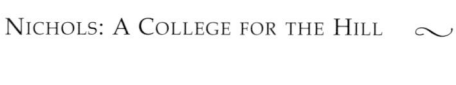

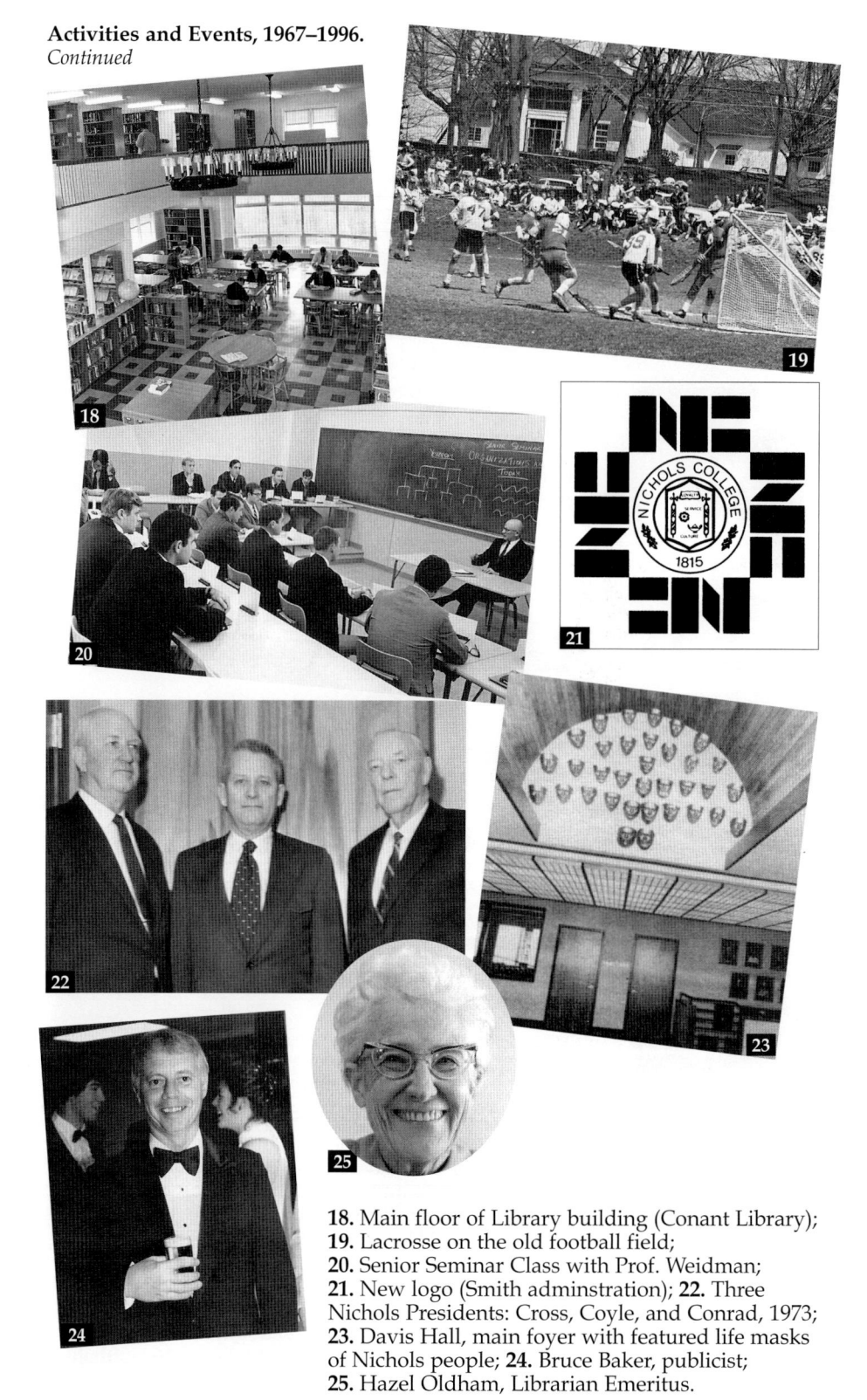

18. Main floor of Library building (Conant Library);
19. Lacrosse on the old football field;
20. Senior Seminar Class with Prof. Weidman;
21. New logo (Smith adminstration); 22. Three Nichols Presidents: Cross, Coyle, and Conrad, 1973;
23. Davis Hall, main foyer with featured life masks of Nichols people; 24. Bruce Baker, publicist;
25. Hazel Oldham, Librarian Emeritus.

∽ OTHER NOTABLE EVENTS, PEOPLE, ITEMS, AND PICTURES 1967~1996

Listing continued from page 215

1971 *Webster Times* salutes Nichols Community Programs and Mayor's Council contributions.
First Annual Earth Day.
U.S. Ambassador to Spain, Robert C. Hill, speaker at Nichols graduation.
Nichols forestry student, "Trooper" Tom Emonds, writes *Because It Is Mine*.
Enrollment about 720.
Nichols' Bruce Ziemski '72 wins New England Intercollegiate Golf Championship.
Work beginning on cleaning and beautifying Conant Pond area.

1972 Joe Namath Football Camp on Nichols campus.
Merrill Hall to be first co-ed dormitory, has seven resident students.
Basketball player Bob Payton scored over 1,000 points in two years.
Peter Bromley undefeated in 33 straight tennis matches.
First Honorary Doctorate from Nichols given to former President James L. Conrad.

1973 Petition for International Honor Society in Economics, Omicron Delta Epsilon chapter, approved.
John Siekierski first Nichols baseball player to throw a no-hitter.
Tuition reduction program with tuition free for those over 65 years of age.
C. Northcote Parkinson, Father of Parkinson's Law, named an honorary Nichols Trustee and scheduled to address College in November 1974.
Football team (8–1) wins New England Football Conference setting 12 team or individual records.
Due to rising energy and fuel expenses, all thermostats to be set lower, expected to save 15–20 percent.
Massachusetts drinking age lowered to 18.

1974 Nichols football team (7–1–1) ranked sixth in New England College Division Schools.
Cost of enrollment (board, room, and tuition): $3,325.
Swim meet held over the phone between Nichols and Cathedral College in New York because of gas shortage.
First Family Weekend to be held in May.
Virginia L. Tierney selected first Nichols woman trustee.

1975 Half-price Family tuition plan adopted.
"Outstanding Educators of America" award to Professors Conrad, Sargent, and Van Leuvan.
Hermann Pool hours: 2:00 p.m. to 5:00 p.m.
Scuba diving classes being held in Hermann Pool.
Newcomen Society of North America honors Nichols.

1976 First Nichols student begins a semester in Washington.
Bison Football team (8–1) 4th consecutive year taking a championship (NEFC). Said to be first team in collegiate football history to win a conference title in four straight years. (Four-year record: 29–5–1.)
Senior Dave French set New England Intercollegiate Lacrosse scoring record – 277 career points (157 goals, 120 assists).
Footballer John Delaney, class of 1976, tries out for NFL position.

NICHOLS: A COLLEGE FOR THE HILL

1977	Nichols Honor Societies: Delta Mu Delta, Zeta Alpha Phi. Yearbook dedicated to Professor Jim Guimond; according to students, "a perfect model for those aspiring to a life in business and dedicated to the maintenance of the free enterprise system."
1978	Dr. M. Mahmood Awan appointed MBA director. New sprinklers installed in most Nichols buildings. Marc Dupuis first player in Nichols basketball history to reach 1,000 pts. in scoring and in rebounds. President Lowell Smith introduced the first all-college employee's Christmas party. Bison statue stolen. MBA program graduates nine in May. (MBA Program enrollment now 71 from 44 in 1975.) Nichols lowers tuition. First Dudley Appreciation Day. Bob Schieffer, CBS reporter, speaks at Nichols. Cost of enrollment (board, room, and tuition): $5,290.
1979	President Smith offers to assist Annhurst College students after dorm fire. Bison returned.
1980	Enrollment: 1,076 (day-820, evening-142, MBA-114).
1981	ROTC to march on Nichols campus. Nichols College Parents' Organization created.
1982	Inaugural Symposium of Institute for American Values speaker was former Governor George Romney. Black Tavern given to Black Tavern Historical Society.
1983	Lisa Kellogg first coed to be elected President of Nichols College Student Government Association. Nancy Rossini, women's basketball, scored 1,000 points. In football, Mike Vendetti's 100th win.
1984	President Lowell Smith said to have canceled classes on April 23, 1984, due to sun shining and it was spring.
1985	Lisa Gionet, Freshman All-American basketball player. Bison's den closed when legal drinking age returned to 21. Full-time Director of Security with full-time professional security officers added to College staff. Frederick Currier's advice to Nichols' students: "Study History." Nichols offers "accelerated" MBA.
1986	Bison's Den reopened in September 1986 as the 21 Club.
1987	Nichols Nighttime goes to Auburn. Rugby Club formed and goes undefeated. "21 Club" needs bartenders. Justinian Council no longer exists.

Other Notable Events, People, Items, and Pictures 1967~1996

1988   WNRC-FM (95.1) back on air.
Formal Security Escort Service begins.
Windfall, Nichols Literary Magazine, introduced.
33% of MBA students, 65% of students in Continuing Education are women.
Admission booklet receives gold medal from American Marketing Report.

1989   Fred Friendly '36 receives Honorary Doctorate at 1989 Commencement.
First Annual Employee Recognition Banquet.
Enrollment: 1,981 (day-848, evening-718, MBA-415).
Cost of enrollment (board, room, and tuition): $11,315.

1990   "Dry House" status considered for two student residences: Chisholm (women) and Houlberg (men).

1992   Shamie Hall opened.

1993   Bazzie passes away. "An institution within an institution."
"Dr. Ice" (Mauri Pelto of Nichols faculty) tracking disappearing glaciers in north west.

1994   Enrollment: 1,766 (day-756, evening-612, MBA-398).
Costs of enrollment (board, room, and tuition): $14,200.

1995   Nichols racquetball team wins men's intercollegiate national championship, Nichols women finish 3rd.

CHAPTER 8

∽

At the End of the Twentieth Century

As this historical review nears the year 2000, a careful summation of the Nichols experience is important. Throughout its existence, Nichols has been a very special and unique school existing in its general form for nearly 200 years. Its course requires a careful reassessment. This effort to summarize 65 years of a remarkable College's existence relies on two different although complementary approaches.

The first is a thoughtful, although brief, review of the College's story taken from an accounting of its progress, achievements and growth over the school's existence between 1931 and 1996. This is relatively basic relying on facts in hand. In contrast, the second approach involves a more in-depth analysis based on less well-defined, more intrinsic and longer-standing features. The result of these approaches – one emphasizing change, the other continuity – taken together, leads to a better understanding of the history of the College on Dudley Hill at the end of the 20th century.

Some aspects of the College's history as noted here are relatively straightforward with changes clearly evident. For instance, for its first 65 years Nichols College was led by four administrations. One lasted 35 years (the presidency of James L. Conrad). Another was in place for 18 years under Dr. Lowell C. Smith, while two (the administrations of Dr. Gordon B. Cross and Dr. Darcy C. Coyle) extended for seven and five years, respectively. The first began in 1931 with a plan for a two-year or junior college program in business administration and executive training for men at a college in a rural area with a commitment to provide intercollegiate athletic competition and extensive recreational opportunities.

Located on the former campus of Nichols Academy, in 1958 Nichols Junior College of Business Administration and Executive Training, became a four-year college of business administration. In 1971, the previously all-male college became coeducational. The College granted the degree of Bachelor of Business Administration (BBA) until 1971, when it awarded the Bachelor of Science in

225

Business Administration degree (BSBA), the Bachelor of Science in Public Administration degree (BSPA), and the Bachelor of Arts degree (BA). Three years later, Nichols was granted permission by the state to award the Master of Business Administration degree (MBA). Those leading the College then termed it a school of administration.

Change also is easily observed in the evolution of the College's curriculum. Beginning with a required set of courses, the curriculum became more flexible and soon provided courses and options leading to a program much different from what had existed in 1931. This change was promoted by an active student body supported by a period of extensive transformation in higher education throughout the 1970s. After offering the degree of Associate of Business Administration as a two-year college, Nichols was the first junior college in Massachusetts granted the opportunity to become a four-year college.

As this was occurring, the campus created by Amasa Nichols and Hezekiah Conant was being redesigned and expanded by President Conrad. The President's office in 1955 moved to Conrad Hall on the "upper campus" from Budleigh Hall on the "lower campus." The athletic facilities were moved from the west side of Center Road and from the former Conant barn to the east side of Dudley Hill to a new field house surrounded by extensive athletic fields and complete outdoor athletic facilities. Many of the older campus buildings were replaced providing essentially modern residential opportunities. This included the construction of new dining facilities all contributing to an entirely new vista for those who graduated after 1960. These were new and logically necessary for further development.

As Nichols evolved over time, the experiences and contributions of the Junior College and the four-year College were significant and path-breaking. The original announcement of the College's beginning in 1931 correctly presented Nichols Junior College of Business Administration and Executive Training as the first eastern junior college exclusively for men. It also was the first junior college in the East to offer a full program of business administration courses and the first to do so as a residential college with a rural campus and full recreational and athletic facilities.[1] Nichols Junior College also was the only two-year college offering a fully transferable program in business administration. After extensive efforts, the school received approval from Massachusetts to grant the state's first Associate of Business Administration degree (ABA) in 1938.

Nearly twenty years later, a formal review of the young college's accomplishments was completed by a Nichols Junior College Trustee Committee led by members with national reputations in higher education. This was done to support the efforts of Nichols to become a four-year college. This committee found that Nichols Junior College was the first college of its classification to require courses in psychology, obtain degree granting privileges, create and develop an operational plan for an advisory council, support a full program of extra-curricular activities and athletics, and offer a Quartermaster Corps Training program. The Junior College also was seen offering new courses in ethics, news analysis, production, and forestry and conservation as well as a full program of business administration.[2] Introduced in 1954, its conservation and forestry program was the first to combine two specialized programs – conservation and forestry courses with business administration courses.

Nichols also was the first institution in the United States to offer its students the opportunity to enlist in the Enlisted Reserve Corps of the U.S. Army for course credit with training on campus. Nichols then became the first junior college in Massachusetts to receive the authority to become a four-year college and to grant the degree of Bachelor of Business Administration (BBA). Interestingly, its new curriculum in 1959 introduced a requirement of two summers of work experience and a thesis for graduation. These were major innovations and the first for this type of institution.

Although the business curriculum was modified with the development of Nichols College in the 1970s, several important innovations were introduced during the next decade. The first was the Institute for American Values (now the Robert C. Fischer Policy and Cultural Institute) intended to focus on student cultural development. This was followed by a personal computer plan (PC Plan) for students intended to familiarize and introduce the student to computer technology and its new culture. Both were on the cutting edge of curriculum and program development.

The nature of athletic competition changed as well for the Dudley college. After competing against a number of college and university freshmen and junior varsity teams in the early years, Nichols, as a four-year college after 1958, began to compete with other four-year colleges as a member of the National Association of Intercollegiate Athletics (NAIA) and the National Collegiate Athletic Association (NCAA), small college division. However, with the development of the NCAA's Division III in 1973, Nichols teams were able to identify and compete with similar small colleges. In 1978, women's teams were added to a significant list of Nichols College teams.

And, as the curriculum was expanding in the 1970s, the College began to develop an evening program. This was new. Its enrollment, including both MBA and evening undergraduate students, became significant and constant. Some off-campus classroom centers were established in Worcester and other central Massachusetts communities. This was all managed by an experienced faculty that was nearly 100 percent tenured by 1996.

In the early days, Nichols alumni provided minor support at best. However, by the late 1980s this group emerged as a major force supporting growth. This was an important development. One of the most critical advancements over the College's past 25 years has occurred due to the increasing contribution of Nichols alumni members as a group and as individuals. Led by Kenneth J. Thompson '39, the Nichols alumni backed the first Nichols Homecoming weekend in 1946, supported the organization of the College's Athletic Hall of Fame, and became involved in other early fund raising opportunities. Several extensive fund raising drives then evolved to help redesign and renew the campus and construct new buildings. Many alumni also became active members of the Nichols Board of Trustees. From this early group, Gerald Fels '66, John and Stephen Davis of the classes of '72 and '80, Robert Kuppenheimer '69, and David Lombard '65 are among those who were both leading individual contributors and campaign organizers.

Nichols College clearly demonstrated significant changes that suggest the leadership role played by the institution as a small college. At the same time, however, the school also experienced the dominating presence of three increasingly persistent, long-existing, and less obvious although powerful forces – location, size, and nature. Altogether they create a very substantial and remarkable institution established at a place, with a purpose, and a "new" plan.

Continuity exists as a significant factor in the history of Nichols. The present College is located on the site of the former Nichols Academy. A number of Academy or pre-college buildings still play an active role in the daily life of the present college. Roger Conant Hall on the upper campus was constructed in 1885 on what was the site of the first Nichols Academy building erected by Amasa Nichols in 1815. It remains on a hilly campus of approximately 200 acres of fields and woodlands in still rural Dudley. In its entirety, this campus is an admixture of older (Academy) buildings and many new college structures reflecting an attractive blending of old and new architecture.

Nichols Academy in the 1880s was composed of three buildings constructed by Hezekiah Conant near the site of Amasa Nichols' original academy building. This was rural New England. These buildings now make up part of the College's upper campus and contribute to an awareness of its 19th century heritage. And, with the construction of a new student center in 2012, the College remains solidly established at the location originally selected in 1815 by Amasa Nichols for his school. In fact, the location of this new student center is on Center Road across from the house where, between 1812 and 1815, Amasa Nichols is said to have created his plans for what became Nichols Academy.[3]

Certainly the specifics of location – on Dudley Hill in rural, south central Massachusetts – are important in the institution's history; they contribute to a statement of continuity. This gives a greater meaning to the place. But, for many, this relationship is as much a matter of heart as it is geography. Such is the way of the small college in America. In 1950, a column in the *Nichols*

Alumnus carried this story about comments made by a Nichols Junior College alumnus at a New York alumni dinner.

> 'I want to say something gang' he said. He went on to say about how after his first year on the Hill he was anxious, as we've all been, to get the hell out and go home. After the summer was over, he drove back to school and about the time he approached the Country Club [golf course] and started up the Hill he got a funny feeling like being home again after being away for a long time. They say that a lot of men gathered there that night agreed with him, some verbally, some with a simple nod of the head.[4]

Aside from its location, another consistent and dominating feature of the College's past has been its size. It is a small, private and independent school. Nichols has been this way since 1819 when it began a brief relationship with New England Universalists. Smallness at Nichols primarily begins with its beginnings as a tiny academy. In later centuries, a series of Nichols College presidents – Cross, Coyle, and Smith – agreed that the Nichols day undergraduate student enrollment should be 1,000. This figure eventually was achieved in 2007, but only after the College became coeducational. Colleges and universities with 800 to 1,500 day students traditionally are labeled as "small."[5] Some educators, however, have now decided that it is necessary to consider 2,500 students as a new goal for a small college enrollment.[6]

Small colleges in rural New England can make specific and vital contributions; the experience of Nichols testifies to this point. To do so they must promote successful internal community building and vigorously develop extracurricular activities including student campus organizations. Events that bring the student body together must be organized and utilized. Then too, the small institution generally seems to easily adjust to certain changes. For instance, this applies to the appearance of larger numbers of women on campus and the presence of diverse groups of students. And smaller institutions generally are better able to focus on the quality of individual attention available to the student. Some educators note the presence of the small college's "value-added" feature. Then too, its graduates generally display a stronger and longer commitment to their institutions than usually is found with graduates of larger schools.

At the same time, the small college obviously cannot do everything that larger institutions might accomplish. This, too, is a feature of size. For instance, athletic associations and conferences are best determined by institutional sizes. And those who work at small institutions will be required to do more and varied tasks and serve on additional committees. The same may be required of students at the small college.

All evidence suggests that the College has kept its commitment to maintain a substantial athletic program for all its students. The investigation and report of the Blue Ribbon Committee on Nichols Athletics in 1988 support the College's continued obligation to make a formal athletic program available for its students. While competitors have changed, the approach of the College to its formal athletic program has not.

One area of long-lasting concern for the small private institution such as Nichols has been the impact of governmental activities – national, state, and local – on private schools beginning with 1827. At that point, the Commonwealth of Massachusetts, by requiring Massachusetts communities to create public secondary schools, condemned the Dudley Hill academy – a private, secondary school – to its eventual closing. This occurred in 1909 and provided the opportunity for a new school – Nichols Junior College – to be established. Much later, in 1957, when the Commonwealth finally created community colleges, the future of private two-year colleges, such as Nichols Junior College, became uncertain. This, in turn, gave further support to the Nichols effort to secure a place as a four-year college. It also is necessary to note that Presidents Coyle and Smith all complained about seemingly endless government reports and oversight. Clearly the small, private college has been vulnerable to decisions by governmental bodies at all levels. This will not change.

Perhaps the best way to see the importance of the small college is through the eyes of a student. A member of the Class of 1956 once asked: "How was it possible that this small college [Nichols] could have such a large impact on our lives?" His answer:

> It's a question I have occasionally thought about and I think it was due in part to Nichols being a close community of friendships, with classes taught in small groups, good instructor/student relationships, sports, school activities, winter carnivals, and just a group of fun-loving guys (lots of laughs). Nichols was home but we also enjoyed our time away from the Hill by getting our burger fix at Bazzies, a beer at Snug Harbor, trips to the lake and weekend journeys to Worcester and Boston.[7]

While small colleges seem quite similar, this is not the case. Certainly Nichols has been unique. This is its nature; it is one of the College's founding and formative features. Although the institution's size, appearance and location make it easy to confuse with the small liberal arts college, accepted definitions of the liberal arts colleges say this is not possible. One set of standards for liberal arts college comes from David M. Breneman in his *Liberal Arts Colleges: Thriving, Surviving or Endangered.* According to Breneman, small liberal arts colleges typically enroll 800 to 1,800 students and award the bachelor of arts degree to full-time students between 18 and 24 years old who have a choice of 20 to 24 majors in the arts, humanities, languages, social sciences, and physical sciences. They are residential.[8] These liberal arts colleges as defined by Breneman offer "virtually no undergraduate professional education." He determined some institutions could be seen as having a liberal arts core curriculum and related traditions, but they could not be considered liberal arts colleges if they awarded more than 60 percent of their undergraduate degrees in professional fields.[9] While some disagree with certain aspects of Breneman's description, most accept his general assessment.

Perhaps the closest acceptable classification for Nichols now is that of a comprehensive college. This term, first introduced in 1972 by the Carnegie Foundation for Advancement of Teaching, was intended to identify and emphasize the importance of diversity in U.S. higher education. To help determine the differences between an increasing number of dissimilar colleges and universities, it sought to include the largest possible number of institutions. According to one source, institutions classified as comprehensive colleges are best identified by what they are "not." Specifically, they "are not research institutions, not liberal arts colleges, not community colleges."[10]

Within the Carnegie classification, Nichols seems closest to fitting into a category labeled "Prof-F/HGC: Professions focus, high graduate coexistence." More precisely, this category applies to institutions where "at least 80 percent of bachelor degree majors are in professional fields, and graduate degrees are observed in at least half of the fields corresponding to undergraduate majors."[11] However, those who rely on these categories must be alert to the shifting and sometimes confusing identifying features and defining characteristics. In situations where institutional classifications are vague and subject to change, the institution's "clarity of purpose" and full development of its mission are crucial for recognizing institutional goals and functions.[12]

Nichols remained small and unique. Over this period, an important factor in the nature of the College has been the relationship or balance in its curriculum between liberal arts courses and professional courses. This contributes both to its uniqueness and to a long-standing dilemma. At all times – through Academy years as a "fitting" school (as in fitting for college) to its college days – the institution evidenced a great respect for the liberal arts. The charter of Nichols Academy written in 1819 made direct mention to its liberal arts requirements. This is important to note. Although the focus of Nichols Junior College after 1931 was on business administration, the College's concern for liberal arts courses and liberal learning – ethics and culture – did exist.

When the Nichols Junior College became the first specialized junior college in Massachusetts and New England in 1931, its emphasis on professional courses had a generally negative impact on its early acceptance. Liberal arts programs were preferred by most. When Nichols became a four-year college in 1958, the nature of its curriculum was carefully examined and approved by the Board of Higher Education of the Commonwealth of Massachusetts and by the then New England Association of Colleges and Secondary Schools. When it entered the 1960s, the new college's curriculum included an equal number of liberal arts courses and professional courses. In 1971, and the widening of the College's curriculum, the ability to award the bachelor of arts degree offered an even broader intellectual path for Nichols students.

The debate in business education in the 1950s and beyond focused on achieving the proper balance between liberal arts courses and professional courses and determining which ones should be offered in an institution's first two years. This debate continued. Since the 1980s, the Institute for American Values (now the Robert C. Fischer Policy and Cultural Institute) has provided an additional opportunity for liberal learning at Nichols unavailable in the early days of the College. By 1996, the College mission statement included the comment that the Nichols curriculum was "rooted in the liberal arts." Perhaps, although this has to be further explained.[13] Nonetheless, this general issue continues to exist as colleges emphasizing professional education decide how to best design liberal learning programs as they seek to develop more effective courses.[14]

Over the past sixty-five years, the Nichols mission has evolved from a broad emphasis on business education and the role of the professional business man to a more specific task of providing students with the ability and skill to secure a job and build their lives as professionals. In the 1930s and 1940s, many Nichols students came from families with businesses. Since 1980, graduates of business programs in the United States outnumber graduates in any other field. Nonetheless, business education has been the strength of Nichols since 1931.

Nichols also has sought to remain a residential college throughout the years. Its rural location so foreign to early business colleges has not changed. Residence halls, substantially upgraded in the past twenty years, still support 80 percent of the student body. However, campus residency no longer is required of Nichols students. Many more students work on and off campus than in the past as they try to meet the rising costs of a college education.

Somewhat surprisingly, however, much of the 1931 "plan" for a Nichols College education remains in place in 1996. This is true of its broadened, but still-existing commitment to business education. It also is true of the College's long-existing and full support for its athletic program and its participants.[15] The Nichols Junior College catalog in 1934 referred to competitive sports as part of the College's educational scheme.[16] This thinking had its origins in 1931; it did not change.

Noticeable, too, is the fact there has been surprisingly little change in the recent geographical distribution of the Nichols student body. In 1974, a 650-member student body saw its largest state representations coming from Massachusetts (57%), followed by Connecticut (20%), New Jersey (8%), New

York (8%), and Pennsylvania (2%). Thirty-five years later, in 2009, the top states representing 309 incoming students again were Massachusetts (54%) and Connecticut (19%), followed by Rhode Island (6%), New York (5%), and New Hampshire (5%). Three of the five states – Massachusetts, Connecticut, and New York – represented at Nichols remained in the "top five" category. "Other" states represented in 1974 numbered 12; in 2009, 17 "other" states could be counted. Six foreign countries were represented in 1974; two were present in 2009.[17] (For further comparisons over time, see Chart 4.1.)

As for the nature of the student population itself, there have been some changes. For instance, recent political positions held by Nichols students are not the same as they were in earlier days. They no longer support Republican candidates as they did Herbert Hoover, Alf Landon, Richard Nixon and Gerald Ford. In 2004, as their backgrounds changed, and more like college students elsewhere, Nichols students believed that John Kerry would easily best eventual winner Republican George Bush. They all were wrong. Four years later they supported Barack Obama in his victory over Republican John McCain.[18]

But other factors have remained constant and important. In 1965, when the College community gathered at an academic convocation to celebrate the institution's 150th anniversary, President Conrad said that "we have a deep obligation to many unknown and unheralded men and women who have been loyal, contributive and dedicated to Nichols."[19] This comment is even more appropriate at this point than it was in 1965. Seven generations, mostly from the Dudley area or the College community, have made Nichols what it is today. The school, now nearing 200 years, is as much a product of their on-going combined efforts as it is the result of planning by a number of Nichols administrations. Their collective contributions provided the substance for an institution much in need of their assistance. Because of them, and those who worked with them, and before them, College administrations have been able to bring Nichols to the beginning of its third century.

It is probable that the roles of Nichols students have slowly evolved, especially if we accept new thinking about this generation. However, a thorough historical analysis of the coming generation, now being referred to as the Millennials (those born between 1982 and 2002), is not yet possible. Nonetheless, one important mid-stream assessment of this present generation's potential is made by Neil Howe and William Strauss in *Millennials Rising: The Next Great Generation*. They suggest that the present young generation gives evidence of being "upbeat and engaged . . . on track to become a powerhouse generation full of technology planners, community shapers, institution builders and world leaders. . . ."[20] It also is seen as a generation that will feature trust, team work, duties before rights, honor over feelings, and action over words.[21] Not surprisingly, everyone does not completely agree with Howe and Strauss. Others see the forthcoming changes as probable, but believe there could be major conflict as in the past.[22]

But much on the Nichols campus at this point suggests that the generational theory of Howe and Strauss will be right. One *Nichols Bison* article in 2004 focused on developing a better environment at Nichols by condemning rowdy and destructive guests and called for fellow students to work together to create a better school.[23] Another expressed concern about a lack of diversity on the campus.[24] In yet another article, a *Bison* editor noted that he had seen three Nichols presidents, six deans and the confusion surrounding these changes. Nonetheless, he concluded: "I can see how great this place really is. Nichols has done nothing but get better and better. . . ." As he saw it in 1998, fellow students, administrators, and faculty had become "my family." His conclusion: "Nichols is the greatest college on the face of the earth because it is my college. . . . The grass is the greenest [here]."[25] This had been a sentiment expressed earlier in the existence of Nichols Junior College.

Nichols, at the end of the twentieth century, remains a product of its past. This is a past that includes both impressive innovations and enduring features. It now sits firmly at peace with its location, size and unique nature. That these features still exist after nearly 200 years gives the institution an important strength for the future. However, where uniqueness exists, it is necessary that the institution always present a clearly identifiable path and purpose – and a plan for the future.[26] This is as much the case with the Nichols College of today as it was for the Universalist Academy in 1819.

Endnotes

Preface

1. James L. Conrad Jr., *Nichols Academy: The Spring on the Hill, 1815–1931* (Dudley, Mass.: Nichols College, 2008).
2. Clark Kerr, *The Great Transformation in Higher Education, 1960–1980* (Albany, N.Y.: State University of New York Press, 1991), xiii.
3. Arthur M. Schlesinger (Arthur Meier), *A Life in the Twentieth Century: Innocent Beginning, 1917–1950* (Boston: Houghton Mifflin Company, 2000), xiv.

Introduction

1. Refer to Ferenc M. Szasz, *The Many Meanings of History*, Parts I-IV, 205.
2. Darcy C. Coyle, D.B.A., *Nichols College; A Brief History* (New York: Newcomen Society in North America, 1975); Elizabeth S. Kelly, *Nichols College: The First 175 Years* (Dudley, Mass.: Nichols College, 1990).
3. Conrad, *Nichols Academy.*
4. *Webster Evening Times*, April 1, 1931.
5. Nichols Junior College, "Announcement," circa May 1931, Folder 513, Nichols College Archives (hereafter cited NCA).
6. Lease Agreement, Trustees of Nichols Academy to Frederick Smith & James L. Conrad, August 20, 1931, Folder 20, NCA.
7. Catalog, *Nichols Junior College, 1931–32*, 7, 14, NCA.
8. Ibid.
9. Ibid.
10. Bertram H. Holland, "A History of the New England Association of Schools and Colleges from 1885–1985," in Robert J. Bradley et al. *The First Hundred Years 1885–1995; New England Association of Schools and Colleges* (Winchester, MA: New England Association of Schools & Colleges, Inc., 1998), 43; Cortright, "Junior Colleges Gain Sway," *New York Times*, May 7, 1933, 8E.
11. Walter E. Eells, *The Junior College* (Boston: Houghton Mifflin Co., 1931), 5, 17.
12. E. Everett Cortright, "Junior College Development in New England," *School and Society* 36 (September 10, 1932), 325–327.
13. Christopher Jencks & David Riesman, *The Academic Revolution* (Garden City, New York: Doubleday & Company, Inc., 1969), 132, 175, 423.
14. Leland P. Medsker, *The Junior College: Progress and Prospect* (New York: McGraw-Hill Book Co.), 234–236.
15. George Hebert Palmer, "The Junior College: An Indictment," *Atlantic Monthly*, April, 1927, 139.

16. Holland, "History of the New England Association of Schools and Colleges from 1885–1985," 33.
17. Cortright, "Junior College Development in New England," 327.
18. Abraham Flexner, *Universities: American, English, German* (New York: Oxford University Press, 1930), 69.
19. Stanley F. Salwak, "Some Factors Significant in the Establishment of Public Junior Colleges in the United States (1940–1951): with special reference to Massachusetts," Diss. for Doctor of Education, August 1953, Pennsylvania State College, 404, 446.
20. Coyle, *Nichols College: A Brief History.*
21. Kelly, *Nichols College: The First 175 Years.*

CHAPTER 1 ~ ROOTS FOR THE BEGINNING

1. "Announcement – A New Educational Plan," 1931, NCA.
2. *Catalog, Nichols Junior College of Business Administration and Executive Training, 1931–1932,* 14.
3. Daniel O. Levine, *The American College and the Culture of Aspiration* (Ithaca and London: Cornell University Press, 1986), 57.
4. "Announcement – A New Educational Plan," 1931, NCA.
5. For a history of Nichols Academy, see Conrad, *Nichols Academy: The Spring on the Hill.*
6. D. Hamilton Hurd, *History of Worcester County, Massachusetts,* (Philadelphia: J.W. Lewis & Co., 1889) II: 1364, 1365.
7. Conrad, *Nichols Academy,* 25–28.
8. See Nichols Academy, *Constitution, Dudley,* 1819, Article 7, NCA.
9. Catalogue . . . *Nichols Academy* . . . 1834, 11, American Antiquarian Society, Worcester, Mass., NCA. See also Conrad, *Nichols Academy,* 66–70.
10. Conrad, *Nichols Academy,* 80–82.
11. A Massachusetts law in 1827 required that communities with more than 500 families provide secondary school education at taxpayer expense. Refer to Conrad, *Nichols Academy,* 35.
12. Ibid., 90–92.
13. Wilcox was a well-known Providence, Rhode Island, architect who designed several Providence area churches.
14. Worcester County Registry of Deeds, September 27, 1888, 1293: 42–44.
15. *Southbridge Journal,* December 26, 1888.
16. "The Summer Residence of Hezekiah Conant, Esq." *Webster Times,* December 25, 1889.
17. Catalog, *Nichols Junior College,* 1931–32.
18. *Webster Times,* June 7, 1889.
19. *Nichols College Bulletin, Alumni Issue,* September, 1966, 4.
20. "Summer Residence," *Webster Times,* December 25, 1889.
21. Catalog, *Nichols Junior College,* 1931–1932, 10.
22. *Catalogue . . . Nichols Academy . . .* 1845, NCA; Ibid, 1846.
23. Conrad, *Nichols Academy,* 123.

ENDNOTES CHAPTER 1

24. The Dudley Bible Institute eventually became Providence-Barrington Bible College in Rhode Island which later merged with Gordon College, Wenham, Massachusetts.
25. *Worcester Gazette*, April 1, 1931; *Webster Times*, April 1, 1931. Leslie R. Bragg, M.D., *The Doctors of Dudley and Webster* (n.p.; n.d.), 155.
26. Worcester County (Mass.) Registry of Deeds, Bethel Bible Institute to Trs. of Nichols Academy, July 28, 1931, 2547: 221–222. See also Academy Trs. to Smith et al, August 20, 1931, 2552: 162–164.
27. Indenture, Trustees of Nichols Academy to Frederick Smith and James L. Conrad, August 20, 1931, Folder 20, NCA; also see Unsigned Agreement Between [Academy] Trustees and Conrad, circa 1936, 2.
28. *Boston Transcript*, April 8, 1931.
29. Announcement, "A New Educational Plan," Nichols Junior College, Folder 513, NCA.
30. R. Freemen Butts and Lawrence A. Cremin, *A History of Education in American Culture* (New York: Henry Holt and Company, 1953), 434–435.
31. Carter. V. Good, ed., *Dictionary of Education* (New York: McGraw-Hill, 1945) 54; Dorothy E. Lee, "Changing Objectives in Business Education on the Collegiate Level in the United States from 1899 to 1954," (Ph.D. diss., New York University, 1957), 9.
32. Good, *Dictionary of Education*, 448; Lee, "Changing Objectives. . . .", 9.
33. Paul A. Moreland, *A History of Business Education* (Toronto: Pitman Publishing, 1977), 44–45.
34. P. George Benson, "The Evolution of Business Education in the U.S.," *Decision Line* (January 2004), 17–20.
35. Benjamin R. Haynes and Harry P. Jackson, *A History of Business Education in the United States*, (Cincinnati: Southwestern Pub. Co., 1936), 25.
36. Benson, "The Evolution of Business Education in the United States," 17–20; Moreland, *History of Business Education*, 47–48.
37. Ibid., 25; Benson, *Evolution of Business History*, 26, 29.
38. Allan Nevins, *Study in Power: John D. Rockefeller; Industrialist and Philanthropist* (New York: Charles Scribner's Sons, 1953), 10; Steven Watts, *The People's Tycoon: Henry Ford and the American Century* (New York: Random House, Inc., 2006) 28.
39. Moreland, *History of Business Education*, 65.
40. Lee, "Changing Objectives," 191.
41. John R. Thelin, *A History of American Higher Education* (Baltimore and London: The Johns Hopkins University Press, 2004), 86.
42. Haynes and Jackson, *History of Business Education*, 85.
43. Edmund J. James, quoted in Moreland, *History of Business Education*, 48.
44. Lee, "Changing Objectives," 3, 190, 192.
45. Ibid.
46. Haynes and Jackson, *History of Business Education*, 93.
47. Benson, "Evolution of Business Education," 18.
48. Eells, *The Junior College*, 44. Eells also mentions "college decapitation" (eliminating a college's third and fourth years leaving the first two years) as another potential contributor to the development of the junior college movement.

49. *Sixty-Third General Catalogue of the Officers and Students of New Hampton Literary and Biblical Institution, 1885–1886* (Laconia, N.H.: Lewis Vaughan & Co., 1886), 22–23, New Hampton School Archives (hereafter cited as NHSA).
50. *Catalogue . . . New Hampton Literary and Biblical Institution, 1868–69* (Concord, N.H.: A.G. Jones, Printer, 1869), 26, NHSA.
51. Ibid.
52. *Catalogue of the New Hampton Literary Institution and Commercial College 1881* (Bristol, N.H.: R.W. Musgrove, 1881), 22–28, NHSA.
53. *Sixty-Third Annual Catalogue . . . New Hampton Literary and Biblical Institution, 1885–1886* (Laconia, N.H.: Lewis, Vaughan & Co., 1886), 22–23, NHSA.
54. *Circular, New Hampton Literary Institute and Commercial College*, New Hampton, 1922, NHSA.
55. Pauline Swain Merrill and John C. Gowan, *A Small Gore of Land: A History of New Hampton, New Hampshire founded in 1777* (prepared under the auspices of the New Hampton Bicentennial Committee, 1976–1977), 170. Also see Norma Jean Moore, "An Academy at New Hampton," *The Hamptonia* 112 (Fall 1996): 14.
56. *Catalog, New Hampton; A New Hampshire School for Boys, 1926–27*, 27, NHSA.
57. Davis Tyack & Elisabeth Hanot, *Learning Together: A History of Coeducation in American Schools* (New Haven and London: Yale University Press, 1990), 146–164.
58. Ibid.
59. Moore, "An Academy at New Hampton," 15.
60. Porter Sargent, *A Handbook of Private Schools for American Boys and Girls* (Boston: Porter Sargent, 1927), 749.
61. *Fitchburg Daily Sentinel*, October 19, 1916.
62. Ibid., June 21, 1918.
63. "Fitchburg Normal Eleven Is Too Fast For The Average Prep School," Ibid., November 6, 1919.
64. "Normal School News," Ibid., November 6, 1919, 2.
65. Villanova College, *Belle Air* 1924 (Villanova College: 1924), 86.
66. www.villanova.edu/business/about/history.htm[1/2/2007].
67. *The Boston University SYLLABUS* (Boston: Boston University College of Business Administration, 1925), 65.
68. *Fitchburg* (Mass.) *Sentinel*, December 6, 1924.
69. "Seniors under Supervised Study," *Boston University SYLLABUS*, 39–44.
70. Catalog, *Nichols Junior College . . . 1931–1932*, 3, NCA; "Col. Wm. Conrad, Formerly Here, Dies in Capital," *Fitchburg Sentinel*, November 29, 1939, 1.
71. *Fitchburg* (Mass.) *Sentinel*, September 9, 1926.
72. *The Belfry* (New Hampton Yearbook), 1927.
73. Ibid., 1929.
74. Ibid., 1930.
75. *Catalog, New Hampton School, 1930–1931*, 31, NHSA.
76. Ibid.
77. Ibid.
78. Ibid.

79. Butts and Cremin, *A History of Education in American Culture*, 404, 424, 586–587; Eells, *The Junior College*, x. For a further discussion of the origins of the junior college in Massachusetts, see Stanley F. Salwak, "Some Factors Significant in the Establishment of Public Junior Colleges in the United States (1940–1951): with special reference to Massachusetts," 59-132.
80. Eells, *The Junior College*, 3.
81. Haynes and Jackson, *History of Business Education*, 116.
82. Ibid., 122.
83. Map 1, "First Map of Nichols Junior College Campus, 1931," Catalog, *Nichols Junior College, 1931–1932*, 12–13, NCA.
84. "New Hampton Junior College of Business Administration" in *Catalog of Officers and Students of New Hampton School, New Hampton School for Boys*, 1930–1931, 33, NHSA.
85. For more on Boyden, see John McPhee, *The Headmaster: Frank L. Boyden of Deerfield* (New York: Farrar, Straus and Giroux, 1966). Frank L. Boyden later became a trustee of Nichols Junior College in the 1950s.

CHAPTER 2 ~ BUILDING THE COLLEGE, 1931~1943

1. Hal Chalmers, quoted in the *Worcester Telegram*, April 20, 1974.
2. Samuel Schuman, *Old Main; Twenty-First Century America* (Baltimore: Johns Hopkins University Press, 2005), 1.
3. Levine, *The American College and the Culture of Aspiration*, 45–48.
4. Bossard and Dewhurst, *University Education for Business: A Study of Existing Needs and Practices* (Philadelphia: University of Pennsylvania Press, 1931), 363.
5. Federal Writers Project of the Works Progress Administration, *Massachusetts*, (Boston: Houghton Mifflin Company, 1937), 544, 475.
6. Nichols Academy Board of Trustees Meeting Minutes, Form of Votes for Record of Meeting, Trustees of Nichols Academy held April 21, 1931, NCA.
7. Nichols Academy Board of Trustees Meeting Minutes, March 24, 1931, NCA.
8. Ibid., September 15, 1931; also see Worcester County Registry of Deeds, Bethel Bible Institute to Trs. of Nichols Academy, July 28, 1931, 2547: 221–222. See also Academy Trs. To Smith et al, August 20, 1931, 2552: 162–164.
9. Ibid.
10. Ibid. The Dudley Bible Institute (formerly Bethel Bible Institute), previous owner of the former Conant estate, closed its summer school, including Budleigh Hall, the second week of August, 1931, and completed its move to Providence, Rhode Island. See *Webster Evening Times* August 13, 1931.
11. Ibid., June 26, 1931; July 7, 1931. Also see Nichols Academy Board of Trustees Meeting Minutes, June 23, 1931, NCA; Worcester County Registry of Deeds, Town of Dudley to Trs. of Nichols Academy, July 22, 1931, 02547: 26–27.
12. "New Hampton Junior College of Business Administration program," in *Catalogue of Officers and Students of New Hampton School, New Hampton School for Boys, 1930–1931*, 33, NHSA.
13. "Announcing – A New Educational Plan" (n.p., n.d.), Folder 513, NCA; Catalog, *Nichols Junior College of Business Administration and Executive Training, Dudley Massachusetts* (1931–1932); *Webster Evening Times*, May 26, 1931.

14. The primary builder for the remodeling was F.X. Laliberte and Son, of Southbridge, Massachusetts. See *Southbridge News*, August 18, 1931; *Boston Transcript*, September 21, 1931.
15. *Webster Evening Times*, April 3, 1931.
16. Nichols Academy Trustees Meeting Minutes, June 23, 1931, NCA.
17. *Webster Evening Times*, April 1, 1931; Ibid., July 30, 1931.
18. Ibid., September 5, 1931.
19. Catalog, *Nichols Junior College, 1931–1932*, 11.
20. "J. L. Conrad, Head of Junior College is Rotary Speaker," *Webster Evening Times*, August 3, 1931.
21. Ibid.
22. Ibid.
23. Ibid.
24. *Webster Evening Times*, September 19, 1931.
25. Ibid., June 4, 1931.
26. Ibid., August 24, 1931.
27. "Scholarship at Nichols Junior College Sponsored by Webster Rotary Club," *Webster Evening Times*, August 24, 1931, 1; *Webster Evening Times*, September 17, 1931, 1.
28. Ibid., August 19, 1931.
29. *Webster Evening Times*, May 23, 1931.
30. Minutes of Incorporators, Nichols, Inc., April 19, 1933. Nichols College, President's Office, NCA.
31. Leslie R. Bragg, M.D., *The Doctors of Dudley and Webster, Massachusetts* (n.p.; circa 1950), 155.
32. *1937 Ledger*, 6.
33. Ibid., 22; *Nichols Budget*, September 21, 1936.
34. Memorial Plaque, "The Merrill Health Center Dedication to Dr. Quincy H. Merrill," mounted on Alumni Hall, Nichols College, Dudley, Mass., circa 1969.
35. *Southbridge News*, September 21, 1931.
36. *Webster Times*, September 19, 1931.
37. *Boston Transcript*, September 21, 1931.
38. Ibid.
39. *Nichols Budget*, November 25, 1931.
40. Catalog, *Nichols Junior College of Business Administration and Executive Training, 1931–1932*, 8.
41. *The Tower*, 1932, published by the Staff of the *Nichols Budget*, 1932.
42. The first published text of the Nichols Alma Mater can be found in the *1942 Ledger*, 1.
43. *Nichols Budget*, June 17, 1939.
44. Ibid.
45. James L. Conrad, to Board of Trustees, Nichols College Board of Trustees, May 12, 1960, filed with Minutes, May 1960, President's Office, Nichols College, Dudley, Mass.

ENDNOTES ~ CHAPTER 2

46. States and foreign countries represented by students at Nichols in 1939 (with numbers in parentheses): Massachusetts (48), New York (25), Connecticut (23), New Jersey (17), Rhode Island (8), Pennsylvania (5), Ohio (4), Maine (1), Vermont (1), Florida (1), Wisconsin (1), Georgia (1), Minnesota (1), Missouri (1), Cuba (4), South America (1), Canada (1). Refer to Nichols *Budget*, October 6, 1939.
47. Nichols *Budget*, October 19, 1936.
48. Catalog, *Nichols Junior College*, 1942–1943, 16.
49. Conrad, *Nichols Academy*, 120–125.
50. Articles of Organization, April 19, 1933, Corporation and Trustee Records, 1933–1942, Administrative Records, Nichols College, President's Office, Conrad Hall, Center Road, Dudley, Mass. Catalog, *Nichols Junior College, 1942–1943*, 2.
51. The large number of specialty programs in the business administration field required that programs be carefully titled. Therefore the need to designate the Nichols program as "Executive Training" was necessary. Another example of the need for proper titles is offered by the case of "Becker Junior College of Business Administration and Secretarial Science." Becker, in Worcester, received the authority to award the degree of Associate in Science from the Commonwealth in 1943. See *Acts and Resolves passed by the General Court 1943* (Boston: Secretary of the Commonwealth, n.d.), Chapter 555, 756.
52. *Nichols Budget*, March 10, 1933, 1, 4.
53. Refer to Catalog, *Nichols Junior College of Business Administration and Executive Training*, Dudley, Massachusetts, for 1931–1932, n.p.
54. Ibid, 1932–1933, 8.
55. Catalog, *Nichols Junior College*, 1933–1934, 8. The General Court of Massachusetts approved the corporate name change from Nichols, Inc., to "Nichols Junior College, Inc.," on March 7, 1933, thus allowing the use of the designation of "college." See *Acts and Resolves passed by the General Court of Massachusetts 1933* (Boston: Secretary of the Commonwealth, n.d.), Chapter 62, 69.
56. *Nichols Budget*, April 26, 1938. See *Acts and Resolves passed by the General Court of Massachusetts 1938* Boston: Secretary of the Commonwealth, n.d.), Chapter 223, 179 (approved April 14, 1938). "New Law Gives Nichols Seniors A.B.A. degree on Graduation," Nichols Newsclip, April 18, 1938, NCA. Students who graduated prior to 1938 were not to receive this degree retroactively. In 1947, however, the Nichols administration awarded members of these earlier classes an A.B.A. degree if they had received an average grade of "C" and completed two years of accounting. Refer to *Nichols Alumnus I*, October 1947, 8.
57. Catalog, *Nichols Junior College*, 1931–1932, 14.
58. *Nichols Budget*, December 2, 1938.
59. Catalog, *Nichols Junior College of Business Administration and Executive Training*, 1932–1933, 7.
60. Sam Munson, "President Hints About New Plan," *Nichols Budget*, January 20, 1939, 1.
61. *1939 Ledger*, 12.
62. *Nichols Budget*, March 25, 1939, 1.
63. Ibid.
64. See Catalog, *Nichols Junior College 1942–43*, 46.

65. In 1943, a large number of colleges went through the Massachusetts legislature to obtain new degrees. Thereafter, the process of approval or accreditation was to become the responsibility of a new state board of higher education.
66. Catalog, *Nichols Junior College, 1933–1934*, 14.
67. Bossard and Dewhurst, *University Education for Business*, 567.
68. *1939 Ledger*, 91, 95.
69. Catalog, *Nichols Junior College, 1933–1934*, 14.
70. Ibid.
71. Catalog, *Nichols Junior College, 1937–38*, 3.
72. Eells, *The Junior College*, 176–183.
73. Catalog, *Nichols Junior College*, circa 1931, 5; Ibid., 1941–42, 12–15.
74. *1938 Ledger*; Ibid., 1939; Ibid., 1941; Ibid., 1980, 12–13.
75. *Nichols Budget*, January 16, 1943.
76. Ibid., October 14, 1938.
77. Winslow, "Junior College in New England – a Contrast," *Junior College Journal* 3 (April 1933), 343.
78. Dorris C. Marcus, "The New England Junior College," A.M. thesis, Brown University, 1939, 20.
79. Ibid., 105, 107.
80. Nichols Academy Board of Trustees Meeting Minutes, June 22, 1936.
81. *Nichols Budget*, December 1, 1942, 1.
82. *Webster Times*, October 8, 1942, 13.
83. www.lituanus.org/1992_3/92_3_01.atm(accessed 3/25/2008).
84. Catalog, *Nichols Junior College 1942–1943*, 4.
85. *Nichols Budget*, December 17, 1931, 1.
86. Ibid., 4.
87. Ibid., April 28, 1937, 3.
88. Ibid., October 15, 1937.
89. Nichols Academy Board of Trustees Meeting Minutes, June 22, 1936.
90. Ibid., September 21, 1936.
91. *Nichols Budget*, December 14, 1936, 2.
92. Worcester County Registry of Deeds, Worcester, Mass., Trustees of Nichols Academy to Conrad et al, March 23, 1935, 2635: 526–527.
93. *Nichols Budget*, November 11, 1938, 1; Catalog, *Nichols Junior College, 1939–1940*.
94. Letter, William J. MacInnis, Jr., to Kristen Kellerher, editor, *Nichols News*, September 13, 1993.
95. *Nichols Budget*, October 14, 1938, 1.
96. Worcester County Registry of Deeds, August 20, 1931, 252: 162–164; March 11, 1932, 02561: 19; October 25, 1933, 2594: 406; November 13, 1933, 2602: 142.
97. Articles of Organization, April 19, 1933, Corporation and Trustee Records, 1933–1942, Administrative Records, Nichols College, President's Office, Conrad Hall, Center Road, Dudley, Mass.
98. Minutes, Meeting of Stockholders of Nichols, Inc., December 17, 1935, President's Office, NCA; Minutes, Nichols Academy Board of Trustees Meeting, September 21, 1936.
99. Unsigned Agreement between Trustees and Conrad, circa 1936, 1–4.

100. Minutes, Meeting of Stockholders of Nichols, Inc., September 21, 1937.
101. Minutes, Nichols Academy Board of Trustees Meeting, June 19, 1935.
102. Memo, from the Committee to Study "The Question of Consideration" to the Trustees of Nichols Academy, filed with Minutes, Nichols Academy Board of Trustees, June 3, 1941, NCA.
103. Ibid.
104. Ibid.
105. Ibid. The members of this Committee included H. Nelson Conant, Earl Goodell, Frederick H. Davis, Dr. Quincy H. Merrill, and Arthur J. C. Underhill.
106. Refer to Nichols Academy Board of Trustees Meeting Minutes, December 23, 1941; See also Ibid., October 21, 1941.
107. Memo, from the Committee to Study "The Question of Consideration" to the Trustees of Nichols Academy, filed with Minutes, Nichols Academy Board of Trustees, June 3, 1941; Worcester County Registry of Deeds, Trs. of Nichols Academy to Nichols Junior College, April 6, 1942, 2850: 373–375.
108. The Charter of Nichols Junior College, dated December 23, 1941, included some of the wording of the Charter of Nichols, Inc., although it went far beyond it. See Administrative Records, Nichols College, President's Office, Conrad Hall, Center Road, Dudley, Mass.; Nichols Academy Board of Trustees Meeting Minutes, October 21, 1941. Refer to Appendix C.
109. Stockholders of Nichols, Inc., Meeting Minutes, May 23, 1942, Administrative Records, Nichols College, President's Office, Conrad Hall, Center Road, Dudley, Mass.
110. This reference to the Academy as being co-educational is misleading. In 1906, the school was advertised as Nichols Academy for Boys. Refer to *Annual Catalog . . . Nichols Academy . . . Dudley, Massachusetts, 1907–1908* (Academy: Davis Press, June 1907). While the Academy accepted only boys for fitting for college, both girls and boys were part of the High School of Dudley at the Academy with all students having the opportunity to take all courses and to graduate. In fact, however, the Academy itself (this does not apply to Dudley High School students at the Academy, many whom were women) was a school only for boys in 1907.
111. Laws of Massachusetts, May, 1819–Feb, 1822, 242. This refers to "An act to establish Nichols Academy in the Town of Dudley" which states that the purpose of their [Academy trustees] action was "the promotion of piety and virtue and for the instruction of youth in such languages, and in such liberal arts and sciences as the Trustees hereinafter provided. . . . Approved by the Governor, June 18, 1819."
112. *Nichols Alumnus I*, January 1947, 9.

Chapter 3 ~ "Ye Strong Sons of Nichols," 1931~1946

1. Charles Dickens, *A Tale of Two Cities* (London: Oxford University Press – Oxford University Illustrated Dickens, 1949), 3.
2. Ibid.
3. *Nichols Budget*, October 31, 1933, 4.
4. *The Tower*, 1933, 16.
5. *Nichols Budget*. November 25, 1931, 2.
6. William O. Kohnke, "Response to Nichols Historical Questionnaire," October 19, 1906, NCA.

7. *The Tower*, 1932, n.p.
8. Roger Geiger, "The Ten Generations of America Higher Education," in *American Higher Education in the Twenty-First Century*, edited by Philip G. Altbach, Robert O. Bemdahl and Patricia Greensport (Baltimore, Johns Hopkins University Press, 1997), 59.
9. *Nichols Budget*, February 2, 1933, 2.
10. Catalog, *Nichols Junior College, 1940–1941*, 47–48.
11. *Nichols Budget*, October 31, 1934.
12. Ibid., April 26, 1938, 2.
13. Ibid., November 3, 1936, 4. This is the result of straw poll results in the *Budget* files for the 1932 election.
14. *Nichols Budget*, October 19, 1936.
15. Catalog, *Nichols Junior College, 1942–1943*, 16.
16. *Nichols Budget*, February 13, 1939, 2.
17. Ibid., January 16, 1942, 2.
18. Catalog, *Nichols Junior College, 1934–35*, 17, and others.
19. Ibid., May 3, 1941.
20. *Nichols Budget*, February 2, 1933, 4.
21. Ibid., November 25, 1931; January 14, 1932.
22. *The Tower*, 1932, (n.p.).
23. *Nichols Budget*, February 16, 1937, 2; Also see *1937 Ledger*, 101, 103, 106.
24. www.dakotadiscovery.com/jamesfraser [accessed April 15, 2009].
25. www.en.wikipedia.org/wiki/Black_Diamond_(buffalo)[accessed May 31, 2009].
26. Perhaps a point of changeover to "Bison" occurred in the *Nichols Budget*, November 11, 1938, 1, 3. This issue of the *Budget* referred to the "Buffaloes" in one sports column and in another, in the same issue, to the "Bisons."
27. *The Tower*, 1932, n.p.
28. *1939 Ledger*, 74.
29. Thomas Gross, "Response to Nichols Historical Questionnaire," 2006. The *Nichols Budget*, February 13, 1939, 2, believed that Gross had handled over 200 shots.
30. *Nichols Budget*, March 17, 1941, 1.
31. *The Tower Yearbook, 1934*, 51. (Refers to 1933 team.)
32. Ibid., October 14, 1938, 3.
33. For more on Friendly, refer to: Jack Fones, "Hey! Who Said That," The *Nichols Alumnus*, Vol. III, No. 2, March 1949, 3–6; "From Nichols to CBS to Columbia, Fred Friendly leaves a Lasting Legacy," *Nichols News*, Vol. 23, No. 3, May 1998, 6–7; Ed Patenaude, "Nichols Grad Fred Friendly a Draw in Morrow Film," *Worcester Telegram & Gazette*, December 8, 2005; Jessica Lafortune, "Fred Friendly, Before and After," *Bison*, April 28, 2006.
34. Catalog, *Nichols Junior College, 1942–43*, Dudley, Massachusetts, 63.
35. *Nichols Budget*, May 3, 1941, 1.
36. Catalog, *Nichols Junior College, 1934–1935*, 19.
37. Ibid., 19–20.
38. Catalog, "College Life Under Sane Control," *Nichols Junior College 1935–1936*, 16.

ENDNOTES ~ CHAPTER 3

39. *Nichols Budget*, November 10, 1932, 2.
40. Nichols Newsclips, 1938–1939, n.d.
41. *Nichols Budget*, October 15, 1937, 2, 4.
42. Ibid., January 14, 1932.
43. Ibid., October 31, 1938, 2.
44. Ibid., October 31, 1934, 1–2.
45. See David E. Krvig, *Revealing National Prohibition* (Chicago: University of Chicago Press, 1979), 201–202.
46. *Nichols Budget*, October 31, 1934, 2.
47. "New Privilege Granted Nichols Students," *Nichols Budget*, October 15, 1937, 2.
48. *Nichols Budget*, November 10, 1932.
49. Nichols Newsclips, 1934–1935, unidentified column, Fall 1934.
50. *Nichols Budget*, June 11, 1938, 1, 5.
51. Ibid., April 26, 1938, 1.
52. Ibid.
53. Ibid., 1, 4.
54. "War Department Recognition," *Budget*, April 26, 1938, 1; "Quartermaster Course at Nichols," *Webster Times*, March 17, 1938.
55. *Nichols Budget*, May 18, 1938; Ibid., December 16, 1938, 1.
56. Ibid., June 1950.
57. Harry A. Marmion, *Selective Service: Conflict and Compromise* (New York: John Wiley & Sons, Inc., 1968), 9.
58. "Automobile Ban Avoided," *Budget*, October 15, 1941, 1.
59. *Fitchburg Daily Sentinel*, April 3, 1918.
60. *Nichols Budget*, November 28, 1941.
61. Ibid.
62. Catalog, *Nichols Junior College, 1942–43*, 17.
63. Ibid., 48–49.
64. *Nichols Budget*, December 12, 1941, 2.
65. "The College Faces the War," *Nichols Budget*, January 16, 1942, 2.
66. Ibid., January 16, 1942, 2.
67. Ibid.
68. "Capt. Conrad speaks to Classes," *Nichols Budget*, March 13, 1942, 1–2.
69. *1942 Ledger*, 82–83.
70. Catalog, *Nichols Junior College, 1942–1943*, 10–11.
71. *Webster Times*, September 24, 1942, 16.
72. Marmion, *Selective Service*, 37.
73. "More Men Needed," *Budget*, November 5, 1942, 2.
74. *Nichols Budget*, December 1, 1942.
75. *Webster Times*, December 3, 1942, 13.
76. *Nichols Budget*, January 16, 1943.
77. *Webster Times*, January 21, 1943.
78. Ibid., February 4, 1943; Ibid., February 25, 1943.
79. Ibid., March 4, 1943.

80. Records of the Registrar's Office, Nichols College, Academy Hall, Center Road, Dudley, Mass., show several members of the Class of 1944 leaving the College between April 30 and June 25, 1943.
81. Catalog, *Nichols Junior College, 1949–50*, 25.
82. "Editorial," *Webster Times*, September 2, 1943.
83. Letter, Herbert L. Plummer, Treasurer, to Dr. Quincy H. Merrill, April 3, 1943, Academy records, NCA.
84. "Dr. Merrill Carried On," *Nichols Budget*, March 21, 1946, 1.
85. Refer to Acts and *Resolves passed by the General Court, 1943*; see Chapter 549 & 557, "An act establishing a Board of Collegiate Authority in the Department of Education. . .," 750–757, and others. See also *Budget*, January 16, 1943.
86. Bertram H. Holland, "A History of the New England Association of Schools & Colleges," in New England Association of Schools and Colleges, *The First Hundred Years, 1885–1985* (Winchester, Massachusetts: New England Association of Schools and Colleges, 1986), 60.
87. *Nichols Budget*, January 5, 1943, 3.
88. *Webster Times*, July 29, 1943.
89. *1975 Ledger*, n.p.
90. *Nichols Budget*, May 28, 1942, 1; Ibid., January 5, 1943, 1.
91. Michael J. Bennett, *When Dreams Come True; the GI Bill and the Making of Modern America* (Washington, London: Brassey's, 1996), xv.

CHAPTER 4 ~ REDESIGNING THE HISTORIC CAMPUS, 1946~1958

1. Martin Trow, "Problems in the Transition from Elite to Mass Higher Education" (Carnegie Commission on Higher Education, 1973), 1.
2. Roger Geiger, "The Ten Generations of American Higher Education," *American Higher Education in the Twenty-First Century*," Philip G. Altbach, Robert O. Berdahl, Patricia J. Greenport, eds. (Baltimore: Johns Hopkins University Press, 1999), 38.
3. Christopher J. Lucas, *American Higher Education: A History* (New York: St. Martin's Press, 1994), xv.
4. Thomas Diener, *Growth of an American Invention: A Documentary History of the Junior and Community College Movement* (New York; Greenwood Press, 1986), 3.
5. Ibid., 3.
6. Nichols Junior College, *Special Catalog, 1946*, 49.
7. "Message from the President," *1947 Ledger*, n.p.
8. Ibid.
9. *Nichols Budget*, March 21, 1946, 1.
10. Ibid., 2.
11. Ibid., September 26, 1946, 1.
12. Ibid.
13. Ibid.
14. "Faculty," Nichols *1947 Ledger*, 9.
15. *The Nichols Alumnus*, I (January 1947), 7.
16. *Nichols Budget*, June 9, 1947; Ibid., January 22, 1948, 1.
17. Ibid., September 1949.

ENDNOTES ~ CHAPTER 4

18. Newsclip, 1940–1941, NCA.
19. *Nichols Budget*, October 25, 1946, 2.
20. *Worcester Evening Gazette*, March 13, 1947.
21. For more details, see "A Family Affair," in *Nichols News*, Vol. 15, Winter, 1990, 2.
22. *The Nichols Alumnus*, I (March 1947), 9.
23. *The Bison*, November 1952, 1; *Nichols Alumnus* IX, January 1955, 3.
24. Ibid.
25. James L. Conrad, *1950 Ledger*.
26. *Nichols Alumnus* II (October 1948), 11.
27. Administrative Records, Nichols College, Memorandum, September 13, 1946.
28. Minutes, Nichols Junior College Board of Trustees, President's Office, March 15, 1947. Also see *Nichols Alumnus*, I (June 1947, 8); Newsclip, Nichols, 1947, NCA.
29. *Nichols Budget*, May 13, 1948.
30. Lucas, *American Higher Education*, xiv.
31. Ibid., xiv–xv.
32. *Nichols Budget*, January 1950, 1.
33. Ibid., February 28, 1948, 2.
34. Ibid., October 24, 1947, 2.
35. Ibid., May 1949, 2.
36. Ibid., November 15, 1948, 2.
37. Ibid, June 1949, 2.
38. Ibid., 1.
39. *1949 Ledger*, n.p.
40. *Nichols Alumnus*, III (July 1949), 7.
41. Nichols Junior College, *Pictorial*, circa 1956, inside front cover.
42. Ibid., 3–11.
43. *Nichols Alumnus*, IV (January 1950), 6.
44. Ibid., III (July 1949), 11.
45. *Nichols Budget*, October 24, 1947, 1.
46. Darcy C. Coyle, DBA, *Nichols College: A Brief History* (New York: The Newcomen Society in North America, 1975), 14.
47. Peter Sammartino, *The President of a Small College* (New York: Cornwall Books, 1982), 11–16.
48. Joseph N. Crowley, *No Equal in this World: An Interpretation of the American Presidency* (Reno: University of Nevada Press, 1944), 97.
49. See summarization of many comments sent on Nichols "Historical Questionnaire," Classes of 1936–2006, NCA.
50. Samuel Schuman, *Old Main: Small Colleges in Twenty-First Century America* (Baltimore: The Johns Hopkins University Press, 2005), 99–102.
51. *1939 Ledger*, 18.
52. *Nichols Budget*, December 17, 1931, 1.
53. Nichols "Historical Questionnaires," from Class files, 1932–1959.
54. Dr. Edward W. Carlson, Speech at Reunion of the Nichols Class of 1940, (Copy sent to James L. Conrad Jr., October 2005, NCA).

55. Memo, from the Committee to Study "The Question of Consideration" to the Trustees of Nichols Academy, filed with Minutes, Nichols Academy Board of Trustees, June 3, 1941, NCA.
56. Crowley, *No Equal in the World*, ix–x.
57. Newsclip, *Worcester Gazette*, June 2, 1972, NCA.
58. Anne Colby, Thomas Ehrlich, et al, *Rethinking Undergraduate Business Education: Liberal Learning for the Profession*, (Sanford, CA.: The Carnegie Foundation for the Advancement of Teaching, published by Jossey-Bass, 2011), 30.
59. Roger L. Martin, *The Opposable Mind; How Successful Leaders Win Through Integrative Thinking* (Boston: Harvard Business School Press, 2007), 23, 191.
60. Schuman, *Old Main: Small Colleges in Twenty-First Century America*, 243.
61. Neil Howe and William Strauss, *Millennials Rising; The Next Great Generation* (New York: Vintage Books, 2000), 366.
62. For more on Dean Charles Edward Leech, see *Nichols Alumnus*, Vol. XI, June 1960, 8.
63. *Nichols College of Business Administration Bulletin*, 1961–1963, 16.
64. *Bison*, November, 1957, 1.
65. *Nichols Alumnus* IV, April 1950, 5–6.
66. *1955 Ledger*, 7.
67. Minutes, Nichols Junior College Board of Trustees, May 9, 1953.
68. Ibid.
69. For a full story, see Joel S. Berger, "Dudley's Bomb-Proof Bank," *Worcester Sunday Telegram, Feature Parade Section*, November 1, 1959, 3–4.
70. *Nichols Alumnus* X, June 1958, 2.
71. Minutes, Dudley Town Meeting, June 6, 1891.
72. *Nichols Budget*, June 1950, 1.
73. Ibid., January 1951, 1.
74. *Nichols Alumnus* IV, October 1950, 3–4.
75. Catalog, *Nichols Junior College*, 1956–1957, 1957–1958, 70–74.
76. *Nichols Budget*, 1950, 1; *1952 Ledger*, 5.
77. *1951 Ledger*, n.p.
78. Minutes, Nichols Junior College Board of Trustees, October 1956, NCA.
79. Catalog, *Nichols Junior College, 1958–59*, 3. This was the last copy of the Nichols Junior College catalog since it became Nichols College of Business Administration in December 1958.
80. *Bison*, March 1957, 3.
81. Minutes, Nichols Junior College Board of Trustees Meeting, May 20, 1950, NCA.
82. Minutes, "Special Committee Report," Nichols Junior College Board of Trustees, May 14, 1955, NCA.
83. "Nichols to Become 3 Year College," *The Bison*, February 1953, 1.
84. *Bison*, March 1953, 1. The three-year program was not unusual. Both Babson Institute (1943) and Bryant College, when in Providence, had three-year programs.
85. *Nichols Alumnus* VII, April 1953, 12.
86. Minutes, Nichols Junior College Board of Trustees Meeting, May 14, 1955, NCA.

87. Ibid., October 5, 1957.
88. Ibid., May 10, 1958.
89. *Bison*, October 28, 1957, 4.
90. *Budget*, October 1950, 1.
91. *Bison.*, November 1954, 7–8.
92. Ibid., May 1952, 3; Ibid., October 1955, 4; Ibid., June 1956, 2; Ibid., January 1956, 4.
93. Ibid., May 1957, 1.
94. Ibid., February 1958, 2.
95. *1955 Ledger*, 47–48.
96. Catalog, *Nichols Junior College, 1956–1958*, 85.
97. *Worcester Gazette*, February 22, 1952, 18; *Bison*, March 1957, 1.
98. *Bison*, December 16, 1958, 5.
99. This discussion took place in the President's Office in the late fall of 1957. The writer was the only other person present.
100. *The Bison*, May 1955, 5.
101. *Nichols Budget*, March 16, 1951, 1; *Bison*, March 29, 1951.
102. *Nichols Alumnus* V, April 1951, 12.
103. Catalog, *Nichols Junior College, 1956–1958*, 81–83.
104. "In Retrospect," *1954 Ledger*, 38; Historical Questionnaire for 1953.
105. *Bison*, October, 1956, 2.
106. Dean Charles E. Leech, quoted in *1959 Ledger*, 8.

CHAPTER 5 ~ NICHOLS COLLEGE OF BUSINESS ADMINISTRATION, 1958~1966

1. Hal Chalmers, "Nichols Graduates First Four-Year Class," *The Nichols Alumnus*, Vol. XI, No. 9, June 1961, 3–7.
2. Ibid.
3. Frank C. Pierson and others, *The Education of American Businessmen: A Study of University-College Programs in Business Administration* (New York: McGraw-Hill Book Company, Inc., 1959), vii; Robert A. Gordon and James E. Howell, *Higher Education for Business* (New York City: Columbia University Press, 1958); Dorothy E. Lee, *Changing Objectives in Business Education on the Collegiate Level in the United States for 1899 and 1954*, Ph.D. diss, New York University, University Microfilms, Ann Arbor, 1957.
4. Memo regarding a meeting held April 23, 1959, filed with Minutes of Nichols Junior College Trustee Meeting, Secretary's Report, May 9, 1959, President's Office, Nichols College, 2.
5. Lee, "Changing Objectives," 190–192.
6. Nichols Junior College Board of Trustees Meeting, April 23, 1959. President's Office, Nichols College.
7. Ibid.
8. Ibid.
9. Memo regarding a meeting held April 23, 1959, filed with Minutes of Nichols Junior College Trustee Meeting, Secretary's Report, May 9, 1959, President's Office, Nichols College, 2.
10. *Nichols College of Business Administration, Bulletin*, College Issue, 1960–1961, 3.

11. "Editorial," *The Bison*, May 25, 1963.
12. *1958 Ledger*, 112.
13. *The Nichols Bison*, December 13, 1957, 1.
14. Ibid., April 30, 1958.
15. Ibid., May 10, 1958, 2.
16. Minutes, Nichols Junior College Trustees, Annual Meeting, October 5, 1957.
17. *Nichols Alumnus*, XI, June 1959, 10, reprinted from *Boston Globe*. See also Ibid., X, November 1958, 3.
18. Ibid., November 1959, 14.
19. Nichols News Clip, 1958.
20. Hal Chalmers, "Nichols Graduates First Four-Year Class," *Nichols Alumnus*, XI, June 1961, 3.
21. *Bulletin of Nichols College of Business Administration*, 1959, 14–16. This is labeled an "interim publication" published prior to the issuance of a formal College Catalog.
22. "Observatory is now a Chapel," *Nichols Alumnus*, XIV, November 1962, 3–5.
23. Ibid., X, November 1958, 11.
24. *Bison*, October, 25, 1963, 1; Ibid., January 10, 1964.
25. *Nichols College Bulletin,* Vol. XVI, September 1965, 4.
26. *Nichols College Bulletin*, Alumni Issue, Vol. XVII, September 1964, 37.
27. *Nichols College Bulletin*, Vol. XVI, September 1965, 4. Also refer to the CPI Inflation Calculation, Bureau of Labor Statistics, United States Department of Labor.
28. "Retired President's Report," Nichols College of Business Administration, effective as of June 30, 1966, Presidential Archives, Conrad Hall, Nichols College.
29. Ibid.
30. Nichols College *Bulletin*, February 1966, 66; *Nichols Alumnus* XI, 1960, 6.
31. "Nichols Students Get a Look at International Scene," *The Bison*, October 20, 1961.
32. *Nichols Alumnus* XI, November 1959, 9.
33. *Bison*, September 13, 1964, 4.
34. *Catalog*, Nichols Junior College, 1931–32, 7, 14, NCA.
35. Nichols College of Business Administration, *Bulletin*, 1959–1960, 85; Ibid., 1965–66, 87.
36. *Bison*, September 13, 1964, 13.
37. C.S. Kolak, "The Director Speaks about Student Activities," *The Bison*, Post-Commencement, 1963, 3.
38. Robert Nemeth, "Student Body of Nichols College has Increased from 11 to 640," *Worcester Telegram*, February 22, 1965, 73.
39. "Students Raid Dean and Becker Dormitories," *The Bison*, February 28, 1959, 1–2.
40. "Editorial," Ibid., 2.
41. Wallace S. Camper, "Letter to the Editor," *Bison*, March 21, 1960, 2.
42. Nichols College Historical Questionnaires, Nichols Alumni, 1957–1966, NCA.
43. See *1960–1966 Ledgers*.
44. *1966 Ledger*, 180.

ENDNOTES ~ CHAPTER 5

45. Hal Chalmers, "Sports Roundup," *Nichols Alumnus*, XI, June 1960, 10.
46. *1966 Ledger*, 171.
47. *Nichols Alumnus*, Vol. XIII, June, 1962, 7.
48. *Bison*, October 25, 1963, 1.
49. *Nichols Alumnus*, XI, June 1961, 9.
50. Nichols College of Business Administration, *Bulletin*, 1959–1960, 85; Ibid., *Catalog Issue*, 1965–66, 87.
51. *Bison*, October 31, 1964.
52. "For Nichols, No More Foresters," *Worcester Telegram*, June 20, 1970, 7.
53. "Nichols Students Aid in State's Forestry Plan," *Nichols Alumnus*, XIII, June 1962, 4.
54. *Nichols Alumnus*, XI, April 1960, 3.
55. Nichols College Historical Questionnaires, 1957–1966. For more on Nichols Foresters, see "They Called Themselves Woodsmen, Nicons, and Lumber Bunnies," *Nichols College Magazine*, Vol. 5, No. 1, Summer 2010, 10–11.
56. President's Report, Nichols College of Business Administration Board of Trustees, April 2, 1966, 3.
57. Nichols College of Business Administration, *Bulletin*, XVI, April 1964, 9.
58. Edward Patenaude, "So I've Heard," *Worcester Gazette*, June 1, 1978, NCA.
59. "Editorial," *Bison*, May 25, 1960.
60. "Dean Hill Commencement Speaker," *The Bison, Special Post-Commencement Issue*, n.d., circa late Spring, 1963, 1.
61. *Bison*, January 21, 1965, 1.
62. Michael G. Ash, "Nichols Sesquicentennial Anniversary Highlighted by Academic Convocation," *Bison*, May 14, 1965, 1; "Loyalty, Service, and Culture," *Bison*, April 24, 1965, 1.
63. Ibid.
64. *Bison*, January 21, 1965, 2; Ibid., May 12, 1965; Ibid., June 4, 1965.
65. Fisher, "The development and recession of the private junior college including Fisher Junior College," 77.
66. Bertram H. Holland, "A History of the New England Association of Schools & Colleges from 1885–1985," in *The First Hundred Years, 1885 – 1985* (Winchester, Mass.: New England Association of Schools and Colleges, Inc., 1986), 70.
67. Secretary's Report, Executive Committee, Nichols College of Business Administration Board of Trustees, February 2, 1963; President's Report, Nichols College of Business Administration, Board of Trustees, April 6, 1963, President's Office, Nichols College.
68. Holland, "History of the New England Association," 92; President's Report, Special Meeting, Nichols College of Business Administration Board of Trustees, February 8, 1964, President's Office, Nichols College.
69. President's Report, Special Meeting, Nichols College of Business Administration Board of Trustees, February 8, 1964, President's Office, Nichols College.
70. President's Report, Nichols College of Business Administration Board of Trustees, October 3, 1964, President's Office, Nichols College.
71. Donald S. Peckrill, "A Dream Realized; a Goal Achieved," *The Nichols Bison*, December 16, 1965, 1.

72. Ibid.
73. *The Nichols Alumnus*, X, June 1957, 3.
74. "Colonel Conrad Honored," *The Nichols College Bulletin, Alumni Issue*, XVII, September 1966, 8.
75. "Retired President's Report," June 30, 1966, Nichols College of Business Administration Board of Trustees, in files of Nichols Trustees, President's Office, Nichols College.

CHAPTER 6 ~ THE COLLEGE "TRANSFORMING," 1966~1978

1. Clark Kerr, *The Great Transformation in Higher Education, 1960–1980* (Albany, N.Y.: State University of New York Press, 1991.).
2. Ibid., xi–xii.
3. Ibid., xii.
4. Ibid., 368–369.
5. Ibid., xii.
6. Ibid.
7. Ibid., xiii–xv.
8. Ibid., xv.
9. Gordon Cross, "President's Message," *Nichols College of Business Administration, Alumni Bulletin*, February 1969, 3.
10. *Nichols College Alumni Issue*, Summer 1967, 10.
11. Gordon Cross, "Nichols will remain an All-Male College," *Nichols College Bulletin, Alumni Issue*, September, 1966, 3.
12. *Nichols College of Business Bulletin*, Catalog Issue, 1966–67, 7–8.
13. Gordon Cross, "President's Message," *Nichols College of Business Administration, Alumni Bulletin*, February 1969, 3.
14. *Bison*, February 11, 1967.
15. Ibid.
16. "For Nichols, No More Foresters," *Worcester Telegram*, June 20, 1970, 7.
17. *Nichols College Bulletin, Alumni Issue*, February 1969, 3.
18. Kerr, *Great Transformation*, 242.
19. Minutes, Nichols Trustees, Executive Committee, December 10, 1966, Nichols College President's Office, Center Road, Dudley, Mass. "Construction Projects started at Nichols, " *Nichols College Bulletin, Alumni Issue*, September 1968, 3.
20. Ibid., 4.
21. *Nichols Alumnus*, Summer 1971, 22.
22. Ibid., April 5, 1969.
23. Minutes, Meeting, Nichols Trustees, received from Long-Range Planning Committee, January 10, 1970.
24. Tyack and Hansot, *Learning Together*, 280.
25. Presidential report to Nichols Trustees, filed with Minutes, March 20, 1970, President' Office, Nichols College.
26. Ibid.
27. College Senate Meeting, (referenced in Trustee Minutes), March 22, 1972, President's Office, Nichols College.

ENDNOTES ~ CHAPTER 6

28. Minutes, Nichols College Board of Trustees Meeting, April 1, 1972.
29. *Nichols Alumnus*, Summer 1971, 6–7.
30. *Nichols College of Business Administration, Catalog Issue*, 1972–73, 106; Ibid., 1967–68, 69.
31. President's letter to Trustees, March 20, 1970 (filed with Nichols Trustee Minutes, this date).
32. *Nichols College Bulletin*, Catalog Issue, 1972–1973, 49.
33. *Nichols College Alumni Association*, April 1971.
34. *Nichols College Bulletin*, Catalog Issue, 1972–73, 8–9.
35. Ibid., 49.
36. Kristen Kelleher, "Women at Nichols," *Nichols News*, (special pull-out section), 1993, 1.
37. Dan Mackowiak, "Nichols on the Move," *Bison*, October 8, 1971, 1.
38. Ibid.
39. Kerr, *Great Transformation*, xiv.
40. Philip G. Altbach, "American Student Politics: Activism in the Age of Apathy" in, *The History of Higher Education*, 2nd ed., edited by Lester F. Goodchild and Harold Wechler (Boston, Mass.: Simon & Schuster Custom Publishing, 1997), 742.
41. Ibid.; also see Jean M. Twenge, *Generation Me* (New York: Free Press, 2006).
42. Roger Geiger, "The Ten Generations of American Higher Education" in *American Higher Education in the Twenty-first Century*, edited by Philip G. Altbach, Robert O. Bendahl and Patricia Greenport (Baltimore: Johns Hopkins University Press, 1997), 38.
43. "Ford Beats Carter at Nichols But Loses Nation," *Bison*, December 9, 1976, 1.
44. "Nichols Supports President; Students Elsewhere Protest," *Southbridge Evening News*, May 11, 1972, 1.
45. *Bison*, October 6, 1967.
46. Ibid., February 24, 1968.
47. Ibid., February 14, 1969, 2–3.
48. *Nichols College Bulletin, Alumni Issue*, February 1969, 8; "Nichols Bar Conceived One Year Ago," *Bison*, March 28, 1969; "Student Lounge," *1969 Ledger*, 192.
49. "Nichols Bar," *Nichols College Bulletin, Alumni Issue*, February 1969, 8.
50. *Bison*, November 29, 1971, 2.
51. John Makely, "Parietal Hours," *Bison*, October 18, 1969, 2; "Nichols to Go Co-Ed," *Bison*, December 14, 1970, 1.
52. Minutes, Nichols College Board of Trustees Meeting, April 4, 1970.
53. "Editorial," *The Worcester Evening Gazette*, April 25, 1970, 6. Also see *Worcester Evening Gazette*, April 22, 1970; "Students Vow to Stand Firm," *Southbridge News*, April 23, 1970.
54. See *Boston Globe, Worcester Telegram* and *Providence Journal*, among others, April 23–25, 1970.
55. "From the President's Desk," *Nichols Alumnus*, Summer 1970.
56. Ibid., Summer 1971, 22.
57. *Worcester Evening Gazette*, April 25, 1970, 6.
58. Minutes, Special Meeting, Nichols Board of Trustees, November 21, 1970.

59. *Bison*, October 12, 1970.
60. "Parietal Hours Extended," *Bison*, October 8, 1971, 1; Minutes, Meeting, Nichols Board of Trustees, June 4, 1971.
61. *Bison*, May 18, 1968.
62. Ibid.
63. "Nichols takes a Stand," *Bison*, January 15, 1970, 3.
64. *Bison*, April 16, 1974, 4.
65. Ibid., October 22, 1971.
66. "Nichols Will Remain All-Male College," *Nichols College Bulletin, Alumni Issue*, September, 1968, 3.
67. Ibid.
68. "From the President's Desk," *Nichols Alumnus*, Summer 1971, 22.
69. *Bison*, December 14, 1970, 1.
70. *Nichols College Bulletin, Catalog Issue*, 1972–1973, 10.
71. Dan Mackowiak, "Nichols on the Move," *Bison*, October 8, 1971, 1.
72. Janice Ducharme, "709 to 6," *Nichols Bison*, October 8, 1971, 4.
73. "Coeds: The Good and the Bad," *Nichols Alumnus*, Winter, 1973, 2.
74. George Winston, "Students Speak Out," *Nichols Alumnus*, Winter 1973, 6.
75. A further look at the experiences of women at Nichols can be found in Kristen Kelleher's article, written in 1993, titled "Women at Nichols: Celebrating 20 years," *Nichols News, Newsletter*, Special Edition, January 1993.
76. *Nichols College of Business Administration, Alumni Issue*, September 1966, 14; Ibid., September 1968, 8; "From the President's Desk," *Nichols Alumnus*, Summer 1971, 22; *The Bison*, March 28, 1969, 1; Ibid., November 24, 1969, 3.
77. See *Nichols College Bulletin, 1993–96*, 13–14, for a list of some additional noteworthy performers.
78. www.2ed.gov/policy/gen/guid/fcpo/ferpa/index.html[8/26/2011].
79. www.unh.edu/registrar/fag/buckley.html[8/26/11]; "Lower Legal Age may Cause Problems for Colleges," *Bison*, February 5, 1974.
80. Mark Alexander, "Response to Nichols History Questionnaire," 2006.
81. Jeffrey Buonforte, "The Nichols Student of Today," *Bison* (beginning of 2nd semester), 1973, 4.
82. *Bison*, March 20, 1975, 1.
83. "The Governance of Nichols College," November 25, 1974, 7, NCA.
84. *Nichols College Bulletin, Alumni Issue*, February 1969, 4.
85. *Nichols News, Alumni Newsletter*, Vol. XXXVIII, No. 2, 5.
86. *Nichols Alumnus*, Winter 1973, 13.
87. This included athletes from eleven different sports in the eleven-year period. Of the classes between 1966 and 1977, the Class of 1976 now has ten athletes in the Hall of Fame; the Classes of 1966, 1972, and 1977 each have seven in the Hall of Fame while the Classes of 1968 and 1975 each have six. These numbers may change as the Hall of Fame Committee adds new honorees. Also see Appendix D.
88. *Webster Times*, February 15, 1978.

ENDNOTES ~ CHAPTER 6

89. *1978 Ledger* (yearbook), 102–103; for the 1977 team, see "Professor William Steglitz, "Nichols Pride . . . . The Women Have It," *Bison*, May 7, 1977. *Nichols News*, June 1977, 5. The *1977 Ledger* did not mention this softball team.
90. Ibid., Winter 1973, 11.
91. Nichols College Trustees Meeting Minutes, August 7, 1972; *Nichols Alumnus*, November 1974, 1.
92. *Nichols Alumni*, Summer 1971, 23.
93. Ibid., November 1974, 1.
94. *Nichols College of Business Administration, Bulletin, Catalog Issue*, 1970–1971, 11.
95. Ibid.
96. "From the President's Desk," *Nichols Alumnus*, Summer 1971, 23.
97. Conrad, *Nichols News*, Vol. 18, No. 1, June 31, 1993, 4.
98. Minutes, Nichols College Trustees, October 7, 1972.
99. Ibid., August 7, 1972.
100. Ibid., January 21, 1973.
101. *Nichols Alumnus, Bulletin*, January 1973, 1.
102. Upper Iowa State University, *The Bridge*, Winter, 2002–2003, 18.
103. Nichols College Board of Trustees Meeting, Minutes, April 7, 1973.
104. Ibid., January 26, 1974; *Nichols Alumnus*, November 1975, 3.
105. See "Presidential Reports" in *Nichols Alumnus*, 1974–1978.
106. Ibid., October 12, 1974, 1–3.
107. *Nichols Alumnus*, November 1976, 3.
108. Darcy Coyle, "Excerpts from President's 1977 Report to Trustees of Nichols College," *Bulletin of Nichols College*, October 22, 1977, 2.
109. Darcy C. Coyle, *Nichols College; A Brief History* (New York: The Newcomen Society in North America, 1975), 7.
110. *Bulletin of Nichols College*, November 1977, 3.
111. Minutes, Nichols Board of Trustees, June 4, 1977.
112. *Nichols College Bulletin, Catalog Issue*, 1977–78, 6.
113. Coyle, *Nichols History*, 18.
114. "President's Report," *Nichols Alumnus*, November 1974, 5.
115. Kelly, *Nichols History*, n.p.
116. *Bulletin of Nichols College*, October 23, 1977, 2.
117. "Coyle Bewilders S.G.A.," *Bison*, November 21, 1974, 1; "Coyle Calls Seniors Illiterate," *Bison*, November 9, 1974, 1; "Student Rights Up for Grabs," *Bison*, February 5, 1974, 2.
118. *Bison*, February 5, 1974, 2.
119. Ibid., May 11, 1974, 5.
120. For more on Thomas McClutchy, *Bison*, September 11, 1975, 2.
121. For more on Michael Vendetti, *Nichols Alumnus*, Vol. XIII, June 1962, 7; and *Bison*, September 11, 1975.
122. *Bulletin of Nichols College*, June 1977, 2.
123. Ibid., 20. For an additional summary of Darcy Coyle's presidency, see "Nichols Mourns Past President," *Nichols News*, Vol. 29, Winter 2003, 11.

Chapter 7 ~ Beyond the Past, 1978~1996

1. Philip G. Altbach, "American Student Politics: Activism in the Midst of Apathy," in *The History of Higher Education*, 2 ed., eds. Lester F. Goodchild and Harold S. Wechsler (Boston: Simon & Schuster Custom Publishing, 1997) 743, 751.
2. Clark Kerr, *The Great Transformation in Higher Education*, 374–375.
3. For an indication of this range of criticisms, see Christopher Lucas, *Crisis in the Academy: Rethinking Higher Education in America* (New York: St. Martin's Press, 1996), x.
4. Rakesh Khurana, *From Higher Aims to Hired Hands; The Social Transformation of American Business School and the Unfulfilled Promise of Management as a Profession* (Princeton & Oxford: Princeton University Press, 2007), 5.
5. George Keller, *Higher Education and the New Society* (Baltimore: The Johns Hopkins University Press, 2008), 6.
6. Lucas, *Crisis in the Academy*, 241; xii.
7. Ibid., 246.
8. Arthur M. Cohen, *The Shaping of American Higher Education: Emergence and Growth of the Contemporary System* (San Francisco: Jossey-Bass, 1998), 497.
9. For additional information, see "Nichols Welcomes Dr. Lowell C. Smith," *Bison*, March 8, 1978, 1.
10. *Nichols College Bulletin, 1978–1979, 1979–1980* (February 1979), 2.
11. Ibid., 1993–1996, 3.
12. Ibid.
13. *Nichols News*, September 1, 1979, 1.
14. Elizabeth S. Kelly, *Nichols College; The First 175 Years* (1990), n.p.
15. Minutes, First Meeting of the Academic Committee, September 1, 1959, NCA; Minutes, Academic Review Committee, 1962–1963, NCA; See Sec. 1.31, "Nichols College Undergraduate College, Academic Policy Manual," September 1977, 3.
16. See my article in the *Bison*: "The Seventy Five Minute Period," May 10, 1975. For a student response to this change, see an editorial in the *Bison*, November 14, 1975.
17. *Faculty Policy Manual*, September 15, 1978, Sec. 8.1–8.5, 16–18, NCA.
18. Ibid., 13 (7.2).
19. *Nichols College Faculty Policy Manual*, January 1986, 8 (2.4) and 29–30 (Exhibit A).
20. Ibid., 26–28 (11.0–11.6).
21. Memo, Warren to Conrad, "Requested Thoughts and Comments on Nichols College, 1978–1997," August 17, 2011, NCA.
22. *Nichols College Bulletin, 1980–1981, 1981–1983*, 6–7.
23. *Webster Evening Times*, August 3, 1931.
24. *Bison*, May 18, 1968, 4.
25. Ibid., February 26, 1974, 1.
26. "Nichols Awarded Consultant Grant," *Bison*, November 30, 1977.
27. *Nichols College Bulletin, 1982–1984*, March 1982, 8.
28. Flyer, "Nichols College Institute for American Values," file #4000, NCA. Also see *Nichols News*, "The Nichols College Institute for American Values," September 9, 1980, 7–9.
29. *Bison*, October 1, 1980, 1.
30. "The Institute for American Values Turns Fifteen," *Nichols News*, Vol. 22, No. 3, July 1997, 3.
31. Ibid.

32. Lowell. C. Smith, "The State of the College 1983," *Alumni News*, 1983 Office of Alumni and Development, Nichols College, Dudley, Mass., n.d., 4.
33. *Nichols College Bulletin, 1984–1987*, 37.
34. Ibid., 1987–1990, 41.
35. *Bison*, May 14, 1990, 3.
36. Ibid., February 15, 1989, 1.
37. Nichols "Historical Questionnaire," 1991.
38. *Bison*, October 6, 1992, 3.
39. *Nichols News, Alumni Newsletter*, XXXVI, No. 3, Summer 1985, 1.
40. Ibid.
41. Merri Ford, "Farewell President Smith," *Bison*, February 3, 1995, 1.
42. *Nichols News, Alumni Newsletter*, Vol. XXXI, No. 1, Winter 1987, 1–2.
43. *Boston Sunday Globe*, October 4, 1987.
44. *Bison*, September 3, 1980, 1; *Nichols College Bulletin, 1993–1996*, 21.
45. "President's Message," *1989 Ledger*, 3.
46. Lowell C. Smith, "A Milestone, Central New England Colleges," *Bison*, October 1988, 2.
47. *Worcester Telegram and Gazette*, June 22, 1990.
48. *1991 Ledger*, 46–47.
49. Nichols "Historical Questionnaire," 2007.
50. *Bison*, October 23, 1990, 1.
51. Ibid., April 17, 1991, 1.
52. Nichols "Historical Questionnaire," 1990; Ibid, 1992.
53. Ibid., 1995.
54. Ibid., 1990–1996, 14; "Campaign of Nichols," *Bison*, November 13, 1989, 9.
55. *Nichols News*, Vol. 21, No. 1, Fall 1995/Winter 1996, 1.
56. Trow, *Problems in the Transition from Elite to Mass Higher Education*, 1–2. Trow's areas of probable growth included: finance, government and administration, recruitment of students, training, socialization of staff, setting-maintenance of standards, forms of examinations, qualifications in housing, job placement, motivation and morale, relation of research to teaching, relation of higher education to secondary education and adult education, to national and state governments.
57. "Dean Eaton Retires," *Bison*, March 15, 1979.
58. Ibid.
59. For more on Dean Carney, see Prof. Edward Warren, "Thank you, Roger," *Nichols Edge*, Vol. 30, Issue Number 5, 2004, 31; also "Roger Carney, A Nichols Icon," *Bison*, February 16, 2004, 1.
60. Ibid., October 14, 1983, 3.
61. See Brianne Callahan, "An Afternoon with a Nichols Legend," *Nichols College Magazine*, Vol. 6, No. 1, Summer 2011, 15.
62. *Nichols College Bulletin*, 1980–1982, 112–116; Ibid., 1990–1993, 103–106.
63. Peter Engh, "End of Semester Enrollment," Office of Associate Dean for Academic Administration and Records, Nichols College, Conrad Hall, Center Road, Dudley, Mass.
64. *Bison*, October 14, 1983, 1; *Nichols News*, Vol. XXXIV, Winter 1980–81, 4.
65. *Nichols News, Alumni Newsletter*, No. 2, Summer 1982, 33.
66. Lucas, *American Higher Education: A History*, xvii.

67. Martin A. Trow, "American Higher Education, Past, Present and Future," in Goodchild and Wechsler, *History of Higher Education*, 577.
68. "Bison Poll," *Bison*, March 15, 1979, 1.
69. "Anderson Vote High," *Bison*, October 22, 1980, 1.
70. Ibid., October 22, 1980, 1.
71. Ibid., May 11, 1988, 10.
72. Ibid., April 21, 1981; *Nichols College Bulletin, 1984–1987*, 65–69.
73. *Nichols College Bulletin, 1984–87*, 30.
74. *Journal*, November 12, 1979, 1.
75. Ibid., 2, 6.
76. *Journal*, September 20, 1979, 2; Ibid., October 12, 1979, 1–3; Ibid., January 24, 1980, 1, 6.
77. *Bison*, November 12, 1980, 1.
78. Ibid., 1, 4.
79. Ibid., March 11, 1981, 3; Ibid., May 2, 1987, 2.
80. "Waiver Waved," *Bison*, April 22, 1981, 1.
81. Ibid., February 9, 1988, 2; Ibid., February 23, 1988, 1; Ibid., December 13, 1988, 1, 3.
82. Ibid., October 9, 1993, 1.
83. Ibid., December 8, 1994, 3.
84. Ibid., February 14, 1994, 4.
85. Ibid., February 12, 1993, 6.
86. Ibid., October 1999, 1, 4.
87. "Alumni Survey Produces Encouraging Results," *Nichols News, Newsletter*, Vol. 21, No. 1, Fall 1995/Winter 1996, 1.
88. Ibid., 2, 3.
89. Kristen Kelleher, "Women at Nichols," *Nichols News* (Special pullout section, 1993, 1–2.).
90. "Mike Vendetti Resigns; Good Luck Mike!" *Nichols News, Alumni Newsletter*, Vol. XXXVIII, No. 2, Spring 1986, 5.
91. "A Farewell Tribute to Mike Vendetti," Ibid., No. 3, Summer 1986, 8.
92. Response to Nichols "Historical Questionnaire," April 29, 2007, NCA.
93. *Bison*, February 10, 1987, 2.
94. *Nichols News*, Vol. 17, No. 4, Fall 1992, 1; *Nichols College Bulletin, 1993–1996*, 21.
95. *Nichols College Bulletin, 1980–1982*, 32–33; Ibid., *1993–1996*, 36–37.
96. "President Smith to retire in 1996," *Nichols News, Newsletter*, Vol. 20, No. 1, Winter 1995, 6.
97. Ibid.
98. Lester F. Goodchild and Harold S. Wechsler, *The History of Higher Education*, 2nd ed. (Boston, Mass.: Simon's Schuster Custom Publishing, 1997), xxv.
99. Ibid.
100. President Lowell C. Smith, "It has been a Year of Change," *Nichols News*, Vol. 13, No. 4, 1988, 1.
101. Ibid.; "Nichols Night Time – The Path to Day Time Success," *Nichols News*, Vol. XXXIII, No. 1, February 1979, 1.
102. *Nichols College Catalog, 1984–1987*, 90.

103. *Nichols College Bulletin, 1982–1984*, 90.
104. Memo, Warren to Conrad, August 17, 2011, NCA.
105. Alumni Survey, 1995–1996, 3.
106. Nichols History Questionnaire, January 31, 2007.
107. Engh, "End of Semester Enrollment," Office of the Associate Dean for Academic Administration and Records, Nichols College, Conrad Hall, Center Road, Dudley, Mass.
108. Lowell C. Smith, "State of the College," *Nichols News*, Vol. 18, No. 1, Winter 1993, 2.
109. "President Smith to Retire in 1996," *Nichols News, Newsletter*, Vol. 20, No. 1, Winter 1995, 1.
110. *Bison*, March 15, 1979, 10.
111. Merri Ford, "Farewell President Smith," *Bison*, February 3, 1995, 1.
112. *Nichols News*, Vol. 21, No. 2, Spring 1996, 2.
113. "The President's Challenge," *Nichols News*, Vol. XXXII, No. 4, December 1979, 10.
114. *The Journal*, March 15, 1979, 10.
115. Ibid., 1.
116. Editor, "Smith Orders SGA Audit of *The Journal*," *Journal*, October 8, 1979, 1.
117. *The Journal*, September 6, 1979, 5.
118. "Academic Freedom and Tenure," ACADEME, May 1980, 207–212.
119. Jean Cardinale, "President Utters Controversial Words," *Bison*, March 12, 1993, 3.
120. Smith, "A Milestone, Central New England Colleges," *Bison*, October 25, 1988, 1–3; "A Tough Lesson for Nichols," *Business Worcester*, August 7, 1989.
121. *Nichols College Bison*, October 25, 1988, 1.
122. Engh, "End of Semester Enrollment,"Office of Associate Dean for Academic Administration and Records, Nichols College, Conrad Hall, Center Road, Dudley, Mass.
123. President Lowell C. Smith, "State of the College, 1983," Alumni Update, 2.
124. "The College's Best Fall," *Nichols News*, Vol. 14, No. 4, Fall 1989, 1.
125. "President Smith to Retire in 1996," *Nichols News, Newsletter*, Vol. 20, No. 1, Winter 1995, 6.
126. Ibid.

CHAPTER 8 ~ AT THE END OF THE TWENTIETH CENTURY

1. Nichols Junior College, "Announcement," May 1931, Folder 513, NCA.
2. Minutes, "Special Committee Report," Nichols Junior College Board of Trustees, May 14, 1955, President's Office, Nichols College, Center Road, Dudley, Mass.
3. Conrad, *Nichols Academy*, 17.
4. "Meet the Professor," *The Nichols Alumnus*, Vol. IV, No. 1, January 1950, 8.
5. David W. Breneman, *Liberal Arts Colleges; Thriving, Surviving, or Endangered* (Washington, D.C.: The Brookings Institution, 1994), 12.
6. James Martin, James E. Samuels & Associates, *Turnaround: Leading Stressed Colleges and Universities to Excellence* (Baltimore: The Johns Hopkins University Press, 2009), 3, 14.
7. Class Notes, John Durney, "Class of 1956," *Nichols College Magazine*, Winter 2007, 36.

8. Breneman, *Liberal Arts Colleges*, 12.
9. Ibid., 13.
10. Dorothy E. Finnegan, "Opportunity Knocked: The Origins of the Contemporary Comprehensive Colleges and Universities," *New England Resource Center for Higher Education Publications*, Paper 6, 1991.
11. "Classification Description," at //classifications,carnegiefoundation.org/descriptions/ugrad_program.php.
12. Ruth B. Cowan, Ph.D., "Prescription for Small-College Turnaround," *Change*, Vol. 25.1 (January - February 1993), 30; see also, www://go.galegroup.com/ps/retrieve.do?sgHitCountType=None&sort=DA-SORT&inPS=tr...,3.
13. *Nichols News*, Vol. 22, No. 1, Fall 1996, 12.
14. For another example, see Anne Colby, Thomas Ehrlich, et al, *Rethinking Undergraduate Business Education; Liberal Learning for the Profession* (San Francisco, CA: Jossey-Bass), 2011.
15. For a review of the athletic program in the first decade of the 21st Century, see "A Decade of Athletics at Nichols College," *Nichols College Magazine*, Spring 2010, 2–7.
16. Catalog, *Nichols Junior College, 1934–35*, 17.
17. *Nichols College Catalog, 1974–75*, 85; "Meet the New Bison," *Nichols College Magazine*, Vol. 4, No. 2, Fall/Winter 2009, 5.
18. *Bison*, December 6, 2004, 1; *The Nichols College Newspaper*, Vol. 1, Issue No. 1, December 2008, 1.
19. Michael G. Ash, "Nichols Sesquicentennial Anniversary Highlighted by Academic Convocation," *Bison*, May 14, 1965, 1; "Loyalty, Service, and Culture," *The Nichols Bison*, April 24, 1965, 1.
20. Neil Howe and William Strauss in *Millennials Rising: The Next Great Generation* (New York: Vintage Books, 2000), 4–5.
21. Ibid., 352.
22. Morley Winagrad and Michael D. Hais, *Millennial Momentum: How a New Generation is Remaking America* (New Brunswick, N.J.: Rutgers University Press, 2011), 25.
23. Joe Guy, "Guests on Campus. . . . The Good, the Bad, the Ugly," *The Bison*, April 12, 2004, 2.
24. The *Bison*, March 1, 2004, 1.
25. Tim Powell, "Stop Complaining! There's Plenty Good to Talk About ," The *Bison*, September 23, 1998, 2.
26. Ruth B. Cowan, Ph.D., "Prescription for Small-College Turnaround," *Change*, Vol. 25.1 (January - February 1993), 30.

APPENDIX A

Programs in Business Administration: New Hampton (1930–1931) and Nichols Junior College (1933–1934 and 1942–1943)

1930–1931 New Hampton Junior College of Business Administration Program

First Year Required Courses	Second Year Required
Accounting I	Accounting II
Business Law I	Business Law II
Economics I	Economics II
Psychology I	Psychology II
Business Administration I	Business Administration II
English I	English II
Finance	

Electives: Salesmanship, Advertising, Credits and Collections

1933–1934 Nichols Junior College of Business Administration and Executive Training

First Year Required Courses		Second Year Required	
Accounting I	3 periods a week	Accounting II	3 periods a week
Business Law I	3	Business Law II	3
Economics I	3	Economics II	2
English I	3	English II	3
Public Speaking	1	Finance I	3
		Ethics	1

Electives: Psychology I & II; Plant Management; Business Administration; Journalism; Salesmanship; Real Estate; Advertising; Insurance; Credits and Collections; French; Spanish; Business Mathematics; Banking; Marketing; Political Science; Contemporary Civilization; Marketing II.

Continued

1942–1943 Nichols Junior College of Business Administration and Executive Training

First Year

Required	First Semester	Second Semester	
Accounting I	3 hours	Accounting II or Financial Statement Analysis	3 hours
Economics I	3	Economics II	3
English I	3	English II	3
Business Law I	3	Business Law II	3
Mathematics I	3	Mathematics II	3
Psychology I	3	Psychology II	3
Public Speaking I	1	Public Speaking II	1
Typewriting *	4	* Elective may be substituted if preliminary test satisfactory.	

Second Year

Required	First Semester	Second Semester	
Accounting III	3	Accounting IV	3 hours
English III	3	English IV	3
Ethics III	1	Ethics IV	1
Finance III or	3	Finance IV or	3
Marketing III	3	Marketing IV	3
News Analysis	1	News Analysis	1
Psychology III	2	Psychology IV	2

Electives: Advertising; American Business Leadership; American Economic History; Banking, Theory and Practice; Cost Accounting; Credit Management; Industrial Management; Insurance; International Economics; Journalism; Labor Problems; Political Science; Real Estate; Recent Economic Trends; Salesmanship; Shorthand; Statistics and Forecasting.

Sources: Catalogues: *New Hampton School, New Hampton Junior College of Business Administration, 1930–1931; Nichols Junior College, 1933–34*, 15; Ibid., 1942–43, 25.

APPENDIX B

Memories of the Hurricane of '38

Ken Thompson '39 contacted his fellow classmates recently to exchange memories of the great hurricane of 1938 which pounded Southern New England mercilessly. Ken penned the following account of the disaster using those anecdotes. The date was Wednesday, Sept. 21.

7:30 a.m. - President James L. Conrad started over to his office in Budleigh, noting that the rain had stopped, finally. Those Nichols students who had volunteered yesterday to help fill sandbags and stack them up along the banks of the Quinebaug River the day before must have done a fine job, by and large, because the ultimate conclusion was that the normally placid stream had stayed within the sandbag dikes.

1:15 p.m. - Coach Waterfield, who lived in Worcester called the soccer team captain, Dick "Red" Whitney to say that practice was cancelled because of the field conditions.

1:30 p.m. - Tommy Gross and Jim Hanan decided that the weather was still too bad to do anything outdoors and that it would be fun to take in the current offering at the Star Theatre in Webster.

2:30 p.m. - Athletic Director Larry Sullivan walked out of the gymnasium, crossed the road, and went down to take a look at the football field to see if the team could practice without chopping up the turf too much. His conclusion: If they stay out of the low corner near the clubhouse, it would be O.K.

3:15 p.m. - Most of the football squad was out on the field: Tex Holloway, Punchy Reddy, Bob Sparks, Bickie White, Reed Shaw, Gig Sanborn, Irv Shiner and Johnny Cole were in the lead as Coach Hal Chalmers ordered a couple of laps to loosen everyone up.

4:15 p.m. - Larry Sullivan was back on the field talking to Hal and Ralph, suggesting perhaps it would be smart to move the team indoors to finish off the practice for the day. The wind was really blowing at gale force. Buck Stark, Dirk Brinckerhoff, Bob Eastwood, Ned Ostby and Bob Union led the squad back to the gym. A shed roof from the house across the street from Pop Cummings' place suddenly came flying off and headed in the general direction of the clubhouse. No more practice this day!

President Conrad arrived at the gym from his Budleigh Hall office and directed everyone back to their dorms as fast as possible. A radio report had just picked up reports of a major hurricane hitting the Long Island and New England coasts and everyone was battening down the hatches.

4:20 p.m. - Tommy Gross and Jim Hana were waiting for the exciting climax to the movie they had gone to. All of a sudden, the screen went dark and the ushers came in with their flashlights to advise everyone to leave the theatre. Tommy and Jim were really ticked off because they didn't even get their quarters back!

4:22 p.m. - Bill Carter decided to move his car out of the old carriage shed turned garage for he felt that the old building with its open front might collapse under the force of the winds. He drove his car out onto the athletic field, but a large branch flew off one of the big trees, smashing into his car. The old garage was unharmed.

4:25 p.m. - Paul "Buck" Glenny, Johnny Cole and Frank Cinquemani, having gotten out of their football gear, showered and rapidly dressed, left the gym to head to Conant Hall (then a dormitory). As they passed the old Academy Building, Johnny called their attention to a strange noise. Looking up, it appeared that the gabled roof over the classroom section was lifting up ever so slightly and coming down on the brick supporting wall. They didn't have time to stay for the winds were building up to 80-90 miles per hour and they simply wanted to reach a safe haven.

4:30 p.m. - "Punchy" Reddy, "Buck" Stark and Ken Thompson made their way out of the gym along with the rest of the football team, and with a unified effort, made it safely to Budleigh. Mr. Conrad grabbed hold of Ken, told him to get some rain gear, and be ready to take messages to the various campus buildings. He figured that Ken, the 250-pound tackle, just couldn't be blown away - even by this storm. The noise outside was getting louder!

The roots of a huge tree dwarf a student after the winds blew through Dudley Hill.

The roof of Academy Hall sustained heavy damage from the storm.

4:35 p.m. Ken was dispatched to Merrill Hall to pass the word on to Ralph Johnson, the resident instructor, that no one was to leave the building. He then fought his way up the hill to Conant and passed on the same word to John Burke. Ken managed to get to the lee side of the wall along the road and got a breather for a moment, after climbing up and over the trunks of two of the great uprooted trees. As Ken passed between the Academy Building and Conant he could see the heavy slate roof tiles flying of the auditorium side of the roof. These flying missiles were in

See page 2

263

From Page 1

many instances burying themselves deep in the wet ground. In fact, the strike area looked like a miniature graveyard with many tombstones askew. He made it to Conant, delivered his message and took a breather.

4:40 p.m.- The large tree on the south side of the dining hall gave up its struggle with the wind and came crashing down on the southwest corner of the building, damaging the roof at that point and blocking the fire escape.

4:45 p.m. - Things were really getting out of hand on Dudley Hill - trees were falling all over campus and on the town road. Other trees had been "topped" by the storm, power and telephone lines were down, debris of all sorts was whipping around. Dudley Hill was an isolated community. Ken Thompson left Conant and started back to Budleigh. As he fought his way past the Academy Building, he looked up in time to see bricks falling out of the wall near the peak of the gable. The roof was actually lifting up and pounding down on the wall. The wind seemed to be peaking now at well over 100 miles per hour. A full 15 minutes was consumed on the return trip.

4:50 p.m. One of the Cellar Rats, listening to his car radio, came back into Budleigh and reported that it was indeed a full-scale hurricane and it had slammed into Long Island and then the coastlines of Connecticut, Rhode Island and Massachusetts, causing untold damage. A tidal wave had hit Providence. A fire raged out of control in downtown New London. Fire Island was totally isolated and had been breached in several places. Train service on the New Haven Railroad was severed by boats, buildings, cars, trucks and other debris on the tracks. Numerous deaths had been reported and rivers and streams, already swollen from days of rain, overflowed their banks.

5 p.m. - Someone in Budleigh yelled out that there was a geyser of water shooting up in the air near the Webster-Dudley Country Club. It was easily seen that a fallen tree had sheared a fire hydrant. Soon water pressure dropped all over campus.

5:45 p.m. The messenger service went into action again. Mr. Conrad recalled previous disasters in the college's past like the fire that destroyed the original Budleigh mansion and the subsequent fire that took out the then-new dining hall. Fire watches were set up in all dormitories. Students were assigned in shifts to keep an eye out for fires or any other major building damage so as to be ready to spread the alarm and evacuate everyone if the need came. When Ken arrived back from his trip he reported that Academy Building had caved in over the classrooms, a lot of the roof had disappeared and the bell tower might go at any time as there was a crack developing through the brick courses on the front and south sides.

6:30 p.m. - The gale forced winds abated a bit, allowing Hal Chalmers and crew to pick up the meals the kitchen had prepared and start deliveries. While it wasn't the most sumptuous meal ever served at Nichols, it was probably the most appreciated.

9 p.m. - The winds dropped considerably and the tension level lowered. No one was allowed out of the dorms, however, as the danger of flying tree limbs and downed power lines presented hazards too great to take a chance in the dark. By 10 p.m., with no power for lights or the radio, everyone settled down for a restless night's sleep.

Thursday morning, Sept. 22, arrived bright and beautiful, as if nothing had happened the day before. But what a mess was to bee seen. Academy Building was a total disaster - the roof was gone over the first floor and the classrooms were smashed to pieces. The bell tower, while still standing, had a very obvious crack all away around near the window level. Over 138 trees were down on campus or along the road in front of the private residences and the Black Tavern. Anything that was not nailed or tied down had been carried off by the wind.

10 a.m. - Road crews could be seen down in the valley, working their way up the road, cutting the big trees with two-man saws. Tractors pushed the big sections of tree trunks to the side of the road. Progress was slow.

The dining hall's fire escape was blocked by a fallen tree

11 a.m. - President Conrad made the announcement that the college was to be closed down for two weeks and suggested that the students go home for that period. The dorms would be closed during that time and and suggested that the students go home for that period. The dorms would be closed during that time and other than the student watchmen - Cinque at Conant and Ken at Budleigh, everyone was to leave unless they wanted to work on cleanup crews. There were few takers.

F.X. Lalibertie started working on the restoration of the Academy Building and other structures. The bell was removed from the old bell tower before it was razed. Plans were rapidly drawn up for a new classroom wing and a small cupola replacing the bell tower.

Classroom space was grabbed where ever it could be found and in two weeks, the college was ready to go back into operation. By the time the students returned to the campus after the Christmas vacation, the redesigned Academy Building was ready to go with its new second floor classrooms and the school was back to normal.

It took a long time for the scars of the storm to disappear. Everyone who was present will always remember that storm!

Several cars were reduced to scrap metal because of falling trees.

Source: *Nichols News*, Vol. 18, No. 3, Summer, 1993, 1–2.

APPENDIX C

Statement of Institutional Purpose as Described in Applicable Charters: 1941, 1958, 1971, 1974

From the Charter of Nichols Junior College, 23rd day of December 1941.

. . . .

To establish and maintain an educational institution of general educational purposes, and more particularly to provide courses for executive and business training; to own, rent, lease, buy or sell real estate for all purposes incidental to the carrying out of all other purposes for which the corporation is organized; to establish and maintain scholarships providing for free tuition in every educational institution established and maintained by the corporation for worthy students, and more particularly those students residing in the Town of Dudley, Massachusetts; to establish and maintain a library for the benefit of the students of any educational institution established and maintained by the corporation and for the gratuitous use of the citizens of the Town of Dudley; to provide lecture courses and other methods of promoting the ethical, social and intellectual culture in the community in which any educational institution established and maintained by the corporation is located; and to do all other acts which may be or are authorized under the provisions of Chapter 180 of the General Laws of the Commonwealth of Massachusetts, as embodied in the Tercentenary Edition and any amendments thereto now existing or which may be hereafter enacted.

For Nichols College of Business Administration, 10th day of May 1958.

. . . .

That the purposes of the corporation be changed by adding the authority to grant the degree of Bachelor in Business Administration to students judged by the Administration and Faculty as having successfully completed the required four year program and having further demonstrated to the Administration and the Faculty, qualities of good character, citizenship and gentlemanliness.

Continued

For Nichols College.

. . . .

1. That the purpose of the corporation be changed by adding thereto the authority to grant the degrees of Bachelor of Science in Business Administration, Bachelor of Science in Public Administration or Bachelor of Arts to students judged by the Faculty and Administration as having completed successfully the appropriate program of studies. (1971)

2. That the purpose of the corporation be changed by adding thereto the authority to grant the degree of Master of Business Administration to students judged by the Faculty and Administration as having completed successfully the appropriate program of studies, and to grant honorary doctorates to individuals deemed by the Board of Trustees to be worthy of that honor. (1974)

Source: Report on "The Governance of Nichols College," November 25, 1974, in the Office of the President of Nichols College, Conrad Hall, Center Road, Dudley, Mass.

APPENDIX D

Nichols College Athletic Hall of Fame Members, 1972–

Name	Class	Sport	Year Inducted
Joseph W. Donahoe	'32	Football, Basketball	1972
Murray T. Potter	'33	Basketball, Baseball	1972
Hal Chalmers	'36	Football, Baseball, Basketball	1972
Edward A. Sherman, Jr.	'36	Football, Basketball, Tennis	1972
John W. Dalzell	'37	Football, Ice Hockey, Baseball	1972
William R. Spilman	'38	Basketball, Baseball	1972
J. Barry Pickford	'38	Football, Baseball	1986
Frank V. Cinquemani	'39	Football, Baseball	1981
Paul A. Glenny	'39	Football, Basketball, Baseball	1984
John Heath	'40	Soccer, Basketball	1988
Alfred E. Monahan	'41	Football, Basketball	1972
Oliver Birckhead	'42	Football, Ice Hockey	2006
Philip C. Gould	'42	Ice Hockey, Baseball	1976
James D. Houston	'47	Ice Hockey, Baseball	1974
James F. Pritchard	'47	Track	1979
Allan P. Dunn	'50	Football, Track	1972
Wilbur W. Whedon	'50	Basketball, Golf	1972
William A. Ward	'50	Lacrosse	1973
Peter Stearns	'50	Football, Baseball	1975
Robert Risk, Jr.	'50	Football, Basketball, Baseball	1975
Donald Coyle	'51	Basketball, Baseball	1979
Donald N. Laboissonniere	'52	Football, Lacrosse	1976
Vincent J. LoBello	'52	JV Basketball, Lacrosse	1978
John P. Howes	'53	Football, Lacrosse	1972
Anthony Venezia	'54	Basketball, Baseball	1978
Alan J. Dwyer	'55	Basketball, Baseball	1981
Jeremiah F. Murphy	'55	Baseball	1983
Leon S. Marshall	'55	Basketball, Baseball	1985
George W. Penniman	'55	Football, Baseball	1994
Richard P. Kowalczyk	'56	Baseball	1993
C. Edward Hjelte, Jr.	'58	Track, Tennis, Basketball	1972
Robert Miller	'61	Basketball	1987
Stephen H. Smith	'61	Basketball, Baseball	1995
Rene T. Langevin	'62	Football, Basketball	1978
Paul E. Zimmerman	'62	Soccer, Ice Hockey	1981
D. Fred O'Connor	'64	Basketball	1974
Edward S. Kunkel, Jr.	'64	Football	1984
Vincent Becker	'64	Football	1988
Henri M. David, Jr.	'64	Ice Hockey	1997
James E. Robinson	'65	Lacrosse, Ice Hockey	1972
Charles T. Kaull, Jr.	'65	Baseball	1991
Robert L. Ansalone	'65	Cross Country, Lacrosse, Football	1992
Curtis A. Burhoe	'66	Football	1973
Jesse Rulli	'66	Basketball, Baesball	1973

Continued

267

Name	Class	Sport	Year Inducted
Jon Gilbert	'66	Football	1975
Phillip E. Collins	'66	Soccer, Ice Hockey, Golf	1980
Alan Malkasian	'66	Baseball	1989
Donn Norton	'66	Soccer	1990
John Cygielnik	'66	Baseball	2011
Robert H. Kullas	'67	Football, Baseball	1993
William Matulewicz	'67	Soccer	2005
Larry G. Crooker	'67	Cross Country, Track, Swimming	1972
Michael J. Carney	'68	Football, Baseball	1976
Robert L. Rulli	'68	Basketball, Baseball	1980
Jeffrey P. Gould	'68	Soccer, Ice Hockey, Tennis	1982
Richard J. Patterson	'68	Track	1983
John R. Schunder	'68	Lacrosse	1992
John A. Nelson	'68	Football, Baseball	1996
J. Clifford Dietrich	'69	Football	2007
Donald A. MacQuarrie	'69	Track	1978
Rodney Swain	'71	Baseball, Soccer	2003
Peter B. Bromley, III	'72	Soccer, Tennis	1977
Bruce Ziemski	'72	Golf	1979
Harvey E. Roberts, Jr.	'72	Soccer, Track	1980
James P. Duchesneau	'72	Football, Track	1981
Bobby G. Payton	'72	Basketball	1983
Mark L. Love	'72	Basketball	1985
David R. Pearson	'72	Lacrosse	1994
Kenneth F. Morris	'73	Ice Hockey	1981
Francis B. Keefe	'73	Baseball, Soccer, Ice Hockey	1982
Eugene Carlo	'73	Football, Track	1984
Frank R. Burns, Jr.	'74	Football	1980
Joseph P. Tokarz	'74	Football, Lacrosse	1982
Gerald N. Millette	'74	Soccer, Baseball	1985
Charles Peterson	'74	Football, Lacrosse	1987
Gary McNulty	'74	Basketball	1989
Mark J. Lempicki	'75	Football	1981
Michael R. Shea	'75	Swimming	1983
Richard M. Ferraro	'75	Football, Baseball	1984
David Hale	'75	Ice Hockey, Lacrosse	1989
Paul F. Hill, Jr.	'75	Football, Baseball	1990
James "Jimmy" Siekierski	'75	Baseball	2001
John Levandowski	'76	Football, Lacrosse	1982
David A. French	'76	Lacrosse	1983
Michael F. Hackenson	'76	Football, Baseball	1985
Donald M. Leonard, Jr.	'76	Baseball, Football	1986
Shawn McAvoy	'76	Football, Ice Hockey, Lacrosse	1987
Don Eklund	'76	Golf, Basketball	1988
Robert J. Daigle	'76	Football	1992
Peter F. Coyle	'76	Football, Baseball	2004
Gary Buma	'76	Baseball	2010
Robert Reynolds	'76	Ice Hockey	2011
Mark F. Brisebois	'77	Football, Track	1985
Edmund H. Fournier	'77	Football, Track, Baseball, Tennis	1986
Michael A. Keefe	'77	Football, Baseball	1986
Peter A. Lieneck	'77	Football, Baseball	1993
John R. Calcagni, Jr.	'77	Football	1998
Frank DeRosa	'77	Football	1999
Pat Clarke	'77	Football, Lacrosse	2011
Marc Dupuis	'78	Basketball	1988

Appendix D

Name	Class	Sport	Year Inducted
Charles 'Wes' Gregory	'78	Football	2012
Martin J. Power	'78	Football	1996
Dave DelMonico	'78	Ice Hockey	2002
William T. Valentas	'78	Ice Hockey	2007
Michael Downing	'79	Ice Hockey, Lacrosse	2006
Gary S. Guglielmello	'79	Football	1991
Michael Villanova	'79	Golf	1998
James Rossini	'79	Football	1999
David P. Hackenson	'79	Football, Baseball	2000
Kevin B. Latraverse	'79	Football	2008
Thomas J. Keefe III	'80	Soccer, Baseball	1990
Dave Rice	'80	Ice Hockey, Baseball	1999
Charles O. Zettergren	'80	Football, Track	1992
Andrew "Andy" Higgins	'80	Football, Baseball	2003
Jack R. Kleminich	'81	Baseball	1991
Christopher J. McWade	'81	Ice Hockey	2008
David M. Whitney	'81	Football	2009
Ellen O'Connor Duggan	'82	Field Hockey, Basketball	1987
Edward J. Zywien	'82	Football	1991
Sandra "Sandy" (Lewis) Crory	'82	Field Hockey, Basketball, Softball	2001
Nancy Rossini	'83	Basketball, Softball	1988
Kim Wentworth Grady	'83	Basketball, Softball	1989
Francis X. Tarpey, Jr.	'83	Football	1994
Richard M. Lengieza	'83	Basketball, Golf	1995
David R. Delisle	'83	Soccer, Basketball	1997
Vincent T. Miller	'83	Basketball	2005
James Gleason	'84	Football, Track	1989
Peter Dodier	'84	Football, Baseball	1990
Peter Holden	'84	Football	1995
Doug Chamblin	'84	Football	2002
Amy B. Bernard	'86	Field Hockey, Basketball, Softball	1991
James R. Giroux	'86	Track	2005
Laura Chalmers Bray	'87	Field Hockey, Softball	1992
Thomas D. Kirby	'87	Baseball	1993
David Gallagher	'88	Football	2001
Lisa M. Gionet	'88	Basketball, Softball	1993
Michelle Sinacola Dick	'88	Field Hockey, Softball	1994
Kevin J. Gabrielian	'88	Basketball	1994
Mark A. Winship	'88	Baseball	1997
Robin L. Provencher O'Laughlin	'88	Softball	2000
Eric Kimes	'89	Football	1998
Steven C. Gallo	'89	Football	2009
Stacey M. Kiely	'89	Women's Basketball, Softball	1995
Kittredge B. Holmes	'90	Football, Lacrosse	1996
Deidra A. Reed Davis	'91	Basketball, Softball	1997
Kristen Allen Belbin	'91	Softball	1998
Jeff Innamorati	'91	Football, Baseball	2001
Christopher Galligan	'91	Basketball	2010
Linda Rose Roseberry	'92	Soccer, Basketball, Softball	1998
John Lamontagne	'92	Football, Baseball	1999
Sandra Rose Regan	'93	Soccer, Basketball, Softball	1999
William J. Malaguti	'93	Football, Basketball	2000
Otis Rankins	'93	Football, Baseball	2003
Mark A. Reino	'93	Lacrosse	2004

Continued

Name	Class	Sport	Year Inducted
Susan E. Drummey Daly	'94	Field Hockey, Basketball, Softball	2000
William Carven	'94	Football, Lacrosse	2002
Dino Campopiano	'94	Football, Baseball	2005
William "Billy" Collins	'95	Basketball	2001
Ed Perrotti	'95	Ice Hockey	2012
Trisha Shimkus	'95	Softball	2002
Kerry Sheehy Randolph	'95	Field Hockey, Softball	2003
Michelle Byrnes	'96	Soccer, Softball	2002
Kendra Cestone	'97	Soccer, Basketball, Softball	2006
Amy M. (Lachenal) Bartlett	'97	Softball	2007
Stacey Rosa	'97	Soccer, Basketball, Softball	2003
David Sokolnicki	'97	Football, Basketball	2004
Anthony DePasquale	'98	Basketball, Baseball	2010
Christie L. (Carlo) Stephos	'98	Field Hockey, Track	2004
Kristina L. Katori	'98	Basketball, Softball	2005
Jen Kinsman	'98	Soccer, Track	2006
Jennifer M. (Eaton) Kilbride	'99	Soccer, Basketball, Track, Softball	2009
Julie M. O'Brien Barker	'00	Field Hockey, Softball	2008
Ryan J. Ankstitus	'01	Basketball, Tennis	2008
Mayles M. Fayle	'01	Football	2007
Matthew Fox	'01	Football	2006
T. LeVar Gary	'02	Football, Track, Lacrosse	2010
Brian Cardoza	'03	Basketball	2012
Kristine O'Coin	'03	Soccer, Basketball	2011
Brian P. St. Peter	'03	Football	2008
Benjamin A. Karter	'04	Football	2009
Natalie (Lavin) Soffen	'04	Basketball, Soccer, Softball	2009
Lisa (Benson) Summers	'05	Soccer	2010
Michael Carven	'06	Football, Lacrosse	2011
2002 Women's Soccer Team	(HOH)	Soccer	2012
Colonel James L. Conrad	(HON)	Founding President	1972
Dr. Samuel B. Wylie	(HON)	Lacrosse Coach, Forestry	1986
Bernard Bazinet	(HON)	Golf Coach, Supporter	1990
Michael J. Vendetti	(HON)	Football Coach, Athletics Director	1996
Richard Scheffler	(HON)	Team Supporter	1999
E. Bates Craver	(HON)	Trainer	2000
Edward J. Socha	(HON)	Men's and Women's Tennis Coach	2004
Kenny Gray	(HON)	Field Maintenance	2006
Bruce Baker	(HON)	Sports Information Director	2007

HOH - Hall of Honor

Source: Nichols College Athletic Hall of Fame, Nichols website.

APPENDIX E

Four-Year Curriculum for Bachelor's Degree in Business Administration (1960)

FRESHMAN YEAR

Required	Hrs.	Sem.
English	3	2
Sociology	3	2
Economic History	3	2
Psychology	3	2
Mathematics of Business	3	2
Public Speaking	1	2
Physical Education	2	2
*Typewriting		
**Developmental Reading		
†Foundation Math of Business		
	18	

*Three periods weekly until qualified
**For students whose tests indicate need
†For students whose tests indicate need (non-credit)

SOPHOMORE YEAR

Required	Hrs.	Sem.
Economics, Principles	3	2
English	3	2
Accounting, Elementary	3	2
Political Science	3	2
Marketing, Principles	3	2
Management, Principles	3	2
	18	

JUNIOR YEAR

Finance Major

Required	Hrs.	Sem.
Financial Institutions	3	2
English	3	2
Accounting	4	2
	10	

Electives - 6 hours	Hrs.	Sem.
Auditing	3	2
Money and Banking	3	1
Statistics	3	2
Investment Analysis	3	2
Credit Management	3	1
Cost Accounting	3	2
Federal Income Tax	3	2
Business Fluctuations	3	2
Financial Statement Anal.	3	2
Business Machine Oper.	3	2

Management Major

Required	Hrs.	Sem.
Principles of Management	3	2
English	3	2
Financial Institutions	3	2
	9	

Electives - 9 hours	Hrs.	Sem.
Personnel Management and Labor Relations	3	2
Insurance	2	2
Transportation	2	2
Statistics	3	2
Purchasing	3	1
Business Fluctuations	3	2
Financial Statement Anal.	3	2
Business Machine Oper.	3	1
Real Estate	2	2
Management Field Trips		

Marketing Major

Required	Hrs.	Sem.
Principals of Marketing	3	2
English	3	2
Financial Institutions	3	2
	9	

Electives - 9 hours	Hrs.	Sem.
Retail Merchandising	3	1
Advertising	2	2
Insurance	2	2
Transportation	2	2
Statistics	3	2
Purchasing	3	1
Mkt. and Sales Research	3	2
Business Fluctuations	3	2
Financial Statement Anal.	3	2
Business Machine Oper.	3	2

Non-Technical Electives

	Hrs.	Sem.
The Sciences in Modern Living	3	2
The Development of the Drama	2	1
Comparative Religions	2	1
Modern Literature	3	1
Art Appreciation	3	1
Ethics	1	1
The Modern Novel	2	1
Human Relations	2	1
News Analysis	1	1

SENIOR YEAR

Required	Hrs.	Sem.
Law	3	2
*Seminar Clinic	3	2
Thesis	2	2
Logic	3	2
Free Electives	6	2
	17	

*Seminar Clinic meets two hours, three times weekly.

Source: *Nichols Alumnus*, June 1960, 6.

APPENDIX F

Major Institutional, Organizational, Academic Restructuring Issues Discussed, 1958~1966

Institutional
1958   Nichols Junior College of Business Administration and Executive Training to Nichols College of Business Administration

Administrative
1959   From an Administrative Committee to two Committees (Administrative and Academic)
1966   Administrative Committee (meeting daily) including
      President, Deans, Director of Forestry School, Administrative Assistant, Treasurer
    Academic Committee
      Foregoing group plus Department Chairmen (meeting weekly)
        "   "   " Dormitory Directors (meeting bi-monthly)
    Faculty (meeting once a month)

Administration
1959   Dean Leech resigns, becomes Chair of Marketing, George F. Chisholm becomes Dean
1961   Position of Dean of Faculty created, filled by Charles M. Quinn, Jr.
1962   Dean Chisholm resigns, becomes Chair of Humanities
1962   Robert H. Eaton becomes Dean of Men

Faculty
1959   Full-Time: 20   Part-Time: 7
1966   Full-Time: 33   Part-Time: 4

Faculty Issues And Benefits Formally Considered
1959   Salary Schedule, Group Life Insurance, Retirement, Medical Insurances
1960   Making land available for Faculty for homes
1961   Determination of Individual Faculty Rankings
1962   Defining Tenure
1963   Strengthening Faculty
1964   Free tuition for dependents
1964   Sabbaticals authorized

Curriculum

1959	Introduced four-year program in Business Administration awarding BBA Majors: Finance, Management, Marketing (Accounting added 1962)
1963	New Forestry majors added: Forest, Park, and Wildlife Management

Additions To Curriculum

1959	Required Summer Work program for two summers
1959	Evening Division with Bachelor Degree courses
1961	European Study Tour begins (can substitute for summer work)
1962	Thesis requirement introduced
1962	Business Clinic becomes part of curriculum

Accreditation

1965	Accreditation received in December 1965, with some minor adjustments

---

Sources: Minutes, Nichols College of Business Administration, Trustee Meetings, 1958–1966; *The Nichols Bison*, 1956–1966; Nichols *Yearbooks*, 1958–1966; Nichols College of Business Administration, *Bulletin*, Catalog Issue, 1958–1966.

INDEX

AACSB. *See* Association to Advance Collegiate Schools of Business (AACSB), also American Association of Collegiate Schools of Business
Academic standards, 70–71
Academy Building, 15, *16, 84, 118*
Academy Hall, *84, 86*
Accounting course, 45, 47, 111, 160
Accreditation
   New England Association of Colleges and Secondary schools later New England Association of Schools and Colleges and, 79
   Nichols College of Business Administration, 122, 134, 137, 154–157, 273
   Nichols Junior College, 141
Accrediting agency for business education programs, 23
Administration
   broadening concept of, 168
   Nichols College, 177–178, *178*, 202–204
   Nichols College of Business Administration, 127, 155, *157*, 272
   Nichols Junior College, 37, 92, 103
   post-World War II, 92
Administrative Building, *142*
Admissions Center, *216*
Adult education program, 111, 128, 156, 209–211, 223, 227
Advisory Council, 69, 99, 120
Advisory Council Day, 103–104, 168
Alcohol, on campus, 70, 166
Alcohol policy, 215
All-male private schools, development of, 24–26

Alpha Phi Chapter of Delta Mu Delta, 215
Alumni Associates, 196
Alumni Bulletin, 154
Alumni Magazine, 115
Alumni Memorial Hall, 93–96, 95, 174
Alumni support, 227–228
Alumni Tower, 106
Amen, Harlan Page, 29, 30
American Association of Collegiate Schools of Business (AACSB), 23, 175
American Association of Junior Colleges, 28–29, 138
American Association of University Professors, 190, 212, 213
American Higher Education; a History (Lucas), 204
American School Foundation, 26
Amos Tuck School of Business Administration, 103, 105, 134
Anderson, John, 205
Annhurst College, 215, 222
Annual Northeastern Intercollegiate Woodmen's competition, 136
Aristotle, 1–2
Arnold, Nason, 83
"Around the Campus" column, 164, *165*
Associate of Business Administration (ABA), 44, 49, 59, 72, 210, 226
Association of American Colleges, 136
Association to Advance Collegiate Schools of Business (AACSB), 152
Athletic and recreational center, Nichols College of Business Administration, 125–127
Athletic Council, 68

Note: Numbers in italics indicate photos.

275

Athletic facilities, 226
Athletic fields, *66, 171, 180*
    construction of Nichols Junior College, 35–36
    off Tanyard Road, 106, *107*, 108
Athletics, 98, 99, 227, 229–230. *See also individual sports*
    blue ribbon committee on, 207–209
    continued importance of, 115
    Nichols College, 171–173
    Nichols College of Business Administration, 130, 157
    Nichols Junior College of Business Administration and Executive Training, 12, 60, 63–68, 83
    team nickname, 64–65
    women and, 171, 173, *173*
Auditorium, 123, *126, 216*
Awan, M. Mahmood, 222

Babson College, 152
Bachelor of Arts (BA), 161, 162, 226
Bachelor of Business Administration (BBA), 95, 117, 225, 227
Bachelor of Science in Business Administration (BSBA), 161, 162, 210, 226
Bachelor of Science in Public Administration (BSPA), 161, 162, 226
Bachelor's degree in business administration
    curriculum for, 271
Baker, Bruce, *220*
Bar, on-campus, 166, 170
Barnard, Henry, 14
Barney School of Business Administration, 154
Baseball team, 99, 130, 141
Basketball Court, *86*
Basketball games, *219*
Basketball teams
    men's, 77–78, 88, 99, 115, 130, 141, *219*
    women's, 171, 173, *173, 219*
Bazinet, Wilfred P., 44–45
Bazinet, Bernard (Bazzie), *146*
"Bazzie's" (Club House), 18, 42, *84, 87,* 106, *142,* 145, *146, 158, 163,* 223
Because It Is Mine (Emonds), 221
Belfry, 27

Bells
    Federal Reserve Bank of Boston, 106–107
    Nichols Academy, 93, *94*
Bennett, James Gordon, 21
Bentley University, 152
Beta Cella Rata, 68
Bethel Bible Institute, 19, 20, 34, 43
Big Brothers Big Sisters type program, 170
Bison Bowl, 123, 145, *147, 148,* 172
Bison (newspaper). *See also Budget* (newspaper); *Journal* (newspaper)
    announcing NCBA, *121*
    "Around the Campus" column, 164, *165*
    on becoming four-year college, 112, 120
    on capital campaign, 199
    on changes on campus, 130
    conflict with President Smith, 212–213
    on Davis Hall's opening, 200
    on end of forestry program, *156*
    name change of, 115
    on new programs 1974-1975, 162
    on PC Plan, 198
    on political leanings of students, 205
    on privilege of attending Nichols, 116
    on state of the College, 234
    on student activism, 167
    on student complaints, 206
    on student interests, 113
    student polls, 206
    on visiting lecturers, 192
"Bison" nickname, 65
"Bison's Den," 166, 222
Bison statue, 158, *158*
Black Tavern, 94–95, *142,* 222
Black Tavern Annex, *142*
Black Tavern Historical Society, 95, 222
Blake, W., 106
Blizzard of 1978, *179*
Blue Ribbon Committee on Nichols Athletics, 208, 230
Board of Collegiate Authority (Massachusetts), 8, 95–96, 112, 118, 120, 161
Booth, Henry, 37

Boston Globe, 198
Boston University College of Business Administration, 27, 28, 36
Bourassa, Annette, 27
Boyden, Elbridge, 15, 107
Boyden, Frank L., 30, 105
Boys Club, 138, 170
Bradford Junior College, 69, 88
Bradway, Edward C., 203
Breneman, David M., 230–231
Brinckerhoff, Dirk, 263
Broderick, Francis L., 192
Bromley, Peter, 221
Brooks, John E., 192, 208
Brothers Four concert, 135, *135*
Brown, Earl, 79–80
Brown University Yacht Club, 64
Bruce, Beulah M., 91
Bryant and Stratton, 21
Bryant College, 186, 187
Bryant University, 152
Buckley, James L., 170
Buckley Amendment, 170
Budget (newspaper), 68
    bridge game problem in, 83
    on extra-curricular activities and athletics
    on Budleigh Towers fire, 51
    on gas shortage and use of cars, 73
    on honors granted Nichols, 72
    lack of discussion of foreign policy in, 74
    name change, 115
    on Nichols as pioneering school, 61, 62
    on post-World War II reopening, 92
    on rules for students, 70, 71
    on student opinions, 96
Budleigh Hall, 17, *17*, 19, 34, 35, 51, 52, *57*, *87*, 107, 156, 200, 226
Budleigh Towers, 35, 40, 41, 43
    fire at, 50–51
"Buffaloes," 64–65
Buffalo nickel, *65*
Burhoe, Kurt, *131*
Burke, John, 263
Burnett, Austin C., 17
Burnett barn, 18
Bush, George, 233

Business curriculum, early
    core courses, 160
    New Hampton Junior College of Business Administration program, 28
    New Hampton's Commercial College, 23–24
    19th century, 21–22
    two-year colleges, 29
Business education
    circa 1958, 119–120
    emergence of, 12
    as higher education segment, 22–23
    19th century, 21–22
Business internship, 128
Business law course, 45
Butterfield, Paul, 169

Cafaro, Thomas R., 208
Calvo, J. Manuel, 39
Camera Club, 68
"Campaign for Nichols," 198–201, 214
Campus, redesign of, 226. *See also* College buildings/campus
Campus signs (1957), *91*
Cape Cod National Seashore Park, 132
Capital campaign, 214
Carlson, Edward, 137
Carnegie Foundation, 119
Carnegie Foundation for Advancement of Teaching, 231
Carney, Roger F. X., 202, *205*
Carter, Bill, 263
Carter, Jimmy, 164, 205
"Casino," 18
Cathedral College, 221
Central Association of Colleges (North Central Association of Colleges and Schools), 49
Central New England College (CNEC), 212, 213
Challenge swim, 211–212, *212*
Chalmers, Hal, *64*, *147*, *148*, *149*, *157*
    administrative committees and, 157
    administrative positions of, 103, *157*
    alumni association and, 104
    arrival at Nichols, 67–68
    Chalmers Circle, 145
    as coach, 115, 130

277

competition with four-year colleges and, 130
death of, 177, 207
dedication of athletic center to, 172
hurricane of 1938 and, 263, 264
military service, 77, 79–80, *80*
in Nichols Athletic Hall of Fame, 173
return to Nichols after war, 79–80, 81, 92
transition to four-year college and, 117, 120
Chalmers, Margaret Conrad, 141
Chalmers Circle, 145
Chalmers Field House, 42, 123, 171, *171, 172, 172, 181, 182,* 201, 208, 215, *219*
Charney, Jack, 208
Charters, 265–266
Cheerleaders, *218*
Chisholm, George F., 100, 127, *128*, 272
Chisholm House, 198, *216*, 223
Cinquemani, Frank, 263
"Circus in America," *195*
Civilian Aeronautics Administration, 75
Civilian Pilot Training Corps, 75, 75, 76, 88
Clark University, 25
Classical Course, Nichols Academy, 13
Club House (Bazzie's), 18, 42, *84, 87,* 106, *142,* 145, 158, *163,* 223
Coeducation
    Nichols Academy and, 57
    at Nichols College, 152, 158, 159, 161, 168–170, 207, 225
    public schools and, 24–25
Cohen, Arthur M., 186
Colby Academy/Colby School for Girls, 25
Colby Junior College, 69, 88
Cole, Johnny, 263
College buildings/campus, 93–96
    for Nichols College of Business Administration, 122–124
    projects (1950-1958), 105–108
College mug, *148*
College of Business Administration, Boston University, 27, 28, 38
College president, responsibilities of, 100
Collegiate Authority Committee, 176

Columbia University, 167
Committee on Committees, 190
Committees, faculty, 190
Community colleges, 7
Community service, 170
Community Union, *218*
Compensation, faculty, 190
Computer center, 196–198
Computers
    IBM 1130, 157, *163*
    PC Plan, 197–198, 211, 227
Conant, Hezekiah
    academy buildings/campus and, 1, 15–18, 41, 107, 122, 199, 226, 228
    death of, 17
    Nichols Academy and, 2, 3, 4, 14–15, 20, 58
    summer residence, 17, 50
Conant, Nelson, 105
Conant, Roger, 17
Conant Commons, well house, *218*
Conant estate, 34
Conant Hall, 15–16, 40, 51, 76, *84,* 124
Conant Library, 19, 20, 56, *87,* 123, *220*
Conant Library and Observatory, *1, 13, 15, 16,* 34, 41, *84,* 123
Conant Library in Academy Hall, *84*
Conant Memorial Church, *1, 13,* 17, 41, 69, 87
Conant Pond, 221
Concerts, 169
Conrad, Annette, 37, 52
Conrad, Catherine Kane, 26
Conrad, James L., 1, *33, 103, 139, 220,* 225
    on accreditation, 137
    administrative approach of, 29–30
    advisors to Nichols Junior College and, 37–38
    building projects, 52, 54, 105–106, 127, 226
    as coach and business program director, 26–27
    commitment to becoming four-year college, 45–46, 95–96, 111–112, 116
    on cultural dimension at Nichols, 192
    death of, 177
    educational philosophy, 36

education of, 26–27
Enlisted Reserve Corps and, 110
extracurricular activities and, 68
as founding head of Nichols Junior College, 3, 4, 5, 8
honorary Nichols doctorate, 221
honors given to, 138
hurricane of 1938 and, 263, 264
leadership style, 100–102
Merrill and, 39
message to Class of 1949, 98–99
at mid-point, 100–105
military service, 72, 73, 75–76, 78, *80*, 80–81, 88, 110
New Hampton Junior College of Business Administration program and, 19–20, 27–30
"New Plan," 32, 46, 101, 132
in Nichols Athletic Hall of Fame, 173
as partner in Nichols, Inc., 43, 54
plan for Nichols Junior College, 32
post-World War II reopening, 91–92
on practicum, 122
promotion of Nichols Junior College, 36
Quartermaster Corps and, 73
relationship between students and business schools, 119
relations with Academy trustees, 55
retirement of, 134, 137–140
ROTC request and, 109
sale of Academy campus to Nichols Junior College and, 57
on sesquicentennial, 135–136, 233
on student conduct and achievement, 70–71
transition to Nichols College of Business Administration and, 122
as trustee, 105
on veterans as students, 96
Conrad, James L., Jr., 177, *178*, 189, 192–193
Conrad, Margaret M., 37, 54, 68, 141
Conrad, Thomas H., 26
Conrad, William L., 27, 73
Conrad Hall, 106, *107*, 107–108, 132, 226
Conservation and forestry program, *110*, 110–111, 132–134, *133*, 145, 156, 227

The Conservative Mind (Kirk), 193
Continuing education program, 111, 128, 156, 209–211, 223, 227
Convocations, 68–69
Cooper, Al, 169
Corbin, Fred E., 38
Council for the Advancement of Small Colleges, 138
Coyle, Darcy C., 8, 100, 151, 174–179, *175, 220*, 225
  approach to presidency, 175–176
  college financial issues and, 175–176, 179, 187
  departure from Nichols, 179
  educational background, 175
  Faculty Policy Manual and, 190
  government regulation and, 230
  MBA program and, 176
  relationship with student body, 176–177
Crisis in the Academy (Lucas), 186
Cross, Gordon B., 8, 151, 153–159, *154, 157, 220*, 225
  approach to student problems, 164
  coeducation and, 168
  college financial issues and, 159, 174, 179
  cultural dimension at Nichols and, 192
  as Dean of the College, 155
  discontinuance of forestry program and, 156
  retirement as president of Nichols, 174
  social rules, 164–168
  use of long-range committees, 157–158
Cross, Melissa, 154
Cross-country team, 99, 130
Cultural dimension at Nichols College, 191–196
Cultural Enrichment Committee, 194, 195
"The Cultural Experience: The Arts, Sciences, and Public Policy," 195
Cummings, Pop, 263
Curfews, 71. *See also* Parietal hours

Curriculum
  for bachelor's degree in business administration, 271
  evolution of, 226
  New Hampton Junior College of Business Administration program, 122, 261
  Nichols College, 162
  Nichols College of Business Administration, 120, 128, 160, 273
  Nichols Junior College, 38, 45–47, 111, 261–262
Currier, Frederick, 222
Currier Center, 108, 145

Daniels, F. Harold, 105, 106, 110, 117
Daniels Auditorium, *18*, 123, *126*
Daniels Forest, 110–111
Daniels Hall, 106, 107, *142*, *182*
Dartmouth College, 23
Davidson, Carter, 136
Davis, John, 197, 228
Davis, Mary and James, 196–197, *197*
Davis, Stephen, 197, 228
Davis Business Information Center, 196–198, 199, 200, 211
Davis Hall, 199, *199*, 200–201, 206, 211, *220*
Dean Eaton Foyer, *216*
Dean of student affairs, 202
Dean of the faculty, 189
Dean's House, *85*, 95
Deerfield Academy, 30, 105
Delaney, John, 221
Delta Mu Delta, 215, 222
deRedon, George, 203, 219
Desautels, Gene, 74
Detroit Business Institute, 22
Detroit Tigers, 115
Dickens, Charles, 59
Dining Hall, 18, *18*, *40*, *43*, *85*, 93, 94, 123, 158, *174*, *183*, 198, 211, *216*
  fire at, 50, 51
Dining Hall in Alumni Hall, *142*
Dirlam, John, 211
Discrimination at Nichols, 206
Division of Continuing Education, 209–211
Dolber's Commercial College, 21

Donahue, Joseph W., 173
Dorman, Ken, 83
Dormitories, 106, 123, 124
Douglas State Forest, 132
Drake, Dorothy, 214
Dramatic Club, *87*, 192
Drawbridge, Jim, 203
Ducharme, Janice, 168
Dudley Appreciation Day, 188, 222
Dudley Bible Institute, 19, 34
Dudley High School, 2, 14
Dudley Hill, *13*, 41
Dudley (Massachusetts), 2, 32–33
Duggan, Ellen O'Connor, 209
Dupuis, Marc, 222
Durfee, Herb, 203
Durkee, Robert, 95

Earth Day, 221
Eastern College Athletic Association, 209
Eastern Collegiate Football Conference, 209
Eastwood, Bob, 263
Eaton, Robert H., *128*, *157*
  on College's purpose, 129
  as Dean, 76, 77, 88, 127, 129, 157, 177, 202, 272
  as faculty, 48
Economics course, 45, 111, 160
Ed Jacobs and the Soulrockers, 169
Educational Commission of the State Legislature, 44
Educational Testing Service, 190
Education program, addition of, 160–161, 162
Eells, Walter, 6
Eichler, Marilyn, *203*
1805 House, *216*
1841 House, *144*
Elbridge Boyden Society, 196
Elbridge Boyden & Son, 15, 41
Eldon C. Grover Cup for Public Speaking, 98
Emonds, Tom, 221
Engh, Peter, 203
English course, 45, 46, 111
English Course, Nichols Academy, 13–14
Enlisted Reserve Corps, *108*, 108–110, *109*, 227

Enrollment
    continuing education programs, 210
    in higher education, 153
    Nichols College, 210, 213–214, 221, 223, 229
    Nichols College of Business Administration, 122, 128, 134, 158–159, 215
    Nichols Junior College (1931-1943), 42, 43
    optimum, 106
    post-World War II, 91, 93
ERC meeting, *149*
EREHWON, 215
Erwin, Fred, *131*
Ethics course, 45
Evening program, 156, 227
Exchange Club, 138
Executive training, emphasis on, 44
Exeter Academy, 29
Extra-curricular activities, 68–72, 98, 115

F. Harold Daniels School of Conservation and Forestry, 105, 110–111
Faculty
    Nichols College, 176, 177, 189–191, 195, 204
    Nichols College of Business Administration, 155–156, 272
    Nichols Junior College, 37, 47–48
    post-World War II, 91, 92
Faculty Policy Manual, 189–190, 191
Family Education Rights and Privary Act of 1974, 170
"Farewell Message," Kingman's, 72
Fasces, 89
Federal Reserve Bank, 106, 123
Feller, Bob, 74
Fels, Gerald, 228
Field house, 125, *126*
Finance course, 160
Financial issues
    Coyle and, 175–176, 179, 187
    Cross and, 159, 174, 179
Firearms on campus, 70
First Congregational Church (Dudley), 13, 41, *85*
Fischer, Robert C., 193–196, *194*, 202, 203

Fischer Institute. *See* Robert C. Fischer Policy and Cultural Institute
Flanagan, Bernard J., 145
Fletcher House, *203*, *217*
Food protests, 71
Football field (Bison Bowl), 123, 145, *147*, *148*, 172
Football team, 61, 63, *86*, 88, 99, 104, 115, 130, *146*, *148*, 173, 215, 221, 263
Ford, Gerald, 164, 205, 233
Ford, Henry, 22
Ford Foundation, 119
Foreign students, 69, 97, 233
Forest Club, 83
Forester trophy, *149*
Forestry Hall, 123, 127, 132, *143*
Forestry program, *110*, 110–111, 132–134, *133*, 145, 156, 227
Foster's Commercial School, 21, 22
Francis W. Robinson, Jr. Tennis Courts, 200, *201*, 208, 211
Franke, Floyd N., 202, *203*, 205
Fraser, James Earl, 65
Fraternities, 68, 83
Free enterprise capitalism, Nichols College and, 188
French, Dave, 221
Freshman initiations/hazing, 70, 170
Freshman seminar, 205
Friendly, Fred (Ferdinand Wachenheimer), 68, 83, 141, 215, *218*, 223
From Higher Aims to Hired Hands (Khurana), 185
Frye, Davis, 169
Fuller House, 198, 199, *216*
Fundraising campaign, 199–201

Gafney, Harry D., 130
Garland, Gilbert C., 92, *92*, 103
Geer, Dave, 145
Generation X, 163
Geographical distribution of student body, 97, 112, 131, 232–233
Gibbons, Floyd, 83
GI Bill of Rights, 81, 89–90, 96, 116
Gionet, Lisa, 222
Glee Club, 68, *86*, 141, *147*, 192

281

Glenny, Paul, 263
Goldwater, Barry, 132
Golf team, 99, *146*
Goodell, Charles L., 41, 94
Goodell, Earl, 105
Goodell, Mary D., 94
Goodell Hall, 123, *143*
Gottfried, Alex, 164, *165*
Government
   impact of legal age of majority change on colleges, 170
   involvement in higher education, 153
   Nichols College and regulation by, 230
Graduate school of business administration, 134
Graduations, 41, 77–78, 83, *87*, 93, *116*, *139*, *218*, 221, 223
Grand March, *147*
Granger, Russell, 172
Grant, Kenneth E., 203, *205*
The Great Plains (Webb), 65
"Great Transformation," 152–153
The Great Transformation in Higher Education (Kerr), 185
Greek fraternities, 68
Green Mountain Junior College, 66, 69, 88
Gromelski, George, 88, 92, 103, 157, *157*, 177
Gross, Tom (Tommy), 65, *66*, 263
Guest (Oldham) House, *217*
Guimond, Jim, *219*, 222
Gurnett House, 198, *216*
Gymnasium, *16*, *18*, 41, 52, *85*, 94
   renovation as auditorium, 123, *126*

Hall, G. Stanley, 25
Hanan, Jim, 263
Hancock Trust Fund, 55, 56
Hart, Jeffrey, 195
Hartman, Richard, 98
Harvard University, 141
Hazing, 170
HEFA. *See* Massachusetts Higher Education Finance Authority (HEFA)
Herbie (security force), *218*
Hermann, Robert, 123, *125*
Hermann Pool, *218*, 221

Hezekiah Conant courtyard, *18*
Higher education
   effects of growth, 201–202
   "Great Transformation" and, 152–153
   growth in following World War II, 89–90
   impact of legal age of majority at 18 and, 170
   junior colleges and, 6–7
   prior to Civil War, 12
   regulation of in Massachusetts, 79
   in 1980s and 1990s, 185–186, 204
Higher Education and the New Society (Keller), 185–186
Hill, Karl A., 48, 134
Hill, Robert C., 221
Hills, Jack, 166
Hilltoppers, 68
"Historical Questionnaire," 200
Hobson, Donald, 98
Hockey team, 65, *66*, 130, 145, *146*
Holloway, Tex, 263
Holy Cross College, 208
Homecoming (1946) weekend, 228
Honor societies, 131, 145, 221, 222
Hoover, Herbert, 40, 62, 233
Houlberg House, *143*, 198, 223
Howe, Neil, 102, 233–234
Hunter, H. Jack, 76
Hurricane of 1938, 41, 44, 89, 93, 106, 263–264
   damage to campus, 50, 52–54, *53*

IBM 1130 computer system, 157, *163*
Infirmary, 123, 124, *126*, 145
in loco parentis, 170
Institute for American Values (Robert C. Fischer Policy and Cultural Institute), 191–196, 211, 214, 222, 227, 232
Institutional purpose, statements of, 265–266
Interfaith Chapel, 123, 124, *125*
International Honor Society in Economics, 221
International Relations Club, 68, 74
Internships, 205
Irene E. and George A. Davis Foundation, 196

James, Edmund J., 22
James L. Conrad Hall, 106, *107*, 107–108
Joe Namath Football Camp, 221
Johnson, Lyndon B., 132
Johnson, Ralph, 263
Journal (newspaper), 212–213
Junior College Athletic Conference, 77
Junior colleges
    emergence of, 12, 28–29
    New England, 6, 48–50
Junior Rose Bowl, 99, 104
Justinian Council, 164, 172, 222
Justinian House, 83, 95, 198
Justinian Society, 68

Kato, Mark, 141
Katori, John, 111
Keg parties, 166
Keller, George, 185–186
Kellogg, Lisa, 222
Kelly, Elizabeth, 188
Kennedy, John F., 132
Kenny Rogers and the First Edition, 169
Keohane, Dennis, 197, 203
Kerr, Clark, 152, 185
Kerry, John, 233
Khurana, Rakesh, 185
Kimball Union Academy, 25
Kingman, Bradford M., 48, *49*, 68, 72
Kirk, Russell, 193
Kisenge, Seth, 145, *149*
Kohnke, William O., 61
Kreuter, Adam, *131*
Kuppenheimer, Robert, 228
Kuppenheimer Hall (New Hall), 174, 198, *217*

Lacrosse, *220*
Lacrosse team, 98, 99, 141, *148*
Lalibertie, F. X., 264
Landon, Alf (Alfred) M., 62, 233
Larson Junior College, 69, 88
Lasher, William R., 190
Learning Resource Center and Writing Lab, 204
Ledger, 68, 89, 110, 145
    on "Nichols man," 113–114
Leech, Edward C., 103, *104*, 127, 272

Leicester Junior College, 138
Lelon, Thomas, 213
Liberal arts, business education and, 119, 231–232
Liberal Arts Colleges: Thriving, Surviving or Endangered (Breneman), 230–231
Liberal arts courses, 6–7, 160, 231–232
    addition of, 159, 160
"A Liberal Education for Business Administration," 136
Library, 123, *124*, 145, *180*, *217*. See also *under* Conant Library
Literary magazine, 204, 223
Literary magazine club, 215
Little Rock Junior College, 99
Logo, *220*
Lombard, David, 228
Lombard Dining Hall, 198, 211, *216*
Lucas, Christopher J., 186, 204

MacLeod, Malcolm, 83
Management course, 160
Managerial revolution, higher education and, 12
Mann, Horace, 14
Marianapolis Junior College, 78
Marianopolis College, 49–50
Marketing course, 160
Marot Junior College, 49–50, 69
Mary and James Davis Business Information Center, 196–198, 199, 200
Maskmakham, 169
Massachusetts
    approval of Nichols becoming four year college, 118, 120
    degree-granting authority given to Nichols Junior College, 31
    junior colleges in, 6–7
    permission to use title "junior college," 44
    petition to change status from two year to four-year college, 95–96
    regulation of higher education in, 79
Massachusetts Association for Intercollegiate Athletics for Women, 209
Massachusetts Board of Higher Education, 159, 161, 176, 231

283

Massachusetts Department of Education Division of Teacher Certification, 160, 161
Massachusetts Higher Education Finance Authority (HEFA), 161, 174
Master of Business Administration (MBA) students, 46
Master of Business Administration (MBA) program, Nichols College, 8, 152, 161, 176, 209–210, 222, 226
Mathematics course, 111
Mayor's Council, 170, 221
McClutchy, Thomas, 177, *178*, 202
McDermott, John, *203*
McQuarrie, Donald A., 172
Men's basketball teams, 77–78, 88, 99, 115, 130, 141, *219*
Mercade, Roberto, 83
Merrill, Quincy H., 19, *33*, 37, 38–39, 52, 105
    as acting President, 78, 79
    death of, 177
Merrill Hall, 42, 52, 52, 55, 77, 83, *182*, *217*, 221
Merrill Infirmary, 123, 124, *126*, 145
Merriman, P. S., 141
Metronomes, 98, 141
Millennials Rising: The Next Great Generation (Howe and Strauss), 233–234
Miller, Arthur, 46
Morat Junior College, 69
Morway, James J., 37
Mount Ida Junior College, 69, 88
MUCK, 68
Munce, George, 88

NAIA. *See* National Association of Intercollegiate Athletics (NAIA)
Nath, Lawrence H., 128, *129*
National Association of Intercollegiate Athletics (NAIA), 119, 127, 171, 227
National Collegiate Athletic Association (NCAA), 119, 127, 134, 137, 171, 172, 209, 227
National Endowment for the Humanities grant, 192–193
Naughton, Richard, *203*
NCAA. *See* National Collegiate Athletic Association (NCAA)

"N" Club, 68
Newcomen Society of North America, 221
New England Association of Colleges and Secondary Schools, also New England Association of Schools and Colleges (NEASC), 6, 79, 134, 137, 141, 154, 155, 156–157, 202, 232
New England Junior College basketball championship, 115
New England Junior College Conference, 66, 88
New England Junior College Council, 138
New England junior colleges, 6, 48–50
New England-Nova Scotia student exchange program, 205
New England Quartermaster Association, 138
New England Universalists, 12, 13, 229
New Hall, 174, *181*, 198, *217*
New Hampton Junior College of Business Administration program
    Conrad at, 27–30
    curriculum, 261
    features of, 20
    move to Nichols Academy, 19–20, 29–30, 33–34
New Hampton Literary and Biblical Institution, 23
New Hampton School, 11
    decision to become all-male, 25
New Hampton School for Boys, 3, 4, 19, 20, 23, 25–26, 32
New Hampton's Commercial College, 23–24
New York University, business education at, 22
Nicholodians, 98, 141, *147*
Nichols, Amasa, 1, 3, 4, 12, 13, 58, 226, 228
Nichols, Inc., 43, 54–55, 57
Nichols Academic Policy Manual, 1978, 213
Nichols Academy, 2, 3, 11, 12–15, 228
    Alumni Hall and, 93
    Conant's new academy buildings, 15–18
    as Dudley High School, 14
    leasing agreement with Nichols, Inc., 55
    leasing campus to Nichols Junior College, 33–34

~ INDEX

sale of campus to Nichols Junior College, 55–57
tenants, 19–20
transfer of New Hampton Junior College of Business Administration program to, 29–30
trustees, 78
Nichols Academy bell, 93, *94*
Nichols Academy Board of Trustees' Committee, 101
Nichols Academy Campus, *1*
Nichols Academy Tower, *31*
Nichols Alma Mater, 59
Nichols Alumni Association, 104
Nichols Alumni Bulletin, 104
Nichols Alumni Magazine, 18
Nichols Alumnus, 57, 117, 159, 168–169, 228–229
Nichols athletic pledge, *148*
Nichols Bar, 166, 170, 222
Nichols College
    administration, 177–178, *178*, 202–204
    adult education program, 128, 156, 209–211, 223
    aerial views of college, *180–183*
    athletic program, 171–173, 207–209
    bicentennial of, 1
    catalog, *219*
    coeducation at, 152, 158, 159, 161, 168–170, 207, 225
    as comprehensive college, 231
    computer center, 196–198
    curriculum, 162
    earlier histories, 8–9
    education program, 160–161
    enrollment, 210, 213–214, 221, 223, 229
    evolution of, 225–234
    faculty, 176, 177, 189–191, 195, 204
    financial issues, 174, 175–176
    geographical distribution of student body, 232–233
    geographic location and, 228–229
    history 1931-1996, 1–9
    internal reorganization and redesign, 189–191
    logo, *220*
    Lowell Smith administration, 8, 186–214
    MBA program, 8, 152, 161, 176, 209–210, 222, 226
    mission of, 232
    new facilities, 198–201
    notable events, 218–223
    reaction to programmatic changes, 162
    size of, 229–230
    social rules, 169–170
    student body, 204–207
    student polls, 206–207
    150th anniversary, 134, 135–136, 233
    trustees, 228
Nichols College; The First 175 Years (Kelly), 188
Nichols College Athletic Hall of Fame, 67, 171, 172–173, 209, 228
    members, 267–270
Nichols College Bulletin, 195
Nichols College European Summer Study Tour, 128, *129*
Nichols College Evening Division, 111, 128, 156, 209–211, 223
Nichols College Golf Course, 123
Nichols College Honor Society, 131, 145
Nichols College of Business Administration
    1958–1971, 152–159
    accreditation, 122, 134, 137, 154–157, 273
    addition of liberal arts program, 159
    addition of new programs, 159–162
    administration, 127, 155, *157*, 272
    athletic and recreational center, 125–127
    athletic program, 127, 130–131, 157, 171–172
    campus map, *140*
    change from all-male to coeducational institution, 152, 158, 159, 161
    change of name to Nichols College, 152, 160, 161
    charter, 265–266
    college seal, 117
    conservation and forestry program, 132–134, 156, 227
    cost of attending, 145
    curriculum, 120, 128, 160, 273

285

enrollment, 128, 134, 158–159, 215
faculty, 155–156, 272
financial problems, 159
geographic distribution of student body, 97, 131
"Great Transformation" and, 152–153
new campus for, 122–124
notable events, 215, 218–219
political leanings of students, 131–132
President Conrad's retirement, 134, 137–140
purpose of, 128–129
restructuring issues, 272–273
seal, 151
Sesquicentennial Celebration, 134 135–136, 233
social rules, 164–168
student activism at, 163–168
transition to, 121–124
trustee vote to become, 120
Nichols College Parents' Organization, 222
Nichols College Woman's Club, 141
Nichols Community Union, 170
Nichols Disciplinary Board, 129
Nichols Executive Training Group, 46
Nichols Fire Department, 68, 145, *218*
Nichols Forestry Club (Nicon), 145
Nichols Junior College, Inc., 54
Nichols Junior College of Business Administration and Executive Training, 2–6
 academic program, 36
 accreditation, 141
 administration, 37
 advisors to, 37–38
 announcement, 3
 athletic program, 60, 63–68, 83
 becoming four-year college, 102–103, 105, 111–112, 116, 121–124, 226
 charter, 265
 college buildings/campus, 34–35, 40–41, 50–55, 93–96, 105–108
 conservation and forestry program, *110*, 110–111
 continuing education program, 111
 cost of attending, 83, 88, 141
 curriculum, 38, 45–47, 261–262

degree-granting privileges, 44–45, 49, 72
elements of, 11–12
Enlisted Reserve Corps at, *108*, 108–110, *109*
enrollment, 42, 43
evolution of, 225–226
extra-curricular activities, 68–72
faculty, 37, 47–48
first campus map, *35*
first graduates, 41, *42*
geographical distribution of student body, 97, 112
goals of, 47
growth of, 59–60
higher education in Massachusetts and, 6–7
leasing campus of Nichols Academy, 4–5, 33–34
local support of, 37
move to Dudley, 33–39
opening of, 40–41
operating philosophies and responsibilities (1940), 38
pioneer period (1931-1938), 61–72
place among New England junior colleges, 48–50
post-World War II reopening, 79, 81, 90–99
prewar years (1938-1941), 72–74
promotion of new educational concept, 42–44
purchase of Dudley campus, 55–57
purpose of, 5
Quartermaster Corps and, 72–73, 74, 76
seals, *11*, *31*, 41, 59, 89
state recognition of, 8
state regulations and, 44
student body (1931-1932), *60*
student conduct rules, 69–70
three-year program, 112
transfer to four-year colleges from, 49
transformation into Nichols College of Business Administration, 117–119
trustees, 37, 39, 54, 56, 78, 104–105, 120
in vanguard of business education expansion, 7
World War II and, 57, 60, 74–81

Nichols News, 198
Nichols "Nighttime," 209, 211
Nichols' seals/emblem, *11, 31*, 41, *59, 89, 151*
Nichols Ski Slope, 215
Nichols Summer Work program, 145
Nichols Yacht Club, 64
Nicon Forestry Club, 133
1958 Yearbook, 120
Nixon, Richard M., 131–132, 164, 233
Nordstrom, Everett, 103, *104*
Northeast Women's Athletic Conference, 209
Norton, Donn, *131*, 138
Notre Dame, 130, 145, *146*

Obama, Barack, 233
Oden, Howard W., 190
O'Kane, Joseph, 45
Oldham, Hazel, 215, *220*
Oldham House, *217*
Olivet College, 193
Olsen, Herluf V., 105, 119
Olsen Hall, *143, 144*, 174, *181*, 215
Omicron Delta Epsilon, 221
Omicron Delta Kappa, 196
O'Neil, Leo D., 105, 119, 120
O'Neil Hall, 123, *143*
Ostby, Ned, 263
Otis Air Force Base, 124
Outing Club, 68, 83

Packard, Robert L., 203
Panty raids, 115, 129
Parietal hours, 166–167, 177
Parkinson, C. Northcote, 221
Parr, Jack, 141
Paterson, Richard "Dick," 145, 166
Payton, Bob, 221
PC Plan, 197–198, 211, 227
Pearl Harbor, attack on, 57, 73, 75
Pelto, Mauri, 223
Penmanship courses, 21, 24
Pfeiffer, Frank, 204
Phelps, Ernest, 215
Phelps, Rob, *148*
Phi Delta Chi, 68
Phi Kappa Epsilon, 68
Phi Sigma Nu, 68, 83

Physical Education Building, 123
Plummer, Herbert L., 78
Political leanings of Nichols students, 62, 131–132, 164, 205, 233
"Pop's," 18
Porter Sargent, 19
Portland Junior College, 69, 88
Post Office, *146*
Potter, Richard, 110
Practicum, 122
Preparatory schools, business courses at, 23
President's Council, 83
President's Home, *85*, 95
Problems in the Transition From Elite to Mass Education (Trow), 201
Proctor Academy, 25
Professional courses, balanced with liberal arts courses, 231–232
Psychology course, 45, 46
Public Affairs Committee, 192
Public schools, 14, 24
Public speaking contest, 97–98
Public speaking course, 45

Quartermaster Corps, U.S. Army, 27, 72–73, 74, 76, 227
Quinn, Charles M., 127, *128*, 155, 157, *157*, 177, 272

Racquetball team, 223
Radio stations, student-run, 68
Ragan, Philip H., 155, 215
Reagan, Ronald, 205
Ream, Norman B., 49
Reddy, Punchy, 263
Red School Building, 145
Red Village School, 106, 108
Regent's University, 205
Regional accreditation, 118, 119
Registrar, 202
Rehabilitation Act of 1973, 176
Renaud, Stanford, 98
Ridings Memorial, 106, *143*
Robert C. Fischer Policy and Cultural Institute (Institute for American Values), 191–196, 211, 214, 222, 227, 232
Robinson, Charles L., 93
Robinson, Francis W., Jr., *201*

287

Rockefeller, John D., 21–22
Roger Conant Hall, *1*, *13*, 34, 37, 228
Roger Conant Inn, 15, *16*
Roger Conant Memorial Window, *87*
Rogers, Kenny, 169
Romney, George, 194, *194*, 222
Roosevelt, Franklin D., 62, 73
Roosevelt, Theodore, 25
Rossini, Nancy, 209, 222
ROTC program, 109, 202, 205, 222
Rutland Forest, 132

Sailing Club, *86*, *146*
Saint Mary's College, 49
Sanborn, Gig, 263
Sargent, Albert, 177, *178*, 221
Satellite campuses, 210, 227
Savage, Peter R., *191*, 204
Schieffer, Bob, 222
Seals, Nichols, *11*, *31*, 41, 59, 89, 151
Searle, George J., 93
Sebastian, John, 169
Senior thesis, 122, 128
Serviceman's Readjustment Act of 1944 (GI Bill of Rights), 81, 89–90
Sesquicentennial Celebration, 119, 134, 135–136, *136*, *146*, 233
Shamie, Ray and Edna, 199, 201
Shamie Hall, *66*, 199–200, *200*, 201, 206, 211, 223
Sha Na Na, 169
The Shaping of American Higher Education (Cohen), 186
Sharpe, Bob, 145
Shaw, Reed, 263
Shiman, Lilian L., 190, 204
Shiner, Irv, 263
Siekierski, John, 221
Slater, Samuel, 3, 4
Smalley, Sterns, 93
Small liberal arts colleges, 230–231
Smith, Eleanor Mann, 187
Smith, Frederick, 4, 19–20, 29, 32
   as advisor to Nichols Junior College, 37
   as partner in Nichols, Inc., 43, 54
   program to expand New Hampton's enrollment, 25–26

Smith, Joseph A., 105
Smith, Lowell C., 8, 9, 177, *187*, *201*, *203*, *212*, 222, 225
   adult education program (Nichols "Nighttime"), 209–211
   athletic program and, 208
   "Campaign for Nichols," 198–201
   computers at Nichols and, 196–198
   conflict with student newspaper, 212–213
   educational background, 186–187
   government regulation and, 230
   Institute for American Values and, 193–196
   internal reorganization and redesign and, 189–191
   reactions to problems of growth, 201–209
   retrospective on, 211–214
   on role and goals of Nichols College, 187–188
Smith, Nora, 211, 214
Smith, Thomas G., 191
Smith College, 69, 71
Smith College Club, 74
Smith Hall, 123, *144*, *182*
Snead, Sam, 141
Soccer, *86*
Soccer team, 88, 99, 115, 130, *148*, *149*
Social Committee, 68
Social life at Nichols College, 206
Social rules, 164–168, 169–170
Softball, *219*
Softball team, 171, 173
Southbridge (Massachusetts), 33
Sparks, Bob, 263
Spencer, Wesley G., 48, *49*, 68, 75
Stancl, Donald L., 191
Stancl, Mildred L., 191
Stark, Buck, 263
Steglitz, William, 204
Stobbs, George R., 54
Stockbridge Aggies, 99
Stoneleigh Junior College, 69, 88
Strauss, William, 102, 233–234
Student body
   1931-1936, 42
   community service, 170

conduct rules for, 69–70, 115, 166–167, 177
geographical distribution of, 97, 112, 131, 232–233
Nichols College, 204–207
pictures of student life (1931-1946), 86–87
pioneer period, 61–63
post-World War II, 96
range of (student) heights (1955), *114*
recruitment of first, 36–37
relationship with President Coyle, 176–177
student activism, 163–168
"the Nichols man," 112–116
Student deferments, 77
Student-Faculty Public Affairs Committee, 192
Student Government Association, 164, 177, 205–206, 212–213
"Student Instructional Report," 190
Student newspaper. *See also Bison* (newspaper); *Budget* (newspaper)
conflict with Student Government Association, 205–206, 212–213
Student polls, 206–207
Student protests, 71, 166–167
Student Services Center, 202, *203*, 217
Sullivan, Larry, 263
Summer session, 215
Summer work program, 128
Surplus Property Act of 1944, 107
Sweet, Tom, 83
Swim meet, *218*, 221
Swimming pool, 125
Swimming team, 130, *147*

Tale of Two Cities (Dickens), 59
Tavern Annex, 94, 141
Tennis courts, 200, *201*, 208, 211, *218*
Tennis team, 99
Thalians, 68
T-Hall, 94, 123, *144*
Thompson, Kenneth J., 228, 263–264
Three-year program, 112
Tierney, Virginia L., 221
Tilton Academy, 25
Tilton Junior College, 48

Tipper, Karen S., 191, 204
Title IX, 176
Tower (yearbook), *31*, 68, 83
Towne, Robert, 95
Townsley, Debra, 2
Track team, *87*, 99, 130
Tesreau, Jeff, 79–80
Tropp, Karen, 208
Trow, Martin, 89–90, 201, 202
Trustees
attempt to create four-year college and, 111–112
Nichols College, 228
Nichols Junior College, 37, 39, 54, 56, 91, 104–105, 120
Tug-of-war, *219*
Tuition plans, 221
Tunney, Gene, 79
21 Club, 222
26th Amendment, 170
Typing class, *147*

Umoja campus group, 206
Underhill, Arthur J. C., 105
Underhill Hall, 123, *144*
Union, Bob, 263
Universalists, Nichols Academy and, 12, 13, 229
University-based business schools, 22–23, 185
University of California business school, 22
University of Chicago business school, 22
University of Pennsylvania, 130
Wharton School of Finance and Commerce, 22, 29
Upper Budleigh Gates, *32*
U.S. Army
Enlisted Reserve Corps, *108*, 108–110, *109*, 227
Quartermaster Corps, 27, 72–73, 74, 76, 227
"Use of Correct English" degree requirement, 205

289

Van Leuvan, Daniel, 160, 221
Vendetti, Michael "Mike," 130, *148*, 173, 178, *178*, 207–208, 222
Vendetti Field, 172
Vermont Academy, 25
Vermont Junior College, 66, 92
Veterans, enrolled at Nichols, 90
Vietnam War, Nichols students' attitude toward, 164, 167–168
Village Grammar School (Dudley), 1
Village School (Dudley), *13*, 17
Villanova College, 26, 28, 36
Villanova University, 138
Visiting lecturers, 192
Vocational education, 21

Wachenheimer, Ferdinand (Fred Friendly), 68, 83, 141, 215, *218*, 223
Walcott, Ray, 99
Wallis, Harry W., 105, 119
Warren, Edward G., 190, *191*, 192, 193, 194, 204, 207, 210
Waterfield, Coach, 263
Way House, 123, *142*
Webb, Walter Prescott, 65
Webster-Dudley Boys Club, 131, 138
Webster-Dudley Chamber of Commerce, 138
Webster-Dudley Golf Course, 95
Webster-Dudley Hockey League, 170
Webster Evening Times, 4
Webster (Massachusetts), 33
Webster Rotary Club, 37
Webster Times, 78, 221
Weidman, Donald J., *220*
Well house, *218*
Western New England College, 138
Wharton School of Finance and Commerce, 22, 29

Whedon, Wilbur, 141
White, Bickie, 263
White, Paul, 132–133, *133*
Whitney, Dick, 263
Wilcox, Charles F., 15, 17, 18, 41
Windfall (literary journal), 204, 223
Winston, George P., 155, 169, 191, 192
Winston House, 198, *217*
Winter Carnival, *87*
Winter Carnival Queen, *147*
WNJC, 68, 98
WNRC-FM, 204, 223
Women
   enrolled in higher education, 153
   number enrolled at Nichols, 213, 223
   in public high schools, 25
   sports teams, 171, 173, *173*, 208–209, 227
   as students at Nichols College, 168–170, *169*, 207
Women's basketball teams, 171, 173, *173*, *219*
Woodmen's Weekend, 133
Worcester Academy, 138
Worcester Evening Gazette, 167
Worcester Museum of Natural History, 110
Worcester Polytechnic Institute, 205
World War II, Nichols Junior College and, 57, 60, 74–81
WVOW, 68

Yacht Club, 68, 99
Yearbooks, 120

Zeta Alpha Phi, 131, 145, 222
Ziemski, Bruce, 221